Money, Banking, & Credit
in the Soviet Union
&
Eastern Europe

ADAM ZWASS

Money,
Banking,
& Credit

M. E. SHARPE INC. WHITE PLAINS

in the Soviet Union & Eastern Europe

Translated by Michel C. Vale

Published simultaneously as Vol. XVII, No. 1-2 of *Eastern European
Economics*.

Library of Congress Catalog Card Number: 78-64910
International Standard Book Number: 0-87332-124-3

Printed in the United States of America

Table of Contents

Preface

The reorganization of the banking system and the evolution of credit policy in the Eastern countries, the intensification of the activities of the international CMEA banks, and, most important, the monetary problems that have arisen due to the rapid expansion of trade and credits in relations between East and West, have made necessary a new evaluation of the possibilities and limits of the monetary and credit system of the planned economies.

Drawing upon my own experience as an official of the Soviet and Polish banking systems and the Department for Financial and Monetary Affairs of the CMEA, I have attempted in this monograph to examine the new developments in this area in light of traditional practice and prevailing theory, and to arrive at some new conclusions. This task is more complicated now than it was before: the Eastern monetary system cannot be considered uniform, for neither the Soviet steering model nor the Soviet credit system can be viewed today as the decisive prototype for the whole Eastern bloc — the Hungarian economic system, for example, differs radically from that of Romania. The task is not easy because official theory, first of all in the Soviet Union — based, as it is, largely on Marxian analysis of the market system of the past century — contrasts more and more with the realities of the market and even moreso with the actualities of the planned economies. Detailed analysis of recent developments in each country in the area of monetary matters, viewed against the backdrop of their evolving

steering systems demonstrates that the monetary systems of the
Eastern industrialized societies of today are confronted with two
problems: in contrast to the conceptions of the first development period, the planned economies cannot steer to a moneyless
society and are forced to enlarge the market features of their
monetary instruments; they cannot hope for success in these endeavors, however, for a state-owned and centrally planned economy sets material limits for money, credit, and prices as instruments of economic activity. The present study shows clearly
that the strong efforts to find a motivated application for credit
relations foundered. So far practice has not given a clear answer to the question as to where the limits between state budget
subsidies and state banking credit could be drawn. The experience of every Eastern country and its results in this regard are
examined here.

Many studies have described the controlling functions of the
Eastern banking system. This book moves a step forward by
trying to assess the effectiveness of these functions. It looks
not at the influence of the banking system on the level or pro-
portions of production, however, for such control never could
be viewed as a serious policy objective. Rather, it examines
the results of banking control in the areas where such monitoring was considered as the banks' decisive task, mainly in the
control of inventories, in the maintenance of a stable currency
and, lately, more and more in the monitoring of the performance
of capital investments. With the help of available data, this
study demonstrates that in these areas the planned economy is
no more — and sometimes less — successful than the market
economy. The investigation makes clear that stability of the
currency in the planned economy is but a fiction. While a
greater than envisaged volume of money in the production
sphere might be neutral, since the possibilities for its application are limited, excessive money in the household sphere
carries an evident inflationary impact. Inflationary pressure
may be offset by budgetary subsidies, but only by limiting the
basic function of price as a cost recovery instrument and equal-
izer of demand and supply; and while inflation in the planned

economies might be given different forms than in market economies, its impact on the consumer is just as great.

This investigation carries forward my earlier endeavors in
Money of Two Markets (1968) and Monetary Cooperation Between
East and West (1974) to assess the monetary problems that have
arisen as a result of the intensification of foreign trade within
the CMEA area as well as between East and West. It shows
clearly that, while a money of limited functions could more or
less satisfy the internal needs of the planned economies, albeit
with immense losses in quality, the Eastern nations have remained unable to develop adequate monetary instruments either
in intra-CMEA trade or in economic relations with the West.
Recent developments inspire the conclusion that while confine-
ment of the currency to the internal sphere might have been adequate during the early stages when the planned economies
tended toward autarky, it comes a severe handicap now, when
the international division of labor is viewed as an important factor in technical progress and comparative cost advantage, as a
precondition for its efficiency.

This study shows in a variety of aspects the consequences of
the limited functions of Eastern curriencies in intra-CMEA relations as well as in East-West trade — first of all, the unsuccessful efforts to multilateralize foreign trade and to make
the transferable ruble attractive for third countries, as well
as the impact of the existing unequal instruments on East-West
trade, which reduces the Eastern countries to the level of the
developing nations.

While the possibility is remote that the planned economies
could introduce money with market-type features in the foreseeable future, the conclusion is drawn that the integration of
Eastern markets into the world economic and monetary system
is a condition sine qua non for further intensification of East-
West economic and political relations.

This book and Monetary Cooperation Between East and
West were written under different circumstances than The
Volume and Structure of Money and Money of Two Markets;
nevertheless, all were written with a single purpose: to make

Money, Banking, and Credit

the Eastern monetary system and its prospects for evolution
more understandable in order to promote the strengthening of
East-West cooperation.

I should like to thank Janet Lincoln for her brilliant editorial
assistance, as well as my wife Friderike for gathering the
source materials and preparing the text.

Adam Zwass

*Money, Banking, & Credit
in the Soviet Union
&
Eastern Europe*

Chapter 1

MONEY IN A PLANNED ECONOMY

1. Inapplicability of Traditional Monetary Theories

The theory of money is tied to the times and reflects the period whose events have shaped it. Money has always been an instrument of accounting, of commerce between individuals and enterprises, the commodity of commodities, the tertium comparationis — and, as such, the universal equivalent in the world of commodities. How money is created and in what quantities, its influence on economic processes, and its pervasiveness have varied considerably from one period to another and from place to place.

Today's nonmaterial money rests on a vast network of banks extending throughout the world, which employs many different clearing and payment procedures (used more and more in the consumer market also) as well as Euromoney, the transferable ruble of the International Bank for Economic Cooperation, and the Special Drawing Rights of the International Monetary Fund; this nonmaterial money bears scarcely any resemblance to the primitive payments activities of yesterday, which relied on money based on the noble metals. A monetary system is as tied to its times as are the theories adduced to explain it.[1]

The monetary system of the planned economies represents a special case; none of the traditional monetary theories is adequate to explain it, since it functions in an economic system that proclaimed its intention to abolish money but proved unable to do so, although it did restrict considerably its use and functions.

3

The first period of Soviet development, War Communism, which approached a moneyless economy[2]; and the second period, the New Economic Policy,[3] with its state-controlled market and monetary relations bearing market features, lasted but a short time. Out of them grew neither an egalitarian natural economy nor a special socialist market, but a centrally administered economy as remote from moneyless distribution as from a market-based money economy.

In the different steering models for a centrally administered economy money is assigned a varying range of functions. Because of features inherent in a planned economy, however, money does not have the integrating function it normally shows. The state sector, with its homogeneous property relations, is coordinated directly with planned targets and steered centrally. Money is not the sole instrument of control; it is one of several whose range and functions are determined by the state as the collective owner of the banks and means of production. The system itself limits the degree to which money may exercise and expand its functions. Money does not give to an economic entity an anonymous, universal purchasing power with which it can acquire any commodity it wishes from any supplier it chooses for its production and investment activities. Possession of money is not the sole "admission ticket to the reservoir of commodities," as Schumpeter put it. In every planned economy, even one that is largely decentralized, the state retains the power to decide on the direction of economic development and on the uses to which the nation's economic assets are to be put. At the private level, an individual may determine how he is going to use his consumer money, but his decision is not as free as it is in a market economy, since the state controls supply. Furthermore, means of production cannot be bought with private money, except in a very few special situations.

But there are limits to how far the functions of money may be restricted. A modern industrial and consumer society — which is where the Eastern countries are headed — needs money that works. Even an extremely centralized planned economy is unable to dispense with money as a unit of accounting or

4

a means of clearing and payments. Since the social order in Eastern Europe is moving in the direction of stratified rather than egalitarian distribution of incomes, the functions of money are increasing, rather than decreasing, in importance. For example, as an incentive to efficiency and a yardstick for costs and profits, money stimulates labor productivity, and hence serves to promote efficiency.

Money will never have the impact it does in a market economy, but it functions in a less disorganizing way. Money mechanisms are not used to boost a stagnating economy or cool an overheated one.

2. The Current Monetary Theory in the Planned Economies

In the Eastern bloc, monetary theory is a much debated topic, in which all sorts of extremes are represented. Some want to extend the Marxist theory of money to the money of a planned economy,[4] while others dispute the need for money in the state sector and are willing to grant it a place only where it mediates the heterogeneous property relations of the nonstate sector.[5] These extreme views, however, lack any true counterpart in the practical reality of the planned economies.

Money in Marx's time was the money of the classical mid-nineteenth century market economy; it still circulated in the form of the noble metals or was based on them. The Marxist theory of money therefore cannot explain how money functions either in today's market economy or in the planned economies, which have little to do with the vision of future society as Marx conceived it. Indeed, he did not foresee any real place for monetary relations in future society, apart from the rather unrealistic "labor money."[6]

In the planned economies, money is neither abstract labor money nor market money. But neither is it essentially different from the money of capitalism, as Brus claims.[7] All the traditional functions of money are found in a planned economy as well, although they have relatively little ability to influence economic events.

3. Why a Planned Economy Needs Money

3.1. The Isolation of Economic Entities

The money of a planned economy is not an imitation of market money. Its functions are not merely to mediate between separately owned economic entities or between the state sector and the population. Its raison d'être lies in the state sector itself.

A steering model took shape in the 1930s in the Soviet Union whose basic features have been retained in Eastern Europe to this day. This model admits of neither market relations nor distribution in natura. Even in the highly centralized planned economies, enterprises have not grown together into one large state cartel, as Lenin had envisioned in 1917.[8] Every enterprise must justify its performance, even when it has no decision-making powers over its own development. Even in the state sector, where all belongs to the state and enterprises are not separately owned, they do not maintain extensive ties with one another. Further, although means of production are rigorously allocated from above, shipments are cleared and paid. Supplier and recipient are bound by contractual terms. Money assets do not give an enterprise the right to buy what it wants; in many cases an official allocation is required. On the other hand, no enterprise can be compelled to accept certain goods. Goods are not only distributed for use, they are also apportioned as value. Labor is also sold as a commodity and paid according to performance; a differentiated pay scale is, of course, best expressed in money terms.

3.2. The Isolation of the State Enterprise from the State

Since the national economy has not taken the form of one large cartel as Lenin envisioned, and capital goods, means of production, and consumer goods are not distributed in natura, the national product must be reapportioned in money form through the state budget. Thus, an enterprise must transfer to the state at least some of its earnings, which are then reallocated to other enterprises by means of the budget.

The ultimate price of a commodity is its cost price plus the surplus value created in its production. This is indispensable for economic growth, and of course the state administration, the health and school systems, and national defense must be paid for as well. The difference between a market economy and a planned economy lies not in the level of performance demanded of the workers, nor in the relation between wages and the value produced, but in the fact that surplus value ends up in state hands rather than private hands.

The redistributive function is much more developed in a planned economy, which assumes total control over economic life and determines the direction of development as well as the allocation of financial resources. Time has brought many changes, however, in the way these functions are exercised and in the relation between the state and the enterprise. While under the earlier, highly centralized steering model, the entire sum of surplus value flowed into the state budget in the form of profits and taxes and was then reapportioned, today an enterprise is permitted to retain a part of its earnings for self-financing. An enterprise can operate independently in pursuit of its own interests to a greater degree than before. But the state still decides on key investments and how they are to be financed. Nevertheless, monetary and fiscal policy has become broader and more variegated.

3.3. Emergence of the Foundations for a Credit System

Quite rightly, credit is regarded as a category of the heterogeneous property relations. In a planned economy, both the enterprise as borrower and the bank as lender are largely or wholly state owned. Credit therefore has a totally different economic import and is used in totally different ways than in a market economy.

A planned economy is still a money economy, however, albeit in a more restricted sense. Goods are paid for in money; taxes and earnings paid into the state budget are expressed in mone-

tary units; and wages and salaries are paid in money. Hence, a
planned economy must also have a currency. Here, too, credit
does the job best; the granting of loans creates the required
amount of money, while their repayment eliminates money that
is no longer needed.

To create money, however, credit must have a place in the
economy. The programmatic Soviet credit reform of 1930-32,
which laid down the basic principles for the credit system of a
centrally administered economy, had a difficult time finding a
way to introduce credits into the economy.

It was clear just what, in a planned economy, credits should
not finance, but it was not so clear what they could finance. At
least in the period where central economic authorities had assumed total power over economic development and over material and financial resources, credits could exercise no capital-
creating functions, nor could they be used to finance capital
projects.

Neither could credits finance the whole of current production,
for an enterprise which had been granted some measure of independence had to have its own resources (own capital) with
which it could carry on its economic activities unimpeded.

Suppliers' credits and discount credits were also impossible,
since in a centralized economy the buyer of every commodity is
determined in advance; moreover, demand is usually greater
than supply, and hence does not need to be stimulated by credits.
The 1930-32 credit reform had good grounds for abolishing
these forms of credit. Suppliers' credits were also unaccept-
able for another reason: they could be used to evade direct
bank control. Yet that should be one of the most important
functions of credit.[9] Thus, the only path open was taken: credit
was to be used as a stopgap measure where there was no basis
for employing strictly regulated budget funds. That is, it was
to be used to finance seasonal production and stockpiling as
well as outstanding supplier claims that could not be foreseen
in setting plan targets.

Since hitches in production and sales inevitably gave rise to
financing lags and these are most easily caught and checked in

8

clearing and payments procedures, credit was viewed as an instrument of state control as well as a means of financing.

4. Money Circulation

4.1. The Creation of Money Through Bank Credits

Lending procedures are many and varied, and we will discuss these in the next chapter. For the present, we shall be concerned simply with describing the ways in which money is created. In a planned economy, every credit is regarded as creating money; this is termed the issuing or monetary function of credit.[10]

Credit injects into the economy the money needed for a growing commodity exchange. Money created can also be eliminated again when the volume of commerce declines or the velocity of money increases. Ordinarily, the volume of both credit and money expands since they not only serve as a medium for economic growth, but also finance it. Credits that have not been paid off within a given planning period finance income, in addition to exercising their money-creating function.[11]

Normally, every credit is recorded in the receiver's own account; Poland, and to a certain extent Czechoslovakia, are exceptions — in these countries, credit is granted by means of overdrafts.

Bank money is issued when the credit appears in the receiver's account. Payments into or withdrawals from a bank account do not constitute creation or elimination of the money issued, but only a restructuring of the circulating money.

4.2. Two Monetary Flows

There are two money flows for money in circulation — enterprise money and private money. The origin of both is the same: both come from bank credit. Cash is diverted from accounting money when it is withdrawn from a bank account for wages and other payments. Wages are a component of enterprise costs

9

and, as such, are tied to the reproduction process. The major portion of the cash money returns to the enterprise accounts by means of trade organizations or is deposited in the savings accounts of the population at large.

The two money flows circulate in completely different markets, kept rigorously separated: one on the capital goods market, the other on the consumer goods market. The rules of the game and the effects of the money flows on economic events differ considerably from one another. Cash is used to settle accounts between enterprises only within strictly controlled limits — in Poland, for payments up to 5,000 zlotys.[12] Private individuals (small entrepreneurs, farmers) can use it to a very limited extent to procure capital goods (means of production). The price basis is also different; consumer goods bear a turnover tax, while capital goods as a rule do not.

Enterprise money is not an allocation factor, nor does it have universal purchasing power.[13] Consequently, price need not necessarily function as a parameter on the capital goods market, even though a price commensurate with cost outlay is an indispensable condition for effective accounting. However desirable it might be, goods may not be produced without approval, even though money for this purpose is available in an enterprise's bank account; conversely, the lack of money does not prevent production once it has been approved.

An enterprise operates according to a totally different concept in a planned economy than in a market economy, and money is creative only in countries where economic reforms have accorded factories some entrepreneurial functions. Otherwise, the state makes all decisions concerning economic development and the allocation of money resources.

Thus, enterprise money is an instrument of accounting as well as of distribution and redistribution of the national product. In a planned economy as well, an inordinate inflow of money cannot be prevented; when it does occur, it is more the consequence of disproportionalities in economic growth, and thus money supply is more automatic here than anywhere and does not operate as a primum movens.[14] Excess enterprise money does not

10

have an inflationary effect, since as we said, it does not have purchasing power of its own.

A bank, which also often creates more money than required, need not worry about its liquidity, since money deposits are not a prior condition for lending, even though the credit plan must see that liabilities balance out assets. This is only at the macro level, however. A bank branch does not have its own balanced credit plan, nor is it compelled to ensure a balance between deposits and credits. Credit backed up by available firm reserves can create good money. Hence, a central function of banks is to make a critical assessment of firm resources offered as collateral. But even a restrictive credit policy is unable to prevent economic mistakes; hence, they too must be financed, although the way this is done varies from country to country.

Household money moves along completely different paths. The person who has it decides how he will use it, but the state influences demand by its employment and wages policy and keeps things in hand by controlling the production of consumer goods and services. Within the overall framework of the state-controlled consumer market, however, the individual may decide on how he wants to use his income.[15]

Prices deviating from intrinsic costs (including an appropriate margin of profit) will effect a redistribution on the capital goods market, although only within the framework of the homogeneous state property domain; on the consumer market, however, such deviating prices will cause a permanent distribution between state and population and place in jeopardy the equilibrium between supply and demand. Enterprise money is relatively neutral, for as such it is not creative. This is not the case with consumer money, however. For this reason, the two money flows are managed differently.

5. The Management of Money Circulation

Since credit is the source of all the money created for enterprise as well as household use, the total amount of money created is regulated in the uniform credit plan of the State Bank.

11

Enterprise money is relatively neutral. Therefore, monetary policy need not be concerned with preventing inflationary pressure from the creation of an excessive amount of money. Rather, its primary aim is to control the economy by controlling credit allocation, and to catch the inevitable disproportionalities through the supervisory functions of the banks. In this way, signals indicating how credit activities are going and the liquidity state of economic units are recognized in good time and the appropriate authorities informed.

Too much money in private hands has a disorganizing effect and disrupts equilibrium. Private money has its own ups and downs. Inflation — although never referred to as such — has already caused appreciable concern on the part of the planning authorities, and special mechanisms have been developed to cope with it. The most important of these are the Balance of Money Income and Expenditures of the Population, the cash plan of the State Bank, and an appropriate monetary policy designed to ensure that these plans are fulfilled. The development plans for household money and the money-creating credit plan for the economy as a whole are organically linked with a unified issue sum of cash.

The liabilities and assets structure of the banking system of a planned economy can be described as follows on the basis of data for the Polish National Bank (see table).

Money in the hands of the state sector covers the greatest portion of the total passive side of the ledger (46.9 percent), although the share of the households is also considerable (29.0 percent); cash represents only 8.3 percent, however (12.6 percent in Hungary). The amount of money saved in cash form is steadily diminishing; the Polish population puts the greater part of its savings in savings accounts. The state budget, which contains the funds for long-term credit activities of the State Bank, has a share of 20 percent on the passive side.

There is a considerable discrepancy between the share of the population and the private sector on the liabilities side (29 percent) and the credits side (7.2 percent). Consumer credits show a 6.8 percent decline over the previous year. On the other hand,

12

Consolidated Brief Balance Sheet of the Polish Credit Institutes,
December 31, 1976 (in billions of zlotys)

ASSETS	Share in %	LIABILITIES	Share in %
1. Credits for		1. Resources	
a. Socialized sector	92.2	a. Socialized sector	52.6
Credits for working capital	48.1		
Credits for investments	44.1		
b. Agricultural sector (private)	3.4	b. Banks' own funds	3.2
Credits for working capital	1.0		
Credits for investments	2.4		
c. Private industry and handicraft	0.1	c. Resources of nonsocialized sectors and households	24.3
		Saving deposits of the population	16.9
		Cash resources of the population	7.4
d. Households	1.7	d. Resources of state budget and budgetary units	19.5
For the purchase of consumer goods	0.7		
Investment credits	1.0		
Total credits	97.4	Total resources	99.6
2. Other assets	2.6	2. Other liabilities	0.4
TOTAL	100.0	TOTAL	100.0

Source: Information Bulletin, Narodowy Bank Polski, 1977, p. 33.

13

about 47 percent of liabilities and 92 percent of credits are in
the hands of the state sector.

5.1. The Management of Enterprise Money

The inflow of money is limited by regulation of resources and
enterprise funds. The size of reserves for the individual components of the working assets (raw materials, finished goods,
etc.) is set as low as possible (minimal reserves) on the basis
of the needs of production. In the earlier steering model, pre-
assigned items had to be approved by higher administrative
authorities; today they must be approved by the enterprise
itself. The state budget allocates the original sum of enterprise
funds in proportion to approved working capital. These funds
are later enlarged in keeping with the production program, formerly from the state budget and now mainly from enterprise
profits. In the reformed model, a portion of the profits is left
in the hands of firms to form their development funds. These
may then be used to build up plant within the framework of
decision-making powers granted to the enterprise, as well as
for investment purposes.

The inflow of money, however, is regulated by the limited allocation of bank credit. The statistics of some of the Eastern
countries indicate that the share of bank credits in the financing
of working capital is larger than the share of enterprise own funds.

Structure of Polish, Czechoslovak, and Soviet
Enterprise Financing Resources (in percent)

	Poland 1974	CSSR 1973	USSR 1973
Enterprise own funds	22.3	26.7	29.5
Bank credits	39.6	38.8	45.0
Obligations to suppliers	21.9	34.5	18.9
Others	16.2		6.6
Total	100.0	100.0	100.0

Source: Information Bulletin, Narodowy Bank Polski, p. 19; Statistická
ročenka ČSSR, 1974, p. 194; Narodnoe khoziaistvo SSSR, 1973, p. 769.

14

Money in a Planned Economy

The share of bank credits in the total funds of the nation's economy is almost the same in Poland and Czechoslovakia, while it is higher in the Soviet Union.

In some Eastern countries, the allocation of credits is still limited by a credit plan approved by the Council of Ministers, or at least is regulated by control parameters. In general, credit is coupled to a specific item of the working capital (raw materials, finished goods, etc.). This practice still exists in Romania and the Soviet Union, although it is now applied more loosely. In the other Eastern countries, credit is originally tied to the growth of total working capital. Credit collateral in the form of enterprise assets is reviewed on the basis of enterprise information and monthly balance sheets, and unsecured credits are paid off from the clearing accounts that exist side by side with credit accounts.

The use of enterprise money is also closely supervised, principally in connection with clearing procedures. Goods deliveries are usually paid for when invoices are submitted to the bank for payment. The banks try to block any demand for money not tied to goods. However, they also control payments operations. Payments must be made within a period stipulated by the state — normally ten days for orders to pay (three days for acknowledgment by the receiver and seven days for the payment itself) — and are accomplished automatically by the bank through deduction from the enterprise account.

Claims that are not met within the stipulated time because of insufficient funds are registered separately and burdened with a penalty interest. They are deducted from the claim files of the supplier, however, to reduce the credit base. (The supplier's claims serve as a banking credit object for the normal collecting time).

As the state's controlling institution, the banks also see that the wages calculated by the enterprise conform with its production performance. The wage fund, approved by higher authorities, is compared with fulfillment of the production target. For instance, in the Soviet Union, the fund is multiplied by a variable coefficient ranging from ± 0.6 percent to ± 0.9 percent, differing for each branch of industry, for every percentage point by which the plan is overfulfilled or underfulfilled. In some Eastern countries — for example, Hungary — the reforms abolished bank supervision of wages. Wage increases are now set in accordance with the level of labor productivity.

If an enterprise becomes insolvent, bank control is brought into full play: the bank takes full control over all accounts. In such cases, wage payments are taken care of first, then payments to the budget, then those to suppliers, and finally payment of overdue credits. The firm is left only a minor sum for its own use. If a firm gets into chronic payments difficulties, it may be declared insolvent; it may then be divested of any unpaid goods it has and refused the right to obtain new credits. Such total bank authority is never exercised consistently, however, even in the Soviet Union, which in August 1954 introduced bank procedures against faltering as well as prospering firms.

5.2. The Effectiveness of the Management of Enterprise Money

The primary objective of management is to prevent disproportionalities in economic development. No suitable criteria are

Share of Growth of Inventories in
Gross National Product (in percent)

	1970	1971	1972	1973
Poland	6.1	7.4	6.8	7.3
USSR	11.4	10.9	9.6	10.9

	1968	1969	1970
Austria	1.2	2.0	2.5
Federal Republic of Germany	2.0	2.3	1.4
Great Britain	0.5	0.8	0.9
United States	0.8	0.8	0.3

Sources: Poland: Życie gospodarcze, October 29, 1974; USSR: Narodnoe khoziaistvo, 1973, p. 605; Austria, Federal Republic of Germany, Great Britain, United States: Encyclopaedia Britannica, Book of the Year 1972, p. 354.

available for assessing whether the amount of money is growing as it should. There are, however, some reference indicators for judging the existence or scope of disproportionalities in economic growth. The growth of inventories is the most clear-cut of these indicators. The editor-in-chief of the Polish economics periodical Życie gospodarcze observed rightly enough that the dynamics of inventories is a barometer of economic management[16]; but this barometer clearly indicates tempests in the planned economy. The figures in the table (page 16) on the growth of inventories in Poland and the Soviet Union as compared with those in some Western countries demonstrates this quite well.

The following comparison of economic growth and inventories shows clearly the true value of the much-prized "growth" in the Eastern European countries. From 1971 to 1973, Polish gross national product increased by 334.1 billion zlotys, while inventories increased by 254.1 billion; in other words, three-fourths of economic growth was not embodied in solid commodities. The total value of inventories in Poland at the end of 1973 (743 billion zlotys, i.e., a reserve of 123 days) was 67.6 percent of the 1973 gross national product.[17] The situation was even worse in the Soviet Union: between 1970 and 1973 inventories (133.3 billion rubles) increased 2.8 times more rapidly than the national product (47.3 billion rubles).[18] All problems in plan fulfillment as well as disproportionalities in the economic structure show up summarily in the state of goods reserves. Here there is no price mechanism that could eliminate the disproportionality, and the central planners seem unable to cope with this problem.

The vast commodity stockpiles are not a result of overproduction in general or surplus over the general amount needed to satisfy the consumers' demand, although overproduction may occur from time to time in some sectors as a result of bad planning or deviation from plan targets. Nowhere are shortages so great and discrepancies between supply and demand so vast as in a planned economy. It is a generally acknowledged fact that plan fulfillment really gathers steam only in the last days of each month; indeed, the stormy activity of these last ten

days has been called the Sturm und Drang period.[19] The command methods of a planned economy are less effective than the
discipline inherent in the market. Production plans must be fulfilled, however, even if at the last moment and with a considerable loss of quality in the goods produced in such a rushed manner.

The statistics given above, although they refer to only the two
largest of the Eastern states, cast the much-acclaimed growth
of the planned economies in a somewhat different light. The
disproportionalities that occur lead not to cyclic recessions accompanied by unemployment, but to enormous stockpiles that
effectively eradicate the efforts of millions of workers.

The credit mechanism, which was supposed to prevent the
occurrence of these phenomena through a restrictive money
policy, becomes helpless; indeed, it is dragged along in the process of waste — and in fact finances it. The halting efforts of
the state sector, which proceed uncontrolled, must be financed
by the State Bank, for in a planned economy only credit has un-
limited possibilities for creating money.

5.3. The Management of Household Money

The primary objective of cash management is to maintain an
equilibrium between supply and demand on the consumer market. Money inflation is a real danger here. The planned economies have always been plagued by galloping inflation — not
only during the war and the postwar period, but also during the
era of rapid economic growth[20] — and creeping inflation has
been an inseparable companion of economic development.

Of course, official Soviet economic theory denies the existence of inflation in a planned economy. By accepting the pos-
tulate that effective demand must be ahead of supply, however,
the imbalance on the consumer market has been made into a
law of economic development. Scarcity is a part of the daily
life of the Eastern European consumer. Heavy industry is given
priority; the production of consumer goods is of secondary importance. It is never planned well enough, and not as much significance is attached to plan fulfillment and supply. The imbal-

ance on the consumer market resulting from insufficient supply
is sharpened further by unreined demand. This is associated
with the growing discrepancy between produced and sold goods,
which shows up in enormous stockpiles. Immoderate, incomplete investments — construction times are especially long in
the planned economies[21] — also lead to imbalance on the consumer market.

Bank control over consumer money is therefore more rigorous than control over enterprise money. The cash plan for the
State Bank approved by the government is regarded more as a state
target than is the credit plan and as such is closely supervised,
with special concentration on the main items of the incomes and
outlays in this plan — namely, payrolls and proceeds from retail sales. The banks coordinate their supervisory activities
with the responsible economic and administrative authorities.

The cash holdings of economic units and observance of cash
limits approved by the banks are monitored closely.[22] Great
importance is attached to saving. Formerly, forced saving was
the rule; every year a state bond was issued, and every worker
was obliged to subscribe to a share equivalent to 10 percent of
his salary. The last compulsory Soviet bond was issued in 1956
in the sum of 32 billion rubles.[23] On April 19, 1957, further issue was discontinued, but so was the redemption of outstanding
bonds. At present, saving is wholly voluntary and is done by
means of savings accounts. The system itself, however, sets
limits on the voluntariness of saving and consumer sovereignty.
A person saves not because he wishes to put off consumption,
but because he cannot always satisfy his desires due to shortages of goods or excessive prices for durable goods.

Every bank branch must draw up a monthly or quarterly cash
plan, in which cash withdrawals of the firms doing business at
that branch (e.g., for wages) and private individuals (withdrawals from savings accounts) are recorded, together with cash deposits of firms (proceeds from retail sales) and private individuals (savings). The balance is counted as either withdrawal or
the creation of cash money.

Some Eastern countries still try to increase control over the

Money, Banking, and Credit

obligatory cash plan by making an issue balance mandatory.
A branch is thus obliged to apply for cash maintenance from a
higher echelon bank in cases where income does not match outlay.

This practice is observed as described above, however, only
in the Soviet Union, though even here in somewhat looser form,
for the republics are empowered to exceed the monthly issue
balances provided they cover the discrepancies in the subsequent periods.

5.4. The Effectiveness of the Management of Household Money

The money in private hands (cash plus savings deposits) is a
real and measurable magnitude whose dynamics parallel that of
the national product. The results of such a comparison is given
in the following table.

Growth Rate of Gross National Product (Nominal)
and Money Volume (in percent)

	German Democratic Republic				Poland				Czechoslovakia			
	1971	1972	1973	1970/73	1971	1972	1973	1970/73	1971	1972	1973	1970/73
National product	4.5	5.7	5.5	16.5	8.1	10.2	11.0	32.2	5.1	5.9	5.2	17.3
Total money supply	7.0	9.2	8.5	26.8	6.9	14.6	19.3	46.7	14.7	15.1	14.4	51.2
Cash	3.7	14.2	4.6	23.5	0.5	13.2	12.7	28.3	9.2	12.9	11.3	37.2
Savings	7.6	8.4	9.2	27.3	10.2	15.2	22.9	56.0	16.3	15.7	15.2	55.0

Source: Statistical yearbooks of the respective countries.

In all these countries, the money supply has increased more
rapidly than the gross national product, although in the German
Democratic Republic, where more stress is placed on equilibrium than in the other Eastern countries, the discrepancy is
less than in Poland and Czechoslovakia. The slight difference
between the growth rate of savings deposits and of cash is also
typical of the German Democratic Republic. In Poland and

20

Money in a Planned Economy

Czechoslovakia, savings rose faster than cash. The difference is due to the high level of savings in the German Democratic Republic. The share in the total money supply is greater than in Poland and Czechoslovakia, although even in the latter countries it shows a yearly increase.

Structure of the Volume of Money in the German Democratic
Republic, Poland, and Czechoslovakia (in percent)

	German Democratic Republic				Poland				Czechoslovakia			
	1960	1965	1970	1973	1960	1965	1970	1973	1960	1965	1970	1973
Total money supply	100	100	100	100	100	100	100	100	100	100	100	100
Cash	20.6	14.2	12.4	14.7	61.9	43.4	33.8	29.6	27.5	22.3	21.9	19.9
Savings	79.4	85.8	87.6	85.3	38.1	56.6	66.2	70.4	72.5	77.7	78.1	80.1

Thus, even in 1960 the share of savings in total money supply in the German Democratic Republic was already quite large, and over the next five years it grew even further, stabilizing at a high level of 85-87 percent. In the other two countries, especially Poland, the share of deposits continued to grow and is now gradually approaching the level in the German Democratic Republic.

Bank supervision of enterprise money is unable to prevent economic mistakes. Bank credits finance them, for this money is more easy to obtain than budget subsidies. Control over household money is not adequate to guarantee the equilibrium between supply and demand aimed for on the consumer market. Relatively more money than consumer goods is fed into the economy, as measured by the increase of the gross national product. The discrepancy between supply and demand is not always bridged by a price rise; when there are price increases, the term "inflation" is carefully avoided. The negative effects, however, are no less severe than in a market economy.

NOTES

1. Schumpeter has this to say: "Monetary relations can differ so greatly in form from epoch to epoch that it would be of no practical use to produce a general theory, which would only be limited to meaningless generalities." Das

Money, Banking, and Credit

Wesen des Geldes, Göttingen, Vandenhoeck, and Ruprecht, 1970, p. 15.

2. The Program of the Russian Communist Party, passed at the Eighth Party Congress in 1919, specified that measures would be taken with the aim of totally abolishing money. See Decisions of Party Congresses, Conferences, and Plenary Sessions of the Central Committee, Moscow, 1953, Vol. I, p. 427.

3. The Ninth Party Congress of April 1922, however, already had its sights set on the gold standard. The decision on this point reads: "Even if measures to restore a gold currency are not undertaken immediately, the country's economic and financial policies will be aimed at restoring gold backing for the currency." Ibid., p. 614.

4. See A. Lemnitz, Das Geld und die Funktion des Geldes im Sozialismus und in der Übergangsperiode vom Kapitalismus zum Sozialismus [Money and the Function of Money under Socialism and During the Transitional Period from Capitalism to Socialism], East Berlin, 1955.

5. Soviet authors I. Malyshev, Obshchestvennyi uchet truda i tsena pri sotsializme [Social Accounting of Labor and Prices under Socialism], Moscow, 1960; and V. Sobol, Ocherki po voprosam balansa narodnogo khoziaistva [Reflections on the Balance Sheet of the National Economy], Moscow, 1960.

6. "The producer may here receive coupons which he can exchange for consumer goods from the social stocks in an amount commensurate with his labor time. These coupons are not money, however; they do not circulate." K. Marx, Das Kapital, Vol. II, Warsaw, 1955, p. 375.

7. W. Brus, "Pieniądz w gospodarce socjalistycznej" [Money in a Socialist Economy], Ekonomista, 5/1963, p. 913.

8. "All citizens will be employees and workers in one state firm. The entire society will be an office and a factory, with the same work and the same compensation for this work." V. I. Lenin, "State and Revolution," Werke, Vol. 25, p. 510.

9. George Garvy rightly observes: "Under a system of administrative allocation of resources, money is relegated to a position of agent of control." Banking, Money and Credit in Eastern Europe, Brussels, January 1973.

10. See Z. Fedorowicz, Pieniądz w gospodarce socjalistycznej [Money in a Socialist Economy], Warsaw, 1962, p. 219; and J. Kronrod, Money in a Socialist Economy, Polish translation from the Russian, Warsaw, 1956, p. 282. Fedorowicz disputes the popular view that the monetary function is exercised solely by means of credit for unpaid orders.

11. Polish economist M. Kucharski says: "The increase in the volume of money requires additional credits, since today's monetary system cannot create money in any other way than through credits. On the other hand, lending is tied to the creation of money income. There is no other way to provide the economy with money." M. Kucharski, Pieniądz dochód, proporcje wzrostu [Money, Income, and Growth Proportions], Warsaw, 1972, p. 106.

12. See E. Wieczorek, "Das Funktionieren des Geldumlaufs in der sozialistischen Wirtschaft" [The Function of Money in a Socialist Economy], Życie gospodarcze, February 16, 1975, p. 11.

13. "In the area of state production, money is not a carrier of options," ob-

Money in a Planned Economy

serves George Garvy correctly. Op. cit., p. 63.

14. Schumpeter's term.

15. "Freedom of consumer choice should not be confounded with consumer sovereignty," observes G. Grossman. See Money and Plan, University of California Press, 1963, p. 5.

16. Życie gospodarcze, October 24, 1974.

17. Życie gospodarcze, October 29, 1974, p. 55. In 1974, Poland's reserves increased by 100 billion zlotys or 15.5 percent over the preceding year, and the national product grew by 10 percent (Gospodarka planowa, 5/1975, p. 286).

18. Narodnoe khoziaistvo, 1973, p. 605.

19. On this point, Pravda of October 20, 1975, quotes a worker on the factory committee of a large factory: "We work unevenly. In the third ten days of the month we produce 40-45 percent of the plan target. Often we even work on holidays with much overtime."

20. During the first Soviet five-year planning period from 1928 to 1932, wages rose by 3.5-fold, while the volume of retail trade rose by only 33 percent and consumer prices by 2.5-fold. See J. Konnik, Den'gi v period stroitel'stva kommunisticheskogo obshchestva [Money in the Period of Construction of Socialist Society], Moscow, 1966, pp. 148-149.

21. See H. Machowski and A. Zwass, "Poland" [Polen], in Die Wirtschaft Osteuropas zu Beginn der siebziger Jahre, Stuttgart, Kohlhammer Verlag, 1972.

22. In Poland, 10 percent of cash money is in the holdings of the enterprises. See E. Wieczorek, in ibid.

23. The bonds are interest free but, like prize loans, have a high redemption premium, although not every bond carries a premium.

Chapter 2

THE PRICE SYSTEM
IN THE PLANNED ECONOMIES

1. The General Problem

The great discussion of the twenties and thirties — namely, whether effective management and accounting of a nation's economy could be established under conditions of common ownership of the means of production as well as abolition of the market and competition, and traditional market steering mechanisms — was resolved in practice by the planned economies.

The view of famed economists Eucken, von Hayek, von Mises, and others that socialism must end up as a natural economy with none of the conditions necessary for economic accounting has turned out to be mistaken. Instead, the long years of development of the Communist nations have confirmed the views of the principal opponents of this theory — Lange and Taylor — if with many qualifications.

Eastern economists are now interested in other problems, such as how prices may be shaped when there is no market and no competition, no interplay between supply and demand, and no direct links to prices on the world market, and the extent to which prices shaped in such a way are necessary for economic development and for overcoming the worst evil of a money economy — inflation. We shall try to develop this problem in what follows.

2. Institutional Background

The planned economies have accepted both the Marxist theory

The Price System

of money and Marxist price theory as a basis for practice.
These theories are joined by the thesis that the value of both
money and commodities is determined by the socially necessary
amount of labor expended in their production.[1]

It was the hard coin of the nineteenth century, however, not
today's symbolic money, which Marxist theory has in mind.
Market economies have been functioning for a long time now
without a currency based on gold to serve as a common measure
of value for real commodities. Planned economies function not
only without a substantive money, but also without a market, at
least in the domain of capital goods — that is, means of production; therefore, in Marxist theory the vehicle of value is less
operative here than anywhere else.

With the elimination of the noble metals as payment media,
there ceased to be any direct connection between the material
value of money and the market value of goods.[2] Other mechanisms evolved to take their place, though even these were interpreted variously in economic theory. Nevertheless, it is an
objective fact that something exists which is the bearer of value,
and no matter how it is interpreted, the most that such a repre-
sentation can do is to influence the manner in and extent to
which the state intervenes in economic processes. The situation is different in the planned economies: there, the state itself steers economic processes, their mechanisms, and prices;
accordingly, not only production and distribution but also economic efficiency is dependent on economic doctrine and the
steering system used.

It would be wrong, however, to say that the central planning
authorities are able to follow their subjective inclinations and
ignore the fundamental laws of economic development with im-
punity. To be effective they, like any other economic entity,
must avoid wasting their resources and must employ them
wisely and circumspectly. Moreover, prices must be allowed
to retain their indicator function — both at the micro level, so that
performance may be assessed adequately and effectively, and
at the macro level, to ensure that adequate account is kept of
the economy and that resources are shifted and reshifted in ac-

25

Money, Banking, and Credit

cordance with economic needs.[3] Polish economist Pohorille is
right in his observation that "the economic mechanism is performing efficiently when it helps prices to exert an effective influence, not when it underestimates them."[4]

3. Factors Determining the Price Structure

Apart from the few cases in which the market is operative,
prices are not market prices in a planned economy. On the
other hand, neither are they merely planning norms nor administratively established accounting units. They must also reflect
adequately the conditions on which improvement in economic
performance is contingent. To the extent they do this, prices
retain their economic content and perform the same functions
they normally would in any economy: they are an instrument
for accounting, for calculating the gross national product, and
for allocating and reapportioning enterprise earnings. One or
another of the functions of money, the purely economic or the
purely accounting, will be more prominent depending on the
steering model. The function of prices is determined primarily
by the nature of commodity-money relations, however. In an
economy based purely on distribution in physical terms, prices
are unable to perform the economic function they would otherwise.
    The economic content of relations between enterprises pro-
ducing means of production is particularly disputed. Soviet and
other economists will frequently claim that means of production
are not commodities in the usual sense.[5] Practice, however,
proves the rule. During the period of forced industrialization,
when distribution of extremely scarce means of production was
strictly centralized and heavy industry was given highest priority, prices were also subordinated to the principal political
task of the times: they were to help promote the rapid and disproportionate growth of heavy industry, whose products had to
be relatively cheap. Since industrialization took place first and
foremost at the expense of agriculture, the prices of agricultural products requisitioned compulsorily by the state had to be
appreciably lower than the actual costs of their production.

26

Consumer goods, on the other hand, were also supposed to realize a portion of the value created in heavy industry and hence were relatively expensive.

The hallmark of this period was chronic scarcity and an unbridgeable gap between supply and demand; in a competitive market economy, prices soon would have pushed skyward, but the planned economies even today hold prices below a level necessary to maintain equilibrium.

Prices, however, far from fulfilled their normal economic function. They were not designed to induce thrift and contribute to equilibrium. The disproportionality in economic development prevented the evolution of an integrated price system that would have reflected actual value relations more adequately, and the system that existed reproduced the disproportionality found in the economy itself. At the time, prices were unable to function either as an accounting instrument or as an objective parameter for choosing between alternative paths of development. Political goals, not value relations, had top priority in the minds of the planning authorities of the time.

The cost of disregarding the objective laws of economic development was much higher than originally assumed. The prices paid by the state for agricultural products, far below what it cost to actually produce them, so severely undermined the performance of Soviet agriculture that even later attempts to back-track — 70 percent of total Soviet investments in agriculture has been made in the last ten years[6] — were unsuccessful in raising its efficiency to a reasonable level. The Soviet population will continue to be dependent on grain imports from the West.

The disproportionate expansion of heavy industry and the defense industry, and the profile this has given to economic development (in 1980, the consumer goods industry will still make up only 26 percent of the total industrial output of the Soviet Union)[7] has meant less goods for the Soviet population and undermines their incentive to work.

The unavoidable side effects of disproportionate and excessive economic growth were accepted as the price that had to be

paid in the belief that industrializing and catching up with the
West would create the conditions necessary for a better social
order — at least, this was the officially proclaimed rationale.
The main reason for this unprecedented growth fetishism, however, was and remains the drive to achieve equality with the West.

During this period, when quantity (measured in tons!) was the
catchword, money, credit, and prices — which are essentially
value categories — could not function in the normal economic
way. The planning system had reduced money to an internal
medium and effectively cut off domestic prices from world market prices. The interplay between domestic prices, exchange
rates, and foreign prices, such as is normal in the market system, was put out of function. The currency was no longer of any
use for business transactions, and prices were shaped independently of the world market. Ups and downs on the world market
were no longer translated directly into effects on the domestic
scene, because the mechanism whereby this occurs — namely,
exchange rates — no longer had any economic reality. Even
today, in a number of Eastern countries, including the Soviet
Union, the traditional monopoly over foreign trade and currency
is still maintained, and the state budget centralizes all foreign
trade earnings, while exporting and importing enterprises do
business abroad in domestic currency at domestic prices with
a foreign trade organization as trading agent.

Further, because the price system is shaped autonomously
and national currencies are nonconvertible, neither is suitable
as a basis for exchange, even for trade among the members of
the Council for Mutual Economic Assistance (CMEA). Trade
within the CMEA is transacted using modified world market
prices and a collective clearing unit.

The basic principles and methods of price formation have undergone change over the course of time, but the laws of a planned
economy retain their force.

4. Methods of Price Formation

Economic theory, so often burdened by unrealistic ideological dogma, has not prevented the quest for the best price concept possible within a given system. The price structure has always been a reflection more of current conceptions of development and the steering model in effect at the time than of the accepted monetary theory.[8] The Marxist labor theory of value has spawned many different notions of prices in the planned economies, but how it was interpreted depended on the pragmatic objectives of the economic planners.

During the first stage of development, there was no room for experimenting with different price systems. The price structure had to be compatible with a centrally steered economy where economic mechanisms played only a minor role. The Soviet model was adopted throughout all the Eastern countries.

At that time, a developed price system that conformed to actual value relations would have been useless at the micro level. Heavy industry normally operated at losses and its potential profits had only a very modest effect on enterprise activity and workers' incomes. Enterprise earnings were calculated in physical terms of gross output, not financial proceeds. A poor financial situation, which need not always be the effect of poor management, did not impair enterprise activity, which was geared to plan targets. Losses, even unplanned ones, and investments in plant and equipment were almost wholly financed directly or indirectly through the state budget. Furthermore, the price structure, shaped centrally with many noneconomic factors taken into account, was of no use at the macroeconomic level as an indicator for valuations or allocations. Prices and expected profitability were incidental to investment decisions, which depended first and foremost on the importance of the project for the economic development of the country, especially for defense. Matters were simplified, however, when prices were transformed from their role as the principal accounting instrument for the overall economy into an instrument for reapportioning enterprise earnings; this was done by attempting to extract the sum total of all the surplus value produced in the economy as a whole through setting excessively high prices on consumer goods. Under such conditions, where the distribution orders of the planning authorities, rather than money and prices, were the crucial factors in interenterprise relations, the price system could not be uniform. Indeed, the purchasing powers of money varied even from one branch of the economy to another. Three price systems based on different principles can be distinguished: (1) industrial prices; (2) prices for procuring agricultural products[9]; and (3) retail prices.

5. Industrial Prices and Their Components

5.1. Costs of Production

The criteria determining prices are intelligible only if one looks at the way their principal components are determined. Pricing begins with the actual costs of production for the industrial enterprise. This cost includes the price of materials (raw materials, fuels, etc.), wages, depreciation, and so on. The following table shows the composition of costs of production, with the Soviet Union and Czechoslovakia as examples.

Components of Industrial Costs (in percent)

	Raw materials, fuels, energy	Depreciation	Wages and Social Security	Other	Total
USSR (1973)	75.3	5.5	14.8	4.4	100
Czechoslovakia (1974)	66.1	5.9	14.5	13.5	100

Sources: USSR: Narodnoe khoziaistvo SSSR, 1973, p. 249; Czechoslovakia: Statistická ročenka ČSSR, 1975, p. 242.

The composition of production costs depends first and foremost on the structure of industry, which is not the same in the

Soviet Union and Czechoslovakia. Nonetheless, there is a broad
similarity, which may seem surprising if one considers that the
net monthly wages of an industrial worker are 20 percent higher
in Czechoslovakia than in the Soviet Union.[10] Many mutually
compensating factors in the industrial structures and cost com-
positions all work together to offset these differences, but their
discussion is beyond the scope of our present study.

Production costs plus enterprise profits — and, in many
branches of industry, plus turnover tax — make up the wholesale price. In the Soviet Union, for instance, the proportion of
the total value of all industrial goods produced in 1973 falling
to production costs was 74.1 percent; profits constituted 12.9
percent; and turnover tax made up 13.0 percent.[11]

The most unique features of price formation in a planned
economy, however, are to be found in the way surplus value is
shaped and put to use.[12]

5.2. Incomes from Enterprises

Just as in competitive market economies based on private
property, unpaid labor[13] in the actual production process is the
source of surplus value. The only difference is that in the planned
economies the state, as the collective owner of the means of
production, has the ultimate say in determining how surplus
value is to be obtained, in what form it should appear, and how
it is to be used.   Hence, an enterprise and its income play different roles in this respect than in a market economy. In no enterprise in the Communist bloc is profit and its maximization
the decisive motor force of economic activity, nor is profit the
sole criterion for determining enterprise efficiency. Rather
than competition for better production and sales returns, it is
the state-set profit rate as a component of prices that is the
crucial factor in determining enterprise profits in each branch
of industry.

5.3. Two Components of Public Income
and the Two-Tiered Price Structure

Surplus value is expressed in profits and turnover tax,[14]

called financial accumulation. In the original model, however, turnover tax — not profits — was the principle item in the state budget income. Nor was this at variance with the system, for the important thing was to find an optimal way to extract surplus value, almost all of which was to go to the state to be redistributed or spent for centrally planned and financed investments and other state purposes.

Profit, as an economic concept, was alien to the realities of the times. An enterprise was an integral part of the national economic plan, dependent on state allocations of resources, producing products destined for recipients specified by the planning authorities at prices set centrally; it could hardly be expected, therefore, that the enterprise would have any essential influence on the formation or utilization of profits.

Thus, it was only consistent that surplus value should not be left in the form of profits, but should be extracted by means of a turnover tax.

In 1940, the composition of financial accumulation in the Soviet Union was 3.3 billion rubles of profit and 10.6 billion rubles of turnover tax,[15] which showed clearly what a great emphasis the state placed on the turnover tax as a means for extracting surplus value during the first stage of development.

At that time, surplus value was regarded as stemming from the economy as a whole, so the point in the economic process at which it was created was of no importance. This also explains why, in accordance with the price concept of the time, surplus value was built into the prices of the different economic branches regardless of what value actually was created in that branch. The general economic conception of surplus value became the foundation for a two-tiered price system; prices in heavy industry were formed differently from those in the consumer goods industry. The view came to prevail that surplus value need not necessarily be tapped at the point at which it was created, but rather should be extracted at the point deemed most expedient from the standpoint of the state budget. It was considered senseless to build into the prices of heavy industry a profit equal to the surplus value created, since that would only

32

inflate trade between enterprises.[16] Net increments created in
heavy industry but not included in their prices were instead built
into the prices of consumer goods. These products, which pass
directly to the consumer, were where, according to the views
of the time, surplus value should ultimately be tapped so as to
avoid its appearance in interenterprise relations.

In fact, this means of extracting profits seemed reasonable
considering the views on the redistribution function of prices;
the surplus value built into consumer prices, which far exceeded
the value created in the consumer goods industry, was extracted
not as profits but as turnover taxes, which — independent of enterprise performance and dependent only on actual turnover —
was then passed on to the state.

The view that prices have a redistributive function (which accounted for the different price levels for the capital goods and
consumer goods industries) has been quite prominent in Soviet
theory and practice. [17]

5.4. Kinds of Prices

Above we have described in rough outline how surplus value
is extracted in a dual price system; this approach became the
foundation for price formation in the Soviet Union, and for many
years in the other Eastern European countries as well. There
are three basic types of industrial prices: (a) the wholesale
prices of an industrial enterprise; (b) the wholesale prices of
an industrial branch; and (c) the settlement prices.

The enterprise price includes the production costs, determined in accordance with the profitability standards set by the
planning authorities; this is the price at which goods are sold
to other state enterprises or sales organizations. It usually
does not include turnover tax.

The wholesale prices of an industrial branch include the enterprise price, as constituted above, and turnover tax. This is
the price at which consumer goods are usually sold to trade
organizations.

The settlement price is a variant of the enterprise price and is used whenever there is a considerable difference between the average costs of an industrial branch and the production costs of an individual enterprise. This was especially true for mining products, for example, because of unfavorable extraction conditions. In this case, the enterprise or mine sells its goods at differentiated settlement prices to specialized sales organizations (coal, metal), which in turn resell them to the ultimate consumer at the uniform price in effect in the particular industry.[18]

5.5. Cost-Induced Prices

In the first phase of development, when profits still did not have their proper economic function and production funds[19] were allocated entirely by the state, prices were first and foremost a reflection of cost expenditures. It would have been meaningless to put profits in any relationship to capital, since capital itself was a concept alien to a socialist economy. This is still true today, although "socialist profit" is gradually acquiring some economic sense, and attempts are being made to use it in the price structure in a way similar to the way it functions in a market system. Prices were originally conceived of as a control instrument of the state to supervise the cost norms and profit targets specified in the plan. This functional concept of prices in interenterprise relations is still operative in the Soviet Union today, although the way prices are formed has been changed somewhat. Not only were cost prices quite suited to the highly centralized economic model used at that time, they were also the best practical solution at a time when a system of accounting for the entire economy was still in its embryonic stages.[20]

The concept of economic accounting which evolved in the first phase of development and has become part of the history of the planned economies under the name "khozraschet," is limited in function not only because of the extremely complicated way in which net increments were dealt with in the different industrial branches, but also because value-creating activity was defined too narrowly. It was wrongly assumed that human labor

34

created value only in production. Neither nonproductive services in, for example, the school system, science, art, and culture,[21] nor values that do not require the expenditure of human labor, such as land, natural resources, or water, were considered value creating, and hence they were given no place in enterprise costs.[22]

5.6. Average Costs Versus Marginal Costs

The "costs principle" provides no precise guidelines as to what standard should be applied to costs in retail prices. Costs are not shaped uniformly; enterprises are equipped with modern technology to differing degrees. Extraction conditions are especially variable in mining. In the Soviet Union there are coal mines whose losses constitute up to 33 percent of the cost expenditures. A 10 percent profitability norm for mines operating in the region of marginal costs would make necessary a price increase of 65 percent for coal.[23] But such a measure would set off a chain reaction throughout the whole of industry, and especially in power plants using coal. A planned economy therefore must also decide whether marginal costs, which also enable low-performance economic units to yield a profit, or average costs, which may also give an enterprise a negative balance, are to be the determining factor in price formation.[24]

Marginal costs are rejected as a basis for determining prices. It was decided that average costs were a better reflection of socially necessary labor, which according to Marxian theory of value is the determinant of value. This view is still heard today, although there is a growing tendency to adapt prices to rising costs and thereby make even enterprises operating on unfavorable conditions profitable. This is done especially through differentiated profit rates. Prices structured on the basis of costs contain, in addition to costs, a profit margin — that is, a sum added to the planned costs, which in the first development phase was supposed to be 3 to 5 percent.

The price formula that fit this cost concept can be written as follows:

$$Pk = c + v + (c + v) \cdot \frac{M}{C + V}$$

where Pk is cost prices; c is consumed means of production; v is labor costs; c + v is average costs for the particular branch of industry; and $\frac{M}{C + V}$ is the profit rate based on production costs. The profit rate is differentiated by industrial branches.

Consumer prices contain a turnover tax in addition to the profit margin. In contrast to a market economy, in which the turnover tax is eliminated as an element in price policy by setting it at a fixed percentage, in a planned economy the tax rate is very differentiated and hence also serves as a "flexible instrument for forming and distributing money income."[25]

Although the turnover tax is being used more and more as an instrument for skimming off excessive profits that arise in cases where production conditions are especially good, it continues to serve as a means for extracting value in light industry and the foodstuffs industry. The table below shows this tendency clearly.

Structure of Basic Prices in Soviet Industry

	1965			1974		
	Total industry	Heavy industry	Light industry and foodstuffs	Total industry	Heavy industry	Light industry and foodstuffs
Wholesale prices	100.0	100.0	100.0	100.0	100.0	100.0
Production costs	74.7	81.3	67.6	74.1	77.4	69.7
Profits	9.4	11.6	7.1	13.0	16.5	8.4
Turnover Taxes	15.9	7.1	25.3	12.9	6.1	21.9

Source: Narodnoe khoziaistvo SSSR 1974, p. 214.

The proportion of profits in the wholesale prices of industry as a whole increased from 9.4 percent in 1965 to 13.0 percent in 1974 — a rise attributable mainly to the development of heavy industry. The consumer goods industry, however, is still the principal payer of turnover tax. Other enterprises pay a turnover tax only if they also produce consumer goods in addition to means of production.

The situation is similar in the other Eastern European countries. In Poland, for example, the turnover tax was the source of 32 percent of the value created in light industry, and as much as 74.6 percent of that created in the foodstuffs industry, while the figure fell to 0.0 percent in mining, 1.7 percent in machine building, and 2.2 percent in the building materials industry.[26]

In the initial phase, industrial prices still had no adequate economic basis as commodity prices. Many extra-economic considerations were attached to them; they were seen as an instrument to redistribute the incomes of enterprises and were shaped on the basis of costs, although by no means all components were taken into account. The profit margin, set by the planning authorities, was related to production costs but not to invested capital. The micro level had no influence on price formation. The entire price structure — in the Soviet Union, this meant 7 to 9 million retail prices[27] — was established by central planning authorities. This concept of prices was practicable only in the "period of consolidation," when value relations had but a very limited range of action. The economic reforms in some of the Eastern states have made some crucial adjustments to this price concept. In the next section, we shall try to describe the effects of economic reforms on the further development of industrial prices.

6. Procurement Prices for Agricultural Products

During the first phase of development (1929-53), price formation for agricultural products was wholly subordinate to the firm decision to accelerate industrialization at the expense of agriculture. During this period, which was extremely trying

37

for the rural population, compulsory deliveries at prices far
under production costs[28] were typical.

In 1936, the price for one ton of wheat was 15 rubles, paid on
delivery; it was compulsory. State purchasing stations sold the
wheat to state mills for 107 rubles a ton, and the difference was
transferred directly to the state in the form of turnover tax. In
1953, purchasing stations were still paying 0.03 rubles for one
kilogram of potatoes, which was not even enough to pay for transport costs to the point of delivery.[29]

Although industrialization was indeed accelerated, agriculture
was ruined: agricultural production in the Soviet Union was
lower in 1953 than forty years previously. The policy that had
produced this result was attenuated in 1953, and finally halted
completely in 1958. The path traversed from symbolic prices
to prices with some economic basis is reflected in the price
indices for the Soviet Union for the period from 1952 to 1959.[30]

	1952	1957	1958	1959
Grain prices	100	614	695	734
Livestock prices	100	420	546	561

A more effective price mechanism has now been introduced
in all the Eastern countries in an effort to raise agricultural
productivity, which in most cases is still inadequate. One of the
most important measures in this direction was the discontinua-
tion of compulsory deliveries and the dismantling of the extremely unfair price structure. Agricultural prices were raised
gradually to a level that not only covered production costs but
also made it possible to self-finance investment projects.

7. Retail prices

Consumer prices have always had a more sound economic
basis than capital goods prices, and were never downgraded to
the status of a mere instrument of state control. Therefore
consumer prices had to assume normal economic properties
very quickly, since together with income structure they deter-

mined the purchasing power of the population and the ultimate distribution of the national income. The guiding principle for the turnover of consumer goods is not their distribution on the basis of resolutions by the state planning authorities, but consumer choice, even when the market is clearly a seller's market. Consumer goods prices have never been left to the free play of supply and demand, although they still have had to contribute to some extent to the attainment of equilibrium on the consumer market.[31]

All the factors determining equilibrium — supply, that is, the production of consumer goods; and demand, that is, income levels and purchasing power — are planned; the automatic result naturally is a preformed price structure. It would be quite wrong, however, to believe that a really effective equilibrium can be achieved by planning these factors. Indeed, equilibrium has become increasingly difficult to achieve over the course of time since, on the one hand, wages have had to be raised to increase labor productivity, which is still lagging, and, on the other, the traditional notion of development giving priority to heavy industry is still being followed, as amply evidenced by the Soviet five-year plan (1976-80). The effect of these two countervailing tendencies is especially obvious in Poland and the Soviet Union.

Planned economies are not spared the problems of disequilibrium. But in contrast to a competitive market economy, they are able to choose between two evils — rising prices, and supply and demand difficulties.[32] A planned economy is not obliged to raise prices in order to rectify disequilibrium and has always preferred excessive demand to price increases. In some cases, when demand could be met, prices actually decreased in the Soviet Union; for example, the price index for foodstuffs declined by 25 percent from 1950 to 1955. This occurred, however, after the drastic price rises that took place in connection with the monetary reform at the end of 1947 (prices for foodstuffs increased by 103 percent between 1940 and 1950).[33]

Food prices have not fluctuated very much since 1965, especially in the Soviet Union, but other consumer goods have become steadily more expensive — generally in a concealed fashion. For example, a new model of an old product is put out which is poorer in quality, and hence more expensive. For political reasons, price stability in the face of rising costs is preferred to a narrowing of the gap between supply and demand. Prices were frozen by a Party and government resolution after the shift of power in Poland in December 1970, and in the German Democratic Republic in February 18, 1971. The state budget must cover the difference between rising costs and stagnant prices. This meant a budget expenditure of 10 billion marks in the GDR in 1973 and of 165 billion zlotys in Poland in 1975.

Vital foodstuffs and services are priced relatively low in the planned economies. Goods earmarked to satisfy increased needs, however — for example, a number of durable consumer goods or items made of new materials such as synthetic fibers — show a much more unfavorable price relation in the East than in the West. In 1973, East German prices for basic food items such as bread, potatoes, and vegetables were only 30-50 percent of the prices these goods fetched in the Federal Republic of Germany, while meat, meat products, and milk were as little as one-sixth the price of these items in the Federal Republic. On the other hand, the prices for flour, eggs, sugar, milk products, fat, imported fruits, cocoa, and sweets were 10 to 320 percent higher than in West Germany.[34] Similar price relations are found between Austria and Hungary. In 1972, the schilling-forint ratio was 2.13 for bread, 1.72 for beef, 2.07-2.21 for veal, 3.5 for streetcar fares, and 2.50 for telephone calls, but only 0.66 for coffee beans, 0.48 for Nescafé, 0.28 for cocoa, 0.92 for butter, and 0.4600 for a Volkswagen (1200 cubic centimeters) (although 3.99 for a one-year auto insurance policy).[35]

The market for consumer goods is also shielded from the world market, since the currencies are not convertible, and commodity prices evolve autonomously. The price structure varies from country to country, and of course tourists within the Eastern bloc try to take advantage of this. Prices have also been affected by the high inflation plaguing the West. Growing production costs are usually covered by budget subsidies, which simply means that the disequilibrium is shifted to other spheres. Attempts have been made to alleviate the acute scarcity of foreign exchange by cutting back on consumer goods imports, but this has only resulted in greater supply problems. Thus, relative price stability can scarcely be considered an intrinsic advantage of the planned economies.

8. "Production" Prices

After the economic reforms, the price system in the planned economies, once uniform, began to differentiate. While in the first phase the Marxist theory of value was embodied in cost-oriented prices, after the reforms "production" prices were the keynote.[36] The Marxist production price, however, is only a subjective interpretation of a process taking place on a real market, in which prices are formed by the competition of economic units for maximum profits. But production price in the planned economy is only the form, not the mechanism, of price formation; it did not appear spontaneously as a result of the development of the market, but was merely another construction of the central planners. In terms of content, it meant that enterprise capital (fixed and working assets) would henceforth serve as the point of reference in setting profit margins and not operating costs as heretofore. According to the concept of production price, profit is neither the sole nor the principal goal of an enterprise, nor the most reliable indicator of its efficiency; it is only a state norm, a component of the overall plan target, although now a more important one than formerly. Profit is built into prices, but it is not maximized by efficient performance as in competition.[37]

In thus appraising a measure that has been introduced in all the Eastern countries except Romania, we do not mean to imply that production price was only a formal change; price serves even more as a steering instrument since the reforms than before. Now, however, production price functions as an efficiency-promoting instrument throughout the economy, even where the economic reform affected only the technical and organizational aspects of the economy, and not its actual inner workings.

The modifications introduced into the principles of price formation were intended to put a stop to indifference on the part of enterprises toward their production equipment, which before the reforms they had received entirely or almost entirely from the state budget without compensation. The reforms made enterprise earnings dependent on the amount of enterprise funds (capital) invested, and the latter dependent on the size of profits, since the profit-distributing procedure also underwent radical reform. While formerly all profits passed entirely or almost entirely to the state, the reforms authorized enterprises to employ part of their profits as a source of financing investments. The modification of the internal accounting system and enterprise bookkeeping relations with the state gave enterprise funds a new role.

The reforms in price formation followed more or less the same lines in all the Eastern countries with the exception of Romania, which retained cost-induced prices. They differed only in the degree to which price formation was contingent on price-determining factors in the new reformed economic model, and models varied from country to country. Hungary went much further in its reforms than, on the average, did the other CMEA countries, where the reforms concentrated primarily on the technical and organizational aspects of the economy. This is also the main reason for variation in the steering instruments, including the price system, so that the way in which price structure is shaped in an Eastern country tells us nothing about the economic content of the reform. How the reformed price system functions will be discernible only in the context of the development of the entire model and in relation to the individual components of price formation.

8.1. Tax on Enterprise Funds as
     a Component of Production Price

Taxes on interest levied on enterprise funds are one of the most important components of internal and external accounting and of price formation. Enterprises, now exercising control over their own funds (production factors), which they have received without compensation or which have been accumulated

from their own resources, can no longer be indifferent to the
size of these funds. They must pay to the state — the collective
owner of means of production — a fee for their use; but in CMEA
countries this does not mean the decentralization of the state's
wealth (the enterprises still function only as administrators of
state property), as it did in the case of Yugoslavia, but only the
delegation of responsibility for how they are to be used. The
idea was to provide an incentive to enterprises to employ their
means of production efficiently. Since the scope of reform
varied considerably from country to country, the function and
impact of this most recent reform event in the economic history
of the East also vary. In any case, it should be viewed as one
steering instrument among many.

The tax levied on enterprise funds was also intended to provide a more effective mechanism for distributing enterprise
earnings, in addition to serving a regulative function. This was
especially the case in heavy industry, which formerly had paid
no turnover taxes at all. Now, however, with this new taxation
on enterprise assets, it too must pay a form of duty (capital assets tax) to the state, the size of which depends upon enterprise
earnings and actual turnover. This interpretation of taxation on
capital — as an incentive to use enterprise funds sparingly and
an effective mechanism for redistributing profits — is represented most conspicuously in the Soviet Union[38] and in Poland.[39]

Hungary had a different view. In the 1968 reform, the tax introduced on enterprise funds was a consequence of the decentralization of economic responsibility, which had already been
carried quite far. Enterprises remained state property, and
their activity was still subordinated to the plan, but they now
had to pay for everything, even items the state formerly had
supplied cost free; all these new expenditures were included in
the calculation of costs. "In the new price system, all resources
used must be taken into account in figuring costs," noted
Csikós-Nagy, principal architect of the Hungarian reform.[40]
Thus enterprises have to pay land rent, which is 5 percent of
the value of the land and grounds, but not more than 0.4 percent
of the value of all plant and equipment; and they have to pay for

the use of other means of production (fixed and current assets). Rates for water, and so on, were doubled and, consistent with this overall pattern, 25 percent of the funds set aside for wages had to be paid to the state for training the labor force. It is clear, then, that the tax on capital was above all an expression of decentralization of economic authority, and in this sense represented a qualitatively new steering instrument, a role that overshadowed its fiscal function.

The degree to which the tax on enterprise funds functions as a steering mechanism is also reflected in the accounting system. In Hungary, this tax is considered a component of production costs. Those countries that subtract the fee for utilization of enterprise funds from the profits passed on to the state, in the belief that this is a better distribution method, are operating according to the dictates of the system, for now heavy industry — and not only the consumer goods industries, as previously — must pay taxes.

The tax base varies as well. In Poland only the plant value (buildings, machinery, and equipment) is taxed, on the grounds that this is the only meaningful way to proceed since its value is two to four times greater than working capital, which are already controlled by the state through the credit system. The other Eastern countries also tax only the part of working capital not financed by bank credits.

Bulgaria, the German Democratic Republic, and the Soviet Union (and, since 1971, Poland as well) tax the original cost of procurement of plant to avoid having to consider this tax as a factor when obsolete and depreciated machinery is replaced. Czechoslovakia, on the other hand, taxes the book value, in order to counteract the influence of variations in enterprise equipment on cost calculations.

The tax rate also varies considerably: in Bulgaria it is 3 percent, in the German Democratic Republic 1-6 percent, in Czechoslovakia and Hungary 5 percent, and in the Soviet Union 3-6 percent. As a rule, however, these rates are meant only as guidelines. Enterprises with below-average profitability are taxed at a commensurately lower rate; they may even be exempted from the tax if it would mean a loss for them or if it would prevent them from paying off premiums or other services. In Poland, branches of industry in which the tax would have no effect on the size of enterprise funds — as, for example in the case of a power plant — are exempted from this tax.

The yield in capital goods taxes is already considerable; in 1973, 20 percent of profits accrued by Soviet industry and 33 percent of profits paid into the state budget were mobilized through this tax[41]; the corresponding tax figure for Poland in 1974 was 39.5 billion zlotys, that is, 30 percent of the profits paid in to the state[42]; while in Hungary 20 percent of the total income of the state budget was accumulated through this tax.[43]

Nonetheless, the effect of this tax on the size of enterprise assets should not be overestimated. Its primary purpose was to induce enterprises to get rid of machinery they did not really need. "No noteworthy efforts in this direction, however, have been discernible as a result of the tax," observe Polish experts. The reduction in the amount of assets tax paid due to elimination of a part of existing plant has increased the profitability of machinery production by only 0.015 percent.[44]

8.2. The Profit Component of Production Price

The enterprise assets tax, which is incorporated into the production price, is different from a turnover tax and is calculated on a different basis; moreover, it must be paid by almost all industries, not only those producing consumer goods. The production price also contains a profit component, which is no longer merely a portion of the net increment independent of the actual value created, as had formerly been the case with cost prices; rather, it is closer to the market conception of profit.

The profit rate contained in the production price is still established officially in the central plan; however, it must correspond to the actual value created in the given branch of industry, since the distributing function of prices, hitherto regarded as a law in the planned economies, is being called increasingly into question. Profit corresponds to market profits in form as well. Production price means, first and foremost, that profits are to be calculated as an officially established percentage of enterprise assets and are no longer a sum to be added onto enterprise costs.

The production price and its profit component (based on enterprise assets) are informative parameters of economic efficiency. As the distributing function of prices is deemphasized, they will be able to move closer to the value of the produced commodity, and profit is already a better indicator of the actual value created by an enterprise. A deviation from the profit target may therefore be seen as a deviation from preset target volumes for production and sales. Today, the profit target is one of the most important indicators in an enterprise's plan. The relationship between profit and fixed assets is also designed to promote efficiency, since both these magnitudes are now under double state control. The capital goods tax as well as profits, calculated on the same basis, oblige an enterprise to keep capital assets as low as possible. The aberrant situation in which capital-intensive goods were usually undervalued was to be abolished.

The emphasis placed on investment goods in the planned economies is a consequence of the chronically low capital efficiency and the enormous stockpiles, whose yearly growth sometimes exceeds more than 10 percent of all created value. In the planned economies, economic categories still function rather primitively. This is true for production price and capital profits, for example. There exists no rational, theoretically grounded, or empirically ascertainable relation between profit and capital investment; but neither is there any autonomously operating interplay between the individual components of the economic system.

The new conceptions of prices and profits vary from country to country in their practical implementation as well.

Two modes of price formation have emerged, which differ in the term of reference used to determine the profit rate: (a) profit rate based only on enterprise capital (fixed and working capital), or (b) profit rate related also to actual costs of production or at least to their wage component.

The first, called a system of "pure production prices," is used in Bulgaria, the German Democratic Republic, and the Soviet Union; the second, a mixed system, is used in Poland, Czechoslovakia, and Hungary.

It is not how price formation works technically, but the mechanism it sets into motion, that is the decisive factor in determining the range over and extent to which the new price model functions. It could function in the traditional economic model as well, but then it would be reduced to a purely technical and organizational instrument of central economic planning — only the refinement in distribution it made possible, not its economic function, would show up. A production price can also be built into a decentralized economic model; in such a case it would form an organic component of the economic mechanism it set into motion.

A clear distinction may be drawn between the function of production price in the centralized economy of the Soviet Union and the other Eastern European countries, on the one hand, and the function it plays in the decentralized model operating in Hungary, on the other.

8.2.1. Production Price in a Centralized Economic Model

Production price and the capital-related profit concept built into the centralized model are first and foremost refined planning and administrative techniques intended to improve the utilization of enterprise assets. A component of the market has been introduced in the planned economies; however, the mechanism that is an inseparable aspect of this component has not been set into motion.[45] The enterprise itself is only one part of a single huge state corporation, and the state still controls its earnings. The way profits are distributed has been modified, however, and the individual enterprise has been given more powers. First, the tax for using enterprise assets is paid along with other taxation payments to the state budget, and the portion of profits remaining constitute a reserve fund for pre-

47

mium payments, social services, and investments. But the state, not the individual enterprise or its association, controls the remainder of the profits. Of the total profits of Soviet industry in 1973, 41 percent was placed at the disposal of enterprises (in 1965, only 29 percent); of this, 16 percent went for the formation of premium reserve funds, 12 percent for investment purposes, and 13 percent for other business affairs. The remaining 59 percent was paid to the state budget (71 percent in 1965), 20 percent as assets tax and 32 percent as residual profits[46] that, because of distribution regulations, could neither be left to the enterprise nor paid into the state budget in another form.

The relation between production price and the centralized, though somewhat reformed, economic model is easy to perceive: the individual enterprise has been allowed to keep relatively more of its earnings for investments and premium funds than previously, but the state has not loosened its control of the allocation of earnings. Indeed, a more effective allocation system than before has been achieved, since a good portion of enterprise earnings is extracted by the state in the form of a capital goods tax which is independent of actual earnings. The state also controls the final apportionment of profits, for even the portion that has not been allocated is paid to it. An enterprise receives no more than officially established norms allow.

The new concept of price and profit has been made part of the same traditional centralized system, albeit somewhat modified, instead of serving as an instrument for creating a qualitatively new system.

8.2.2. Production Price in a Decentralized Model

We shall be speaking here primarily of the Hungarian economic model introduced in 1968. In this model, production price is regarded as an organic component of a decentralized economic model that gives increasing room to the market mechanism.[47] The difference is that in Hungary production price, together with all the other mechanisms of the economy, form an integral economic package; sights have been set on transition from a system of centrally fixed prices to a flexible price mechanism. At the micro level, in fact, enterprises have been granted the right to set prices for some products.[48] The aim is to create conditions under which the forint can function as a uniform measure of value. The discrepancy between the relative overpricing of consumer goods and the relatively low prices of means of production, conceded to have been built into the system, is gradually to be overcome.

The goal of the reforms was kept within bounds set by existing conditions. It is accepted that, during the current phase, the forint will continue to be inconvertible into hard currencies. For this reason, no direct relation between the internal price structure and foreign prices was established by way of exchange rates, nor has any effort been made to achieve a complete equilibrium between the supply and the demand. A bridge between internal and foreign price relations has been fashioned, however, initially on the basis of the fixed conversion coefficients for the forint and later on the basis of exchange rates corresponding better to real conditions.[49] Furthermore, sights are set on a price system that will be able to adjust to the shifting relations among foreign currencies and to accommodate continuously to costs without immoderate budget subsidies. Although this may not always be successful — due among other things to imported inflation — Hungary still has managed to establish a more flexible price system now than have the other Eastern countries.

8.2.3. The Profit Component in Hungarian Production Prices

The Hungarian system, however, still has retained most of the basic principles of a planned economy. Profit is still not profit in the market sense; it continues to be set centrally. In the quest for a maximally effective criterion for measuring profit, the relation between the cost of wages and the value of the means of production employed was hit upon. The principal difference between this system and a highly centralized model, however, lies in the fact that in Hungary it is the enterprise

that essentially controls profit accrued; the actual way in which
profits are defined is secondary. The state budget still receives
its assigned share, but the remainder is left wholly to the disposal of the enterprise. To give investment more flexibility,
enterprises have also been granted strong powers of decision
over their investment ventures; and to make financing possible,
a larger portion of profits is left in the hands of the enterprises.

The set-profit rate in Hungary is about half that in the Soviet
Union, because, among other reasons, in Hungary enterprises
must pay the state for all goods received from the state, for
land, for water, and so on, which is not the case in the Soviet Union.

The relation of profit rate to enterprise assets is highly differentiated: the overall average for industry is 6.5 percent but
the share varies, amounting to 1.6 percent in mining, 2.5 percent in power production, 3.4 percent in the iron and steel industry, 9.5 percent in the chemical industry, 9.2 percent in
light industry, 9.8 percent in machine construction, and 5.6 percent in the foodstuffs industry.[50]

8.2.4. Modifications of the Price Structure

Prices gradually are being released from the function they
served in the old system, namely, as an instrument for the distribution of income — a function for which they are unsuited.
A prime target, however, is to eliminate the price differential
between the consumer goods sector and heavy industry. Turnover tax is paid by the trade organizations, instead of by the
consumer goods industry as formerly, and now constitutes only
a negligible share of total accumulation (profit + tax). The
share of turnover tax in total revenue to the state budget was
reduced from 53 percent in 1965 to 7 percent the first year after
the reforms went into effect.[51]

As the initial groundwork toward establishing an economic
basis for price formation, an ideal price was fashioned, defined
as actual production costs plus a supplement (12 percent of the
cost of wages + 10 percent of the value of plant).

A comparison of prereform and postreform prices (1965 and

1968) with the ideal price shows how far the economic reform reshuffled the price structure: prices for the products of heavy industry, which before the reform were 40 percent undervalued, are 10 percent above the "ideal" price, on the average; prices for light industry were 5 percent lower than the 1956 level, but still 15 percent over the fictitious price; prices for foodstuffs, which were 30 percent undervalued in 1956 if turnover tax is left out of account, were only 6 percent lower than the fictitious price after the reform; finally, agricultural prices were still 17 percent undervalued after the 1968 reform.

For some products actual prices are considerably lower than the fictitious price: coal, 45 percent; meat, milk, bakery goods, and so on, 10-30 percent; rents, 70 percent; tobacco and beverages, 20-50 percent.

The reformers were quite aware that the price system could not be transformed overnight; accordingly, the goal was set at bringing consumer prices into equilibrium within 10 to 15 years. Until that time, subsidies would be granted for some products, while others would be burdened with above-average taxes. The turnover tax was retained for the most part only for monopoly products (alcoholic beverages and tobacco) and a few others, mainly luxury and semiluxury items, and was to serve as the source of financing subsidies for consumer goods that required supports. Eventually, however, both were to be eliminated. So far, unfortunately, no reductions have occurred because of a worsening in the terms of trade, and in fact subsidies have had to be increased in some cases. To counteract this trend, price rises were instituted in early 1976.

8.2.5. Liberalization of Price Formation

The outstanding characteristic of the Hungarian price system — the feature that really identifies it as a mechanism of a decentralized economy — is the liberalization of pricing, especially for foods. Prices for foodstuffs are set centrally for only 31 percent of the total turnover; ceiling prices are fixed for 29 percent of the turnover; prices are steered by the state for

27 percent; and prices are set freely by the producer or vendor for 13 percent.

In trade between enterprises — especially in the energy sector — prices are mostly fixed (75 percent) or else ceiling prices are set centrally. In the chemical industry and machine building, prices are arrived at freely by the trading partners themselves for 35 to 65 percent of the total trade volume.

Although the somewhat decentralized economic system in Hungary might be said to create better preconditions for prices to regain their economic function than does a centralized system, one must still take into account the fact that either system can lead to a simplification of the price-forming procedure. Both systems are homogeneous. Hungary's price structure is shaped autonomously,[52] without organic interplay between the forint exchange rate and world market prices, although the latter have been allowed greater influence than before. On the other hand, the system in Poland or the German Democratic Republic could be described neither as highly centralized nor as decentralized.

In any planned economy, budget subsidies will always be an alternative to cost-covering prices, and supply shortfalls an alternative to equilibrium prices.

Although Schumpeter was undoubtedly right when he said that accounting at the enterprise level was logically possible in a planned economy,[53] compromise with political priorities will always be necessary. The planned economy, which has placed principled restrictions on the traditional economic process, has so far been unable to create an adequate price system that, by creating an equivalence between prices and value in every area, could serve as an effective instrument of internal accounting and clearing with the state and hence as a reliable parameter for choosing between alternative paths of development.[54] A few connecting links between plan and market have not been enough to create harmony between quantity and value as envisioned by the Czech economist Soukop. Not only is there no self-contained price system adequate to the needs of a planned economy, the planned economies have so far been unable to develop a model

The Price System

that would fit the present state of development.

Although their price systems are more stable than those in market economies, the discrepancies brought about by inherent instability, which persists despite all measures to combat it, are no fewer — they just take on different forms.

NOTES

1. "A unit of labor in one form is transformed into the same amount of labor in another form." K. Marx, Kritik des Gothaer Programms, 4th ed., East Berlin, 1965, p. 23.

2. "We have seen that the economic process can determine only price relations, not absolute prices." J. A. Schumpeter, Das Wesen des Geldes, Göttingen-Wandenhoeck and Ruprecht, 1970, p. 258.

3. Prices must say something if Garvy's position is correct: "The extent to which planners may want to use changes in retail or wholesale prices (or both) as a means of shifting resources, is a matter of strategic choice in which political considerations as well as the cost of alternative courses of action (including enforcement) enter." G. Garvy, "Price Stabilization Policies in Some Eastern European Countries," Tenth International Seminar, Venice, August 29-31, 1974, p. 11.

4. M. Pohorille, "Funkcje ceny i warunki działania ich systemu" [Price Functions and Their Conditions of Operation], Życie gospodarcze, August 3, 1975, p. 11.

5. This thesis was argued in detail by Stalin in his book Economic Problems of Socialism in the USSR (1951).

6. From the proceedings of the Twenty-fifth Congress of the CPSU.

7. From the speech of the prime minister at the Twenty-fifth Congress of the CPSU.

8. "In the socialist countries, the conditions of production — known to varying degrees — distribution, and commodity exchange are taken as the basis for price setting, not the value of money, which could be determined automatically by comparing the values of goods." Z. Fedorowicz, Podstawy teorii pieniądza w gospodarce socjalistycznej [Basic Principles of Monetary Theory in a Socialist Economy], Warsaw, 1975, p. 104.

9. Price paid by the state to the manufacturer.

10. See Monatsberichte des Öster. Inst. f. Wirtschaftsforschung, 1/1976, p.42.

11. Narodnoe khoziaistvo, 1973, p. 253.

12. "Payment for labor to those employed in production reflects only a portion of the value created by the labor power employed. The rest constitutes surplus value" (also called product for society as a whole). Z. Fedorowicz, Finanse w gospodarce socialistycznej [Finance in a Socialist Economy], Warsaw, 1970, p. 198.

13. Ibid.

Money, Banking, and Credit

14. The turnover tax has some of the characteristics of cost — it is levied on enterprise earnings independent of the product — but at the same time it functions as an instrument for eliminating enterprise surplus (surplus value) since through its prescription the actual profit, every bit of which must be transferred to the state, is kept at a low level.

15. Narodnoe khoziaistvo SSSR, 1973, p. 763.

16. The profit accruing to a factory from the sale of goods to another does not expand the supply of money at the disposal of the state. T. Kierczynski and U. Wojciechowska, Finanse przedsiebiorstw socjalistycznych [The Financing of Socialist Enterprises], Warsaw, 1973, p. 30.

17. For instance, a textbook edited by V. V. Lavrov states: "A society's net income is created in all spheres of material production. However, depending on the existing system of price formation, a portion of the net income of some branches of industry is realized in the commodity prices of others. Through the turnover tax, which is collected on foods and the products of light industry, the portion of net income obtained from the manufacture of means of production is also transferred to the state budget." Finansy i kredit SSSR [Finance and Credit in the USSR], Moscow, 1972, p. 152.

18. In Poland, for example, the coal mines clear their above-average profits or deficits resulting from above or below average conditions with the sales organization of the coal industry. The negative differences are financed by the positive differences, and the total excess or total deficit is transferred to the state budget or covered by it. Until 1960, the coal industry as a whole was operating at a deficit. During 1957-61 every coal mine received a budget subsidy from 22 to 769 zlotys per ton. See Kierczynski and Wojciechowska, op. cit., p. 71.

19. Plant capacity and raw materials, auxiliary materials, and fuels.

20. Professor H. Raupach says on this point: "In view of the general indeterminacy of the Soviet price system, all that exists is a pragmatic approximation of prices to costs." System der Sowjetwirtschaft, 1968, Munich, p. 138.

21. This conception is still used today in the Eastern nations as the basis for calculating the gross national product, which does not take into account nonmaterial services.

22. A. Bergson: "The industrial enterprise is charged systematically for labor, materials and depreciation on fixed capital, but not for rent for material resources." See The Economics of Soviet Planning, New Haven and London, Yale University Press, 1964, p. 166.

23. See D. Walowoj, "O planowym vykorzystaniu stosunków towarowo — pienieznych" [Planned Utilization of the Commodity-Money Relationship], Życie gospodarcze, August 11, 1977.

24. "Up to now, our [Soviet] prices have been constructed on the basis of a formula of average value." V. V. Novozhilov, "Problems of Planned Pricing and the Reform of Industrial Management," in Socialist Economics, edited by Alec Nove and D. M. Nuti, 1972, p. 388.

25. S. Sitarian, Chistii dokhod i biudzhet [Net Income and State Budget], Moscow, 1964, p. 153.

26. Rocznik statystyczny, 1975, p. 160.

27. See Raupach, op. cit., p. 141.

28. Alec Nove: "These were confiscatory prices, or a species of hardly disguised tax in kind." The Soviet Economy, New York and Washington, 1969, p. 153.

29. Ibid., pp. 113, 153.

30. Raupach, op. cit., p. 147.

31. A. Bergson observes rightly: "Where the open market prevails for consumer goods, prices ideally are such as to limit demand for each product to available supplies." Op. cit., p. 53.

32. M. Kasers has the following opinion on this: "Evidently, if they do not exercise their power to vary prices, they are faced with the alternatives of changing quantities offered at retail or tolerating maladjustment, i.e., a non-concordance of real and money flows exhibited in lengthening queues, and frustrated shoppers for some goods...." Soviet Economics, New York and Toronto, 1970, p. 124.

33. Sovetskaia torgovlia, Moscow, 1957.

34. See DDR-Wirtschaft, Berlin, Deutsches Institut für Wirtschaftsforschung (DIW), 1974, p. 250-251.

35. See Adam Marton, Consumer Prices in Austria and Hungary 1945-1972, Wiener Institut für Internationale Wirtschaftsvergleiche, December 1974, pp. 87-98.

36. Marx considered the production price as a modified form of the market price. It is formed by approximating enterprise profits to the average profitability of capital throughout the economy as a whole. See Marx, Das Kapital, Vol. III, 7th ed., East Berlin, 1959, Chaps. 9-12.

37. J. Schumpeter rightly observes: "Income formation there (in the socialist community) is not tied to the price formation of productive services, but since this is the only tie which gives prices some quantitative definition in an economy based on private property, income formation is indeterminate in a socialist society." Op. cit., p. 88.

38. "The interest is supposed to help ensure that enterprise funds are used effectively. But at the same time it is also a means to redistribute profit and a stable source for budget revenue. This source may now be planned on the basis of the production fund, which varies only negligibly over time." Finansy i kredit SSSR, p. 165-166.

39. "The interest burden on enterprise funds is a kind of fee (tax) which the enterprise must pay to the state for the use of social property." Kierczynski and Wojciechowska, op. cit., p. 91.

40. See Reform of the Economic Mechanism in Hungary, Budapest, 1969, p. 143.

41. Narodnoe khoziaistvo SSSR, 1973, p. 764.

42. Rocznik statystyczny, 1975, p. 502.

43. Reform of the Economic Mechanism in Hungary, p. 136.

44. Kierczynski and Wojciechowska, op. cit., p. 95.

45. P. Samuelson interprets this reform as follows: "The Soviets are moving a small step toward reconciliation with the economic tools of modern analysis.

Money, Banking, and Credit

This is not meant to suggest in the least that the Russians are turning to capitalistic enterprise systems.".... "Rather the notions of scarcity, production cost, substitution and resource allocation have to be objectively regarded as fundamentals in almost any economic system." Economics, 8th ed., New York, 1971, p. 828.

46. Narodnoe khoziaistvo SSSR, 1973, p. 764.

47. Thus Csikós-Nagy observes: "It was part of the general form concerning the system of economic control that intended to improve efficiency as a condition of quicker development by relying on the market mechanism." In Reform of the Economic Mechanism in Hungary, p. 133.

48. Csikós-Nagy says: "[The price reform of 1968] was no simple price adjustment but also a transition from the system of officially set prices to a more flexible price mechanism accounting for market conditions." Ibid., p. 134.

49. On January 1, 1976, the official forint exchange rate was raised from 8.51 to the dollar to 41.35 to the dollar, equaling the former conversion factor.

50. See Csikós-Nagy, op. cit., p. 146.

51. See ibid., p. 136.

52. Csikós-Nagy, the price architect, said at a speech at the International Seminar in Venice, August 29-31, 1974: "The price reform did not change the administrative price system into a market price system."

53. "Thus we see that rational economic accounting is the primary prerequisite for rational economic management, and in a socialist society is not only logical, but thoroughly possible...." J. Schumpeter, op. cit., p. 104.

54. "To create the preconditions for a price system that would perform the economic functions of prices is a task which must be solved at the present stage of development," says Czech economist P. Soukup, "In What Direction Must Our Efforts Be Directed to Perfect the Price System?" See Hospodarske noviny, November 14, 1975.

Chapter 3

ARE THE PLANNED ECONOMIES
SHIELDED FROM INFLATION?

1. The Monetary System and Inherent Inflationary Tendencies

In any economy inflation, regardless of the form it takes, is
a kind of adulteration of the value of money. In antiquity and the
Middle Ages, when the noble metals were the major form of
money in circulation, inflation resulted from the debasement of
coin; in modern industrial society, it has been caused by rising
prices and hence a decline in purchasing power.

Whether the result of deliberate intent or elemental market
forces, inflation is always undesirable both socially and economically, even though it may temporarily stimulate economic
growth and help bring about full employment. It is no accident,
then, that the term "inflation" is absent from the official jargon
of the planned economies, for its existence is not recognized.
Although it is not denied that signs of inflation do occur despite
planning, it is stressed again and again that nonfulfillment of the
plan target is exclusively responsible, the argument being that
a decline would never be deliberately planned in a socialist
country.

In fact, if inflation is measured in terms of price rises, official theory is correct for, with the exception of Yugoslavia, not
even relatively low inflation rates such as occurred in the Federal Republic of Germany and Austria were recorded in the
East, to say nothing of the inflation rates in Italy or Great Britain. (In Yugoslavia, with its decentralized planned economy,
the inflation rate was 22.5 percent in 1974 and 23.0 percent in

1975, among the highest rates in Europe. But Yugoslavia's economy is largely decentralized, and enterprises must make their way competitively.)

But even the highly centralized planned economies are not shielded from inflation, although economic factors such as production — including production of consumer goods — income of the population, prices, and the money supply are all planned and mechanisms are operative that are supposed to ensure equilibrium. There is, after all, no perfect plan able to make all components of economic activity work together harmoniously, and no ideal mechanisms that can ensure optimal plan fulfillment.[1] In actuality, however, it is the particular conception of development which has existed in the East that has been the major cause of chronic disequilibrium.

Long years of experience have demonstrated without doubt that, although price rises may be smaller in the planned economies than in market economies, the former have not been any more successful in achieving equilibrium. The state has greater influence in the economic process and therefore may be able to disguise disequilibrium in different forms, but its impact on the population is just as great.

Thus factors other than price rises, apparently inherent to the system, also work to cause inflation in the East; but, in addition, the monetary system in the East operates under far more constraints than in the West, giving disequilibrium other forms and other dimensions.

Money is used far less in dealings between enterprises than on the consumer market. An individual enterprise cannot have a surplus of money, nor can it use its liquid funds however and for whatever purpose it wishes. The what, when, and how of production and the scope of economic activity in general are determined not by monetary processes but by plan targets, set by planning authorities, who also allocate capital goods. Therefore inflation, rather than extending throughout the entire economy, generally is confined to the consumer sector.

As the collective owner of social wealth, the state has greater control of budget inputs and expenditures and hence can better avoid budget deficits than in market economies. If a deficit occurs nonetheless, negative repercussions on the value of money can by and large be prevented. There is no economic or social partner with contrary interests whose demands the state must take into consideration.

Development priorities have institutionalized disequilibrium. For years they have determined the direction of growth and thus may, with full justification, be regarded as inherent to the system.

The plan target cannot eliminate the institutionalized causes of disequilibrium; indeed, it must take them into account and calculate them into the parameters for growth. Inevitable divergences from plan targets are not the cause of inflation but only one factor aggravating the inflationary tendencies already inherent in a planned economy.

Inflationary disequilibrium is fully apparent, if not always measurable, in a planned economy. As far as its impact on the population is concerned, whether inflation is a factor calculated into plan targets or a consequence of failure to meet them, makes no difference. It is important, however, to distinguish between factors inherent in the system and others that are only secondary and are not always calculable.

2. Disequilibrium Calculated into Plan Targets

Disequilibrium is rooted in a conception of development that, from the very beginning down to the present, has given priority to heavy industry, including armaments. Inevitably, as a result the population has had to suffer chronic shortages of vital goods.[2] This does not mean just that plan targets for consumer goods are set too low to meet growing needs; even more important is the fact that the priority given to heavy industry has determined the overall structure of the economy. The plans for heavy industry are more realistic, and it can count on better supply of the means of production than can the consumer goods industry.

Time and again, during periods of relatively smooth functioning or acute supply difficulties, the resolve is expressed to put an end to the lopsided economic growth; but the traditional notion of development again wins out in the end, as is shown quite clearly by the 1976-80 Soviet five-year plan.

In no other economic system in history, or in the world today, has growth fetishism assumed such broad dimensions as in the planned economies. One-sided growth with continual priority to heavy industry means also priority to investments over the needs of consumption. An inordinately high rate of investment has become an invariant feature of every planned economy, without exception.

This emphasis on heavy industry has another consequence as well: capital creation is much more intense in the Eastern bloc than in the West, as the following table shows. The figure for the German Democratic Republic (an average of 28.7 percent for 1971 to 1975) is rather low compared to those for the other Eastern bloc countries.

Relation of Capital Creation to
Nominal Gross National Product

Country	1973	1974	1975
		%	
USSR	29.2	29.9	31.1
Bulgaria	34.1	35.4	32.4*
Poland	35.9	39.8	41.6
Romania	36.2	36.5	39.7
Hungary	34.1	34.5	n.a.
Federal Republic of Germany	24.6	22.5	25.7
Great Britain	19.5	20.1	20.4
Sweden	21.9	22.0	21.3
USA	18.2	17.5	19.3

Sources: Eastern countries: Economic Survey of Europe, United Nations, 1976, Table 3; Western countries: Monthly Bulletin of Statistics, United Nations, May 1976, pp. 191-197, 1975 estimates.
*Plan.

Priorities in production mean parallel priorities in investment. In the five-year period from 1966 to 1970, 5.6 rubles (and in 1973 as much as 6.2 rubles) were invested in Soviet heavy industry for each ruble invested in the consumer goods industry.[3]

The priority given to heavy industry and the burden of lop-

sided investments have been dictated by high defense spending,
a policy point from the outset and perhaps the main reason for
the disproportionate growth that has made inflation an inherent
feature of the planned economies. Defense spending is considerable — which is only to be expected, since the Soviet Union
must compete in this domain with the greatest economic power
in the world, the United States. The official figures for defense
spending were 17.9 billion rubles (about $24 billion); this amount
has remained constant since 1970, representing a little less than
10 percent of the Soviet budget and only 3.7 percent of the nominal gross national product; there is no evidence, however, that
actual expenditures on defense are less in the Soviet Union than
in the USA, where in 1975-76 they ran to $112 billion — an amount
totaling more than 16 percent of the nominal gross national product
of the Soviet Union (corrected by the Western criterion to $699
billion).[4] Some Western experts estimate defense expenditures
of the Soviet Union at 13-15 percent of the gross national product, corrected by the Western criterion of measurement.

The per capita nominal gross national product is $2,110 in the
Soviet Union,[5] that is, less than one-third the figure for the USA
($7,020), where defense spending amounts to 7.5 percent of the
national product.

The reason for shortages of consumer goods is not difficult
to see considering this overemphasis on heavy industry and defense, which absorbs most of invested capital and means of production. The general purchasing power of the population at
large can find no outlet on the inadequately supplied consumer
market. The gap between supply and demand has become a
hallmark of the planned economies because of this excessively
high growth rate in heavy industry as compared with the consumer goods industry.

In the five-year period from 1966 to 1970, growth in the foodstuffs industry amounted to 54 percent in Bulgaria, 57 percent
in Czechoslovakia, 69 percent in the German Democratic Republic, 31 percent in Poland, 53 percent in Romania, 71 percent
in Hungary, and 67 percent in the USSR (where total industrial
growth = 100).[6] The increase in food supply was definitely not
great enough to satisfy the increased purchasing power. This

discrepancy has been greatest in Poland, and toward the end of the five-year period attempts were made to plug the inflationary gaps by means of the usual market methods — that is, price increases. The uprisings on the Baltic put a stop to these attempts, and the supply and demand gap has remained.

These sharp differences diminished to some degree in the Soviet Union in the five-year period from 1971 to 1975: the ratio of the growth rates in heavy industry to that in the consumer goods industry was 1:0.87 in 1974 and 1:0.82 in 1975; this trend will not continue, however, and in 1976 the ratio will be only 1:0.55, while by 1980 the share of consumer goods in total industrial production will amount to only 24 percent.[7] The five-year plan for 1976-80, issued by the Fifteenth Party Congress of Czechoslovakia, provides for a growth rate of 58-51 percent for heavy industry but only 25 percent for the consumer goods industry.

Steering mechanisms are unable, as on a free market, to adjust supply to demand on the basis of prices and profits. All the mechanisms in operation favor heavy industry: the most highly skilled and best paid workers are employed in this industry, and it is given priority in deliveries of scarce capital goods. Plan fulfillment is also pushed more vigorously in heavy industry than in the other sectors. The consumer goods sector experiences more frequent divergences from plan targets, since not only is it placed in a disadvantageous position by the planning authorities, but it is also vulnerable to the effects of poor performance in the agricultural sector.

3. Disequilibrium as a Consequence of Deviation from the Plan Target

It is an oversimplification, of course, to divide inflationary factors into two groups, those that are automatically calculated into the plan target and those that are caused by deviations from it. Indeed, rather than determining the economic process, the plan hobbles along in its footsteps.

The economic structures that have evolved in the Eastern

countries are now firmly rooted in reality. No one-year or five-year plans can make any basic changes in them. Only a radical shift in the notion of what economic development means could effect a fundamental change in the present economic situation, and nothing of the sort can be expected in the foreseeable future. For the present, both plan targets and deviations from them are here to stay.

Agriculture affords a good example of how misleading the artificial distinctions between different kinds of inflationary factors can often be. During the initial period of consolidation of Soviet power, the task of agriculture was to finance rapid industrialization; to do this, it had to deliver its planned quotas at prices that were far below the actual costs of production. Forced collectivization had the same goal. Although prices for agricultural products have risen steadily since the fifties, agriculture in the Soviet Union — and in other Eastern bloc countries as well — has grown much more slowly than its elementary needs would require. Countries like the Soviet Union and Poland which once exported grain, today are net importers.

The insufficient growth rate in the consumer goods industries have causes rooted in the system; it makes no difference whether they are planned too high or too low. In addition, they are probably more inflationary than other factors of economic development. Deviations from plan targets are probably greater in agriculture than in any other sector of the economy, since the targets set for agriculture reflect actual needs more than concrete possibilities.

The wide gap between the overall economic growth rate and that for agriculture for the years 1971 to 1975 are shown in the following table.

Annual Growth Rates (in percent)

	Bulgaria	GDR*	Poland	Romania	Hungary	Czechoslovakia	USSR
Gross national product	7.9	5.4	9.7	11.2	6.3	5.7	5.6
Agriculture	2.1	2.4	3.2	4.6	3.4	2.9	2.5

Source: Economic Survey of Europe 1976, Table 1.1.
*Plan.

The harvest failure in the Soviet Union in 1975 (a short-fall of more than one-third of the planned target) hit the population especially hard, although 16 million tons of grain were imported. The relatively high percentage of agricultural workers among the total number of employed (Soviet Union, 25.2 percent; Bulgaria, 31.5 percent; Poland, 34.6 percent; Romania, 42.1 percent; Hungary, 24.4 percent) is one of the reasons that harvest failures, all too frequent, shift the apportionment of the meager yields in favor of the rural population (the peasants keep relatively more for their own use) and disrupt supply to the town more than usual. The German Democratic Republic and Czechoslovakia enjoy a relatively more favorable position, with 11.5 percent and 15.9 percent of the working population, respectively, engaged in agriculture, though they too have been forced to import grain.[8]

The United States is a good example of what a developed agricultural sector can do: it was able to provide the Soviet Union with 30 million tons of grain in 1972-73 and 26 million tons in 1975-76, although the share of its population employed in agriculture is only one-sixth of the figure for the Soviet Union.

The inherent weaknesses of the system make it especially difficult to adjust supply to demand in this very sensitive area, which more than any other needs the stimulus of the market to right itself. The trends and mechanisms that operate are rooted in the system and tied to the plan, and the most important equilibrating instrument — prices — are tardy in their effect, if indeed they have any effect at all. Between producer and consumer stands the state with its priorities.

Delays in getting new investment projects into operation because of the long time required to produce plant and equipment are also inflationary factors. The annual report for the Twenty-fifth Party Congress of the CPSU tells us that the target for new production capacities completed and in operation was only 60 to 80 percent fulfilled in the 1971-75 five-year period.

During the period from 1970 to 1974, the production time needed for plant in Poland was 2.6 to 14.4 percent higher than planned. Losses from delays in getting new plant into operation amounted to 8.5 billion zlotys during this period.[9]

From 1970 through 1973, the total value of unfinished projects in the Soviet Union rose steadily from 52.5 to 67.1 billion rubles because of delays in starting. This averaged 75 percent of the total sum invested annually during this period.[10]

Since new investment projects are begun regardless of the state of unfinished projects, the sum of funds invested is always higher than provided in the plan, since outlays for projects still uncompleted are not taken into account in the new plans.

The excess purchasing power generated by new investment projects widens the gap between supply and demand.

An analogous negative factor affecting equilibrium is the excessive stockpiling, which — like its opposite, chronic shortages — has become a hallmark of the planned economies. Hoarding is a way to get around shortages. Neither the stiff lending terms nor high interest rates are able to alter this situation at all. Ways are always found to circumvent the meager allocations of the planning authorities.[11]

The value of accumulated stocks in proportion to total value created is excessively high in the Soviet Union: for the years from 1970 to 1973, it amounted to 11.4 percent, 10.9 percent, 9.6 percent, and 10.9 percent. During this period stockpiles grew by 133.7 billion rubles, a figure 2.8 times as high as the growth of gross national product for this period.[12]

In Poland's state sector, stockpiles grew in value by 14.4 percent, 5.8 percent, 9.8 percent, and 15.5 percent for the years 1971 to 1974. At the end of 1974, the value of Poland's industrial stockpiles (356 billion zlotys) was 20 percent of the total industrial production for that year. The growth in stockpiles amounted to 6 percent of the gross national product in 1970 and had risen to 8.8 percent by 1974.[13]

In Czechoslovakia, stockpiles at year's end constituted 63 percent (230 billion koruny) of the gross national product for 1973.[14] Turnover time was 77 days for raw materials, 26 days for semifinished goods, and 103 days overall — much too long.[15]

The inordinate pileups summarize all that is wrong with planning and all the disproportionalities in plan fulfillment. It is the consumer, however, who is most adversely affected. Moreover, the system itself acts as an obstacle to eliminating these disproportionalities. A large part of these stores could find buyers, if the price mechanism was made more elastic.

4. The Importation of Inflation

Csikós-Nagy rated the role of external factors in price rises in Hungary at 45 percent in industrial production, 18 percent in agriculture, and 8 percent in the consumer goods industry for 1968 through 1973.[16] Thirty percent of the price rises were covered by state subsidies in 1972, and 60 percent in 1973. Losses due to increased prices for imported goods (including those originating within the CMEA) were 6 percent of the national gross product in 1974 and 9 percent in 1975.[17]

In Czechoslovakia, the increase in world market prices caused losses of 4.5 billion koruny in 1973, which was 29 percent of the value of imports from the West. In 1974, losses due to price rises were 8 billion koruny.[18]

In Poland, import prices rose 8.8 percent in 1973 and 16.9 percent in 1974. Imported grain cost 70 percent as much in 1974 as in 1971, fodder almost twice as much, wool 90 percent as much, and leather 120 percent as much. In terms of quantity, 43 percent more grain was imported in 1974 than in 1971, although the amount paid was 125 percent higher.[19]

In 1974, the Soviet Union paid 41 percent more for steel, 42 percent more for pipeline, 171 percent more for chemical products, and 45 percent more for grain than in the previous year.

Although the unfavorable terms of trade have only slight influence, if any, on internal prices, they are still inflationary. Larger budget subsidies than contemplated must be provided, and the ailing payments balance requires a tightening of imports, with consumer goods being the first affected.

We have not attempted a complete inventory of inflationary factors; we have wished merely to point out that inordinate cost increases are also inflationary, since they are due mainly to rising wages, which are not matched by a commensurate increase in supply to absorb the added purchasing power thus created (18 percent of Soviet factories did not meet their profit target for the preceding five-year period). Even perfect planning — which, of course, is impossible — could not eliminate the imbalances inherent in the system, since they are a consequence of the prevailing conception of development and the economic structures it has created. Prices neither reflect the degree of actual inflation, nor act as a safety valve for systematic tensions on the market. In all probability, disequilibrium could largely be remedied by planning a sufficient supply, as Csikós-Nagy correctly states. But before this can happen, the present notion of development must be changed, and the economic structures emended accordingly. If this were to happen — that is, if the stress on heavy industry and defense were lessened, and correspondingly greater effort was invested in the consumer goods industry — tensions on the market, not only in the Eastern bloc but the world over, could be eased considerably.

5. Inflation and the Capital Goods Market

Inflation shows up in a variety of ways in a planned economy, since price rises do not eliminate disproportionalities. In contrast to the way things are in a market economy, price increases, especially in the capital goods industry, are the result not of a gap between supply and demand (demand pull), but of a cost push. In a restrictive distributive economy, where excess demand is an inherent feature, it would in fact be meaningless to try to eliminate this excess demand by raising prices. A measure of this sort has meaning only if enterprises can choose among alternative sources of supply. Then the price mechanism can be used to induce firms — to the extent they can act autonomously — to employ new, more advanced materials instead of traditional ones.

The rapid increases, which have been quite abrupt in some cases, have their origins not only in growing production costs, as mentioned above, but also in gradual abandonment of the traditional notion of the distributive function of prices. This conception of prices had given birth to a chaotic price structure with relatively low prices for capital goods subsidized by the budget.

The principal reason for increasing costs is the growing view that low incomes are not conducive to efficiency over the long term. An attempt was made to escape from the vicious circle of low wages for low productivity by importing technical progress, raising wages, and in some cases reforming the steering model. These trends continue, however, to one degree or another, in all the planned economies. A few figures from Soviet statistics offer confirmation. In 1950, the real monthly average wage was 64.2 rubles, while it was 146.0 rubles in 1975. In the five-year period from 1950 to 1955, the average wage increased by only 11.8 percent; during 1955-60 it rose by 12.3 percent; but over the next three five-year periods it grew by 19.7 percent, 26.4 percent, and 19.7 percent, respectively.[20]

In the planned economies, price rises do not parallel rising costs. Price changes are sporadic and usually occur in connection with other, more radical economic reforms. In the Soviet Union the first price reform in the capital goods industry after World War II was instituted on January 1, 1949. Wholesale prices were increased by 58 percent to cover, at least partially, the cost rises that had occurred during the war. The next comprehensive price reform took place in 1967; wholesale prices were increased by 9 percent (in heavy industry, by 17.5 percent). On January 1, 1973, wholesale prices in light industry were increased by 8 percent, while prices in machinery and equipment were reduced by 8 percent. Price rises were considerable in the other industrial branches between 1948 and 1973: 371 percent in coal mining, 399 percent in the lumber industry, 142 percent in iron and steel, 123 percent in the cellulose and paper industry, 350 percent in construction materials, and so on.[21]

Prices have moved more closely in line with costs in the other Eastern countries as well. A major price reform was introduced in Czechoslovakia in 1966. But in 1974 the average price index for industry as a whole was only 6.4 percent higher than before the reform. Major price increases have occurred

in the iron industry (46.3 percent), construction materials industry (21.0 percent), leather and footwear industries (11.4 percent), and textile industry (9.9 percent).[22] The next price reform
was carried out on January 1, 1976. Prices for raw materials
were raised by 62 percent. Still, price levels overall remained
essentially unchanged, since prices were raised for 41 percent
of industrial goods but lowered for 59 percent.

An ambitious price reform was instituted in Hungary in 1959
in the capital goods industry. Its purpose was to set more realistic prices for imported goods and gradually eliminate budget subsidies to factories operating at a loss. Csikós-Nagy,
architect of this reform, claimed that it relieved the disproportionalities that had arisen in the period from 1952 to 1958.[23]
Again, however, the reform was limited to adjustments in a few
branches of industry. The overall wholesale price index in Hungary has risen only negligibly: it grew by 1.1 percent in 1953,
0.8 percent in 1954, 0.6 percent in 1955, and 0.2 percent in
1956; over the decade 1957-67, it rose by an average of 4.4 percent annually and during 1968-73 by 2.7 percent annually.[24]

In all cases, however, reform has been limited to the adjustment of price levels, rather than the introduction of the market
price mechanism. The intention has been to adjust prices to
costs and render budget subsidies unnecessary. The instrument
of economic accounting (khozrashchet) has been perfected, but
profits in the capital goods industry still have not been promoted to the status of a price component. Planning authorities,
which still allocate capital goods, still control prices as well.
The internal price structure is still shielded for the most part
from foreign trade prices, even in cases where exporting and
importing firms have felt some of the impact of events on the
world market, as reflected in the use of conversion factors, and
where external prices are taken into consideration in setting
domestic prices (for example, in Poland and Hungary). As long
as there are no exchange rates, the automatic interplay between
domestic and external prices which exchange rates make possible, cannot exist. Price adjustments bear no relation to the
market type of inflation. The disproportionalities that inevita-

bly arise are remedied by the plan wherever possible; when this cannot be done, they are pushed further into the background.

6. The Consumer Market

Demand pull, in addition to cost push, contributes to inflation on the consumer market, although perhaps not as intensely. But consumer goods prices are still not equilibrium prices, even where attempts have been made to use prices as an instrument of equilibrium. Price increases on the consumer market have been steadier and more dramatic than those in the capital goods sector.

In the Soviet Union, the monetary reform of 1947 brought retail prices into line with costs, which had risen during the war. In 1950, the retail price index rose to 186 (prewar level in 1940 = 100), the food price index (excluding alcoholic beverages) to 133, alcoholic beverages to 258, and industrial consumer goods to 165. The price reductions of 1949-52 returned the overall index to 140. It changed little over the following years and measured 139 in 1975, although the prices of some goods, notably alcoholic beverages, had risen considerably.

The Soviet Union, however, places little importance on the equilibrium function of prices, and therefore price rises do not reflect the inflationary tensions that exist overall, as, for example, in the gap between prices on the free market and on the state market. Prices on the so-called kolkhoz markets are two and often three times as high as in the state stores. The discrepancy between supply and demand shows up in chronic shortages, queues, and under-the-counter sales (waiting time for a car is at least two years, and the price of a used car on the free market is at least twice as high as the price of a new car). The amount of time people lose and the extra money they must pay to obtain what they need are incalculable. Adjustments of prices to many changes in product grading or packaging — undertaken solely to effect a (concealed) price increase without improving quality — are likewise beyond estimation.

Signs of inflation are clearly visible, but they are reflected

in no statistics. It seems to have been decided that a tripling of
rents (which were especially low in the Soviet Union, covering
no more than one-third of the costs of maintenance and depreciation) was not enough to solve the severe housing problem,
just as a doubling of prices for some consumer goods was unable to bring the chronic undersupply in line with the ever growing and widening demand. The only solution is a fundamental
change in the prevailing conception of development and in the
political and economic steering mechanism.

The price mechanism is now being used more actively in other
Eastern countries to eliminate imbalance. In Poland retail
prices in 1974 were 21.5 percent higher than in 1960, and 5.9
percent higher than in the preceding year[25]; they rose by 5 percent in both 1975 and 1976. Prices for basic foods, including
meat, were frozen, which resulted in considerable supply shortages, especially in meat and meat products.[26] The December
13, 1970, price increases — from 36 to 50 zlotys for one kilogram of pork, from 26 to 40 zlotys for beef, from 40 to 60 zlotys
for veal, and so on — were rescinded by the new Party and
government leadership after the events on the Baltic coast on
February 28, 1971. The shortages were relieved for only a few
months, however; later they intensified again. Of course, meat
could be imported, or at least exports of better-quality meats
could be reduced. Nevertheless, since the balance of payments
deficit continued to be large and the import of capital goods still
took priority, there was a reluctance to lose the foreign market
for Polish meat products that had become established. Shortages were patently reflected in the long queues and empty meat
shops, and aptly captured by Polish humor in a number of jokes.[27]
The government arrived at the curious conclusion that it was
the consumer structure, not the supply structure, which was at
fault. Thus, the prime minister of the newly elected Sejm declared on March 28, 1976: "We will need price increases that
will enable us to adjust demand to the economic realities of today. A modified price structure should help to shape consumption more efficiently and counteract the pressure of demand for
foods whose supply can be increased only slowly owing to pro-

duction conditions.[28]

In Poland, where about three-fourths of agriculture is in private hands, the gap between prices on the state market and those on the private market is even more clearly manifest than in the other Eastern countries. Moreover, it can be measured statistically: in 1974 the prices for foods rose by 3.9 percent on the state market, while they rose by 18.2 percent on the free market, including 60.7 percent for vegetables and 15.2 percent for fruits. Price increases on the free market have affected the prices for services, which in Poland are mainly part of the private sector. Thus, in 1974 tailors' prices rose by 36.4 percent, shoemakers' by 22.0 percent, barbers' by 28.8 percent, and so on.[29]

The patent but price-frozen inflation in Poland is occurring in a period of economic growth propelled by high investment rates and above-average production of capital goods. Above-average increases in wages have also contributed to economic growth, although they have not been matched by sufficient rise in the production of consumer goods. The difference between the cost increases of the last five-year period and unchanged state prices for foods is financed by budget subsidies. The state supplements consumer spending with an annual average of 2,870 zlotys per capita. A retail shop buys one liter of milk for 3.60 to 4.0 zlotys, but sells it to the consumer for 2.90 zlotys. In 1976, the budget subsidy for milk was 1.45 billion zlotys, while for sugar it amounted to 5.6 billion zlotys.[30] Altogether, price subsidies totaled 165 billion zlotys in 1975.[31] The Polish leadership has finally come to realize that the damage caused by maintaining existing prices through large subsidies while the gap between supply and demand widens, is greater than its advantages.

On June 24, 1976, price increases of 69 percent for meat and meat products, 50 percent for dairy products, 100 percent for sugar, and so on, were announced. These increases were almost twice as great as those announced and then rescinded at the end of 1970. Popular discontent was just as great in 1976 as before, and the very next day the prime minister was obliged to cancel the scheduled rises for the present. At the same time, procurement prices were increased for wheat (40 percent), potatoes (20 to 30 percent), cattle (20.2 percent), swine (19.2 percent), and delivery prices rose for fodder (45 percent) and fertilizer (20 to 25 percent).[32]

Hungary would also like to reduce its enormous food subsidies (28 billion forints in 1975), and with this end in mind has raised the price of beef and meat products, poultry, and fish by 30 percent, 20 percent, and 30 percent, respectively.[33]

Prices in the German Democratic Republic, on the other hand, remain stable, although they are highly subsidized as well.[34] The state had to contribute subsidies of 26.90 marks for each 100 marks' worth of purchases in 1975. Over the last five-year plan period, the GDR government paid out a total of 45.1 billion marks in price supports, and East German economists expect a further rise of over 20 percent by 1980.

7. Growth in the Volume of Money in Circulation

No exact figures on the volume of currency in circulation have been published, for the Soviet Union and some of the other Eastern countries regard this as a state secret. Moreover, cash holdings of state enterprises are not a measure of the adequacy of supplies, since the latter depends on lending terms among other things. In countries such as Poland, where credit is advanced as current account overdraft, firm deposits are very low. Furthermore, economic units may not have excess currency. Allocation of monetary resources from the state budget is always earmarked and meager.

Some idea of the adequacy of cash flow can be gained from the relation between the volume of loans and economic growth. In the Soviet Union, the gross national product increased by 45 percent between 1965 and 1970, while loans rose by 58.8 percent; in the period from 1970 to 1973, gross national product rose by 20 percent and credit by 24 percent.[35] This discrepancy is easy to explain if one recalls the disproportionate share of increases in stocks in the total amount of value created.

Money for private use is also put into circulation through

credits. The Soviet Union does not publish any statistics on cash circulation. Statistics are available, however, on savings deposits, which have grown enormously: from 1.85 billion rubles in 1950 to 10.9 billion in 1960, 46.6 billion rubles ten years later, 68.7 billion rubles in 1973, and 80.1 billion rubles in 1976.[36] It is interesting that a portion of these deposits represents an outcrop of surplus money in the hands of certain strata of the population, mainly in the cities.

Given the chronic shortages, there can be scarcely any doubt that the growth in savings is due to the broad gap between supply and demand.[37] It is no coincidence that "forced saving" is a frequent term in the economic jargon on the East.

Although the volume of consumer goods supply in the Soviet Union has increased considerably, the ratio between this volume and savings deposits has contracted from 5.3 : 1 in 1950 to 0.76 : 1 by the end of 1973.[38]

A similar trend can be observed in Poland, where the ratio between consumer goods supply and money in the hands of the population (cash and savings deposits) has contracted from 1.4 : 1 in 1960 to 0.46 in 1974.[39] The ratio of volume of currency in the hands of the population to economic growth can also be used as an indicator of how this volume has grown: from 1960 to 1974, cash plus savings increased by almost ninefold, while the gross national product increased by 2.7-fold.[40] This ratio is better in the German Democratic Republic, where money increased by 237 percent and the gross national product by 78 percent during the same period.[41]

Forced saving in the most literal sense of the term — that is, in the form of forced loans to the state — was halted in the Soviet Union in 1956 and the redemption of bonds was frozen for twenty years. However, if one considers, for example, the difficulties experienced in trying to buy a house or a car — since prices are either too high or the supply too short — there is really no adequate range of uses to which saved money could be put. It is not that the purchasing power of the population is too great; there are just not enough goods to buy.

To sum up, then: Inflation is an inherent part of the system

Inflation in the Planned Economies

in the planned economies, but not, as is usually claimed, because — or at least not only because — mistakes are made in
planning or the plan targets are not always fulfilled. The crucial factor in the chronic disequilibrium is the prevailing notion
of development, which has given precedence to investment in
heavy industry and defense at the expense of consumption as a
precondition for accelerated growth and transformed the consumer market into a state market and hence a seller's market.
The state is not only the collective owner of the means of production, which determines the direction development will take
and controls distribution. It also sets prices, which are subordinated to the needs of growth. Price increases are therefore neither a signal of disequilibrium nor an instrument to
remedy it. Inflation, usually price-curbed, is still patent everywhere. It is no less socially harmful than in a market economy,
and perhaps is even more so, since no indexing procedures and
no other safeguards are available.

NOTES

1. Keith Bush correctly observes: "It would be unwise to assume that everything can be planned in a planned economy or that all commands in a command economy are obeyed." See "Soviet Inflation" in Banking, Money and
Credit in Eastern Europe, 1973, Brussels, p. 97.
2. G. Garvy notes correctly: "In the Soviet economy inflationary pressures
arise basically because of shortages in supply rather than excesses in aggregate
demand as in nonsocialist countries." Talk given at the CESES seminar in
Venice, August 29-30, 1974, p. 2.
3. Narodnoe khoziaistvo, 1973, p. 549.
4. A report by John M. Collins and John S. Chwat, recently presented to the
U.S. Congress (a study by the Library of Congress, January 1976) estimates
armaments expenditures in 1974 at $124 billion in the Soviet Union and $21 billion in the other Eastern countries. See H. Block, "Die wachsende sowjetische
Militarmächt erfordert grosse wirtschaftliche Opfer" [The Growing Soviet
Military Power Requires Considerable Economic Sacrifice], FAZ, April 20,
1976, p. 12.
5. Handelsblatt, April 6, 1976.
6. "Die Wirtschaft Osteuropas und der UdSSR 1971 bis 1973" [The Economy
of Eastern Europe and the USSR from 1971 to 1973], in Monatsberichte d.
Öesterr. Institutes für Wirtschaftsforschung, 3/1974.

Money, Banking, and Credit

7. Taken from the annual report for the Twenty-fifth Party Congress of the CPSU.

8. Rocznik statystyczny 1975, p. 561, data for 1974.

9. St. Albinowski, "Cena opoznienia" [Delay Costs], Trybuna ludu, April 14, 1976.

10. Narodnoe khoziaistvo, p. 558.

11. In the Soviet Union it is a generally known fact that in 1951 the minister for agricultural machinery and equipment issued an order that all metal stock be cut up in order to meet the gross production target (scrapped metal is considered a part of gross production) and to reduce the stocks of commodities so as to be able to requisition new stocks.

12. Narodnoe khoziaistvo, p. 605.

13. Rocznik statystyczny, p. 74, 157, and 186.

14. Rude pravo, June 26, 1974.

15. Statistická ročenka 1975, p. 241.

16. Symposium in Venice, August 1974, 29-31, p. 11.

17. Andor Laszlo in his talk in Vienna, February 10, 1976.

18. "Bleibt der Ostblock von Inflation verschont?" [Will the Eastern Bloc Be Spared Inflation?], Die Presse, June 27, 1974.

19. Rocznik statystyczny, pp. 336 and 346.

20. Narodnoe khoziaistvo, p. 586.

21. Narodnoe khoziaistvo SSSR, pp. 252 and 253. It should be noted that coal mining, which was still operating at a loss of 1.58 billion rubles in 1965, had a profit of 718,000 rubles in 1973. Ibid., p. 765.

22. Statistická ročenka, p. 497.

23. Talk at Venice symposium, p. 7.

24. Ibid., p. 9.

25. Rocznik statystyczny, 1975, p. 392.

26. Because of the limited supply of consumer goods, added buying power affects especially the demand for meat and meat products.

27. Here is one of many examples: To the question, "Is meat available here?" the salesgirl answers in perfect English, "Yes sir." But in Polish phonetically this means, "There's cheese."

28. Trybuna ludu, March 29, 1976.

29. Rocznik statystyczny, p. 394.

30. Trybuna ludu, June 23, 1976, p. 5.

31. Rocznik statystyczny, 1976.

32. Trybuna ludu, July 14, 1976.

33. Le Monde, July 6, 1976.

34. Spiegel, May 24, 1976, p. 34.

35. Narodnoe khoziaistvo SSSR, pp. 782 and 604.

36. Ibid., p. 634, and Narodnoe khoziaistvo SSSR, 1977, p. 515.

37. The quality of goods in the Soviet Union is rated none too highly; referrin to Literaturnaia gazeta, Time, March 8, 1976, reported that only 6 percent of the shoes and 1 percent of the clothing produced in 1974 met international standards.

Inflation in the Planned Economies

38. Narodnoe khoziaistvo, 1973, pp. 634 and 664.
39. Rocznik statystyczny, pp. 509, 512, and 371.
40. Ibid., p. 69.
41. Statistisches Jahrbuch der DDR, 1974, pp. 313, 40.

Chapter 4

THE BANKING SYSTEM
IN A PLANNED ECONOMY

1. Introduction

The banking system in the planned economies developed along
the same contradictory lines as did the economy as a whole.
The conceptions of how the economic system should function and
what money and credit relations the society should aim toward
after the successful revolution were unclear at the very least,
and ideas on how the future economy was to be steered had not
at all matured.

Marx had not anticipated that communist society would need
money. He wrote: "He [the individual producer] receives a
certificate from society that he has furnished such and such an
amount of labor (after deducting his labor for the common funds)
and with this certificate he draws from the social stock of
means of consumption as much as costs this amount of labor." [1]
These certificates were not to circulate, however, and hence
would not function as money. A viable banking system could not
develop on the basis of certificates.

In 1917, Lenin was still visualizing future society as a single,
countrywide state "syndicate," with equal pay; for him, however,
"a single State Bank, the biggest of the big, with branches in every
rural district, in every factory, will constitute as much as nine-
tenths of the socialist apparatus. There will be country-wide
bookkeeping, country-wide accounting of the production and distribution of goods; this will form, so to speak, the skeleton of
socialist society." [2]

78

The Banking System

How right G. Garvy is when he comments: "It is likely that
his [Lenin's] advocacy in 1917 of using the banking system as
a tool for the socialist transformation of society was more directly related to the discussion in the pre-World War I social
democratic literature."[3] O. Bauer, leader of the Austrian Social Democrats, declared: "If all banks are nationalized and amal-
gamated into a single central bank, then its administrative board
becomes the supreme economic authority, the chief administrative
organ of the whole economy. Only by nationalization of the banks
does society obtain the power to regulate its labor according to a
plan and to distribute its resources rationally among the various
branches of production, so as to adapt them to the nations needs."[4]

The banking system in the Soviet Union has taken a different
path, however. After the socialist revolution in Russia, the
banks resumed their activities. The Russian State Bank was
subordinated to the new state, and on December 27, 1917, private banks were nationalized. During the civil war, however,
money lost all its value. A barter economy evolved in which
money had no significance, and the nationalized banks carried
out none of the usual bank activities. The State Bank was abolished by government decree on January 19, 1920. The reason
given — that "the financing of industry and trade by state budget
funds rendered the State Bank unnecessary in its function as a
state credit institution"[5] — suggests that this step was more
than a technical and organizational measure and indeed represented a fundamental restructuring of the system. Confirmation
that this was so is given by the Party program adopted by the
Eighth Party Congress in 1919, which speaks of the development
of a moneyless society. The report of the Finance Commissariat to the Eighth Soviet Congress (the predecessor of the Supreme Soviet) on December 22-29, 1920, also seems to be aim-
ing in this direction: "A unified economic plan will be possible
only when the chains that bind the financial apparatus to the
bourgeois order — that is, the issuing and monetary system —
are cut asunder and the way is paved for a transition to direct
commodity exchange."[6]

It was soon realized, however, that War Communism and a

79

barter economy (in 1919 money wages made up only 20 percent
of total compensation) provided no foundation for the restoration
and development of a severely devastated and backward economy.
Labor productivity was 70 percent lower in 1919 than in 1913.[7]

The ill-conceived experiment of building up a barter economy
was finally abandoned, and in 1921 the New Economic Policy
(NEP), which bore a number of market features, was instituted.
At the end of 1920 the Finance Commissariat had prepared the
way for the introduction of a suitable labor unit (a unit of accounting expressed in terms of labor hours), but on October 7,
1921, the State Bank was restored and the Ninth Party Congress
of April 1922 outlined a viable monetary system to be based on
gold.[8]

The State Bank and some of the other banks revived or founded
in the period from 1922 to 1928 were tailored to the NEP, which
had permitted private agriculture and, to a limited extent, even
private enterprises in industry and trade. Neither this system
nor its banking apparatus was to last long, however. By the beginning of the thirties, the model that has come to be known as
a centrally administered economy had emerged to take its place
in the history of the Soviet Union. After World War II it was introduced into the other Eastern European countries as well.
The banking apparatus of this system produced the credit reform of 1931-32.

Although economic reforms have altered many features of the
banking system and credit policy since that time, the basic
principles, which derive from the nature of the system, have
remained intact.

2. Basic Principles of the Banking System

The distinctive feature of the banking system in a planned
economy is the fact that nationalized banks are state and cooperative property, and function on that basis. Banks are not a
special kind of firm such as Schumpeter described them to be
in market economies. They are only one of the instruments of
economic control, one link in the state steering mechanism, a

state-owned money institution in a state-run economy. The banking system does not pursue its own course with its own objectives. Banks are wholly in the service of the economy, and its goals are their goals.[9] Neither high profits nor an uncommonly large volume of credit activity are indicators of success in the banking system; indeed, failures in the economy would be more likely to produce such effects than efficient bank performance.

Total subordination of the banking system to economic objectives has left its mark on the banking structure, of course. There is no place in the planned economies for commercial banks nor a market type of competition among them to win customers. As the universal owner of the banking system and economic assets, the state has tailored bank functions to fulfill economic needs, defined the range of lending and credit activities, and decreed any divergences from the norm to be an infringement of socialist law.

An enterprise must keep its accounts, clear its business transactions, and obtain loans only with the bank assigned to it. A customer may not deal with the bank of his choice, nor can banks attract customers by offering more favorable terms. A centralized economy requires a centralized banking system that is an integral part of the administrative apparatus and pursues no separate goals; with no interests of its own, the State (National) Bank is the absolute center of the banking system, and at once serves and protects state interests. It is not a "bank of banks," however, for it alone exercises the most essential functions of the banking system. The central administration plans and steers money and credit flows. Branches make loans, clear giro accounts, and manage cash circulation. The State Bank is not the only state banking institution, but it is the only one that sets into motion money and credit activities and channels commercial activities outside the state bank into the mainstream. The State Bank refinances credits granted by other banks or backs up their money deposits.

Later attempts to build market features into the banking system of a planned economy (Bulgaria, German Democratic Republic) foundered because of the established steering system.

81

Money, Banking, and Credit

2.1. The Restricted Range of Bank Activities

In the ordinary sense, credit is a relationship between economic entities with different owners. But in a planned economy, both the economy itself and the banks are state property. There are no money and capital markets, nor could there be. Therefore, neither is there any natural room for credit relations to develop. There is no natural price in the form of an interest rate that keeps supply and demand for credit in equilibrium or permits the earning of a fair profit. The planning authorities are responsible for maintaining equilibrium, and they also set the price of credit and the interest rates. Like commodity prices, the price of credit is not an effective instrument for maintaining equilibrium; for this reason, in discussing credit and interest — and, indeed, the entire monetary system of the planned economies — we must keep certain reservations in mind.

Thus, it was not easy for the authors of the 1930-32 credit reform to introduce credit into the economy, or to define its limits or its terms. Initially, the attempt was made to activate credit automatically by means of a current account system, so that money needed for clearing could be provided at any moment to the economic enterprises. The results, however, were not inspiring. The volume of money brought into circulation in this way increased by a factor of 3.5 from 1928 to 1932,[10] and it was decided in 1932 that the basic principles of lending needed a fundamental redefinition.

The guidelines laid down at that time still provide the framework for credit relations in the planned economies, though there are some variations from country to country.

2.2. The Range of Application of Credit

Since there is no way in a state economy for state credit to evolve naturally, its scope had to be defined and lines drawn between areas where enterprises should use their own funds and those where credit could be used. These limits have been variously expanded and contracted over the course of time, although conventional boundaries of the area where financing may be used have been maintained.

When an enterprise commences production, it receives an endowment, a founding capital, its "own funds" which are supposed to finance its fixed and working assets. The source of this money is the state budget or the higher-level economic department to which it belongs. These funds are later augmented with some of the enterprise's own earnings.

The size of an enterprise's own funds is determined on the basis of rotation norms set by the planning authorities for the enterprise's stocks (raw materials, unfinished products, semi-finished and finished products, etc.). The function of credit is to finance inventories exceeding the norm and other assets affected by seasonal fluctuations, as well as gaps in funds that cannot be controlled or planned beforehand, for example, clearing documents en route from the supplier to the receiver or a percentage of commodity turnover in the trade organizations.

Over the course of time, the narrow scope of bank credits set by the credit reform has been widened considerably in both the Soviet Union and the other Eastern countries. The way was prepared for introducing credits into heavy industry (which was not subject to seasonal fluctuations), and credits were allowed to finance a specified percentage of current input. In several Eastern countries, however, credit also finances unplanned stocks and bridges over payments gaps, as well as temporary drains on an enterprises' own funds caused by miscalculations, until the enterprise is able to replenish them from its earnings.

2.3. Banks as the Only Credit and Clearing Institutions

The centralized economy has created a centralized banking system. All the state's money flows begin and end in it. Banks are the only state lending institutions. This was the only way that a set of unified lending principles could be adopted throughout the economy.

There are no interenterprise lending, bills of exchange, or discount credit in the planned economies. Automatic payment of suppliers' claims from the receiver's account without prior authorization to pay has also been discontinued. To control payments transactions, all clearing is centralized in banks.[11] An account holder may present his claims for redemption only to his assigned bank. Fixed rules have been established for clearing transactions. A supplier with a buyer in another city must present his claims in the form of a collection document submitted to its bank for collection. A buyer may use a money order to pay a bill for goods received only if the supplier is in the same locality. Generally checks are accepted for settlement only in relations between enterprises and transport firms.

Bank collections are the predominant form of settlement procedure, as can be seen from the table below.

Settlement Transactions in the Soviet Union

	1971	1974
Bank collection	60.1	63.8
Money orders	28.1	27.5
Checks	8.6	5.4
Letters of credit	3.2	3.3
	100.0	100.0

Den'gi i kredit, 9/1975, p. 34.

The bank pays the supplier's claim from the buyer's clearing account if there is enough money in it, grants an earmarked payments credit, or waits until the buyer has enough money in the account before redeeming a claim. Payment is usually effected only when the buyer accepts the supplier's claim.

If funds are short, there is an established sequence for payment in the Soviet Union and some other Eastern countries that banks are obliged to follow: first wages are paid, then money owed to the state budget; second are suppliers' claims; third, amortization writeoffs are paid into a special account; fourth, bank credits are paid (except for credits granted to meet suppliers' demands, which are paid in second); and fifth are all other payments.[12]

Banks are obligated to verify the invoices of a supplier's

claim. A claim without invoice is not paid. A supplier presents his claim for payment and, until it is cleared, receives a bank credit — limited in time by law, but usually for ten days after the collection order arrives at the buyer's bank. The procedure is similar to that followed when a firm sells a bill of exchange to a bank, thereby transforming a goods credit into a bank credit, to use Schumpeter's apt description.[13]

Current regulations have abolished commercial credit, but not obligations between firms. Payments are usually effected when the prescribed term of payment has expired. (Other regulations exist in the German Democratic Republic and Romania, where payment is made as soon as a claim is presented.) Payment is not always made on time, and often a bank will refuse a buyer's application for a payments credit. Obligations to suppliers therefore represent a rather high amount, as is evident from the following table showing the structure of working funds of enterprises in the Soviet Union and Poland.

	Poland	Soviet Union
Working funds	100.0%	100.0%
Own funds and similar	22.3	28.0
Bank credits	39.6	45.0
Creditors	21.9	20.4
Other	16.2	6.6

Sources: Narodnoe khoziaistvo SSSR 1974, p. 74; Information Bulletin, Narodowy Bank Polski, 1975, p. 19.

We see that, in both Poland and the Soviet Union, obligations to creditors comprise more than one-fifth of the total. The share of enterprise funds and bank credits is higher in the Soviet Union than in Poland. Poland makes up for this difference with other resources (development funds, etc.).

2.4. Differentiation of Capital Funds from Working Funds

There is a strict line of demarcation between an enterprise's own funds and bank credits, between the funds of individual economic units, and between capital funds and working funds. This was especially true in the first phase of development. If one considers that, at that time, the central authorities viewed it as their primary task to organize the economy over which they had assumed almost exclusive control, a strict demarcation between the funds of different enterprises would seem wholly warranted. The state, not the enterprises, disposed over profits, almost all of which were transferred to the state budget to be used for purposes defined by state planning authorities.

Centralization of profits in the state budget, however, was merely a corollary of the state's assumption of sole power in determining the direction of development of the overall economy. The individual enterprise, shorn of all decision-making powers, has no need to control the funds it has itself earned. It cannot utilize for investment purposes any of its own profits, nor any other funds accruing from its production and sales operations, since that would be illegal under prevailing conditions.

Hence, the strict separation of funds financing working assets from fixed assets and the unavailability of the former for investments flows logically from the prohibition on independent investment projects. Indeed, the use of production funds for investments was even liable to legal prosecution.

The 1930-32 credit reform, which separated fixed assets from working assets, had a crucial influence on the initial structure given to the banking system, just as the later relaxation of this rigid distinction was instrumental in the restructuring of the system.

3. The Structure of the Banking System

Various banks were encharged with ensuring that the separation between investment and productive activities, and hence between fixed assets and working assets, was maintained. Short-term credit and clearing operations in the production sphere, as well as control over the amount of money in circulation, were placed in the hands of the State Bank. Long-term credits — rarely granted in the first stage of development —

and the financing of investment projects were put in the hands of investment banks, established specifically for that purpose. The intention was that an extensive network of investment banks would prevent the occurrence and financing of unplanned investment projects. The Soviet Union has four investment banks: the Bank for Industry and Energy, the Agricultural Bank, the Bank for Domestic Trade and Cooperatives, and the Communal Bank. These banks financed and supervised investments until 1960. Most of the other Eastern countries have only two investment banks: one for financing industrial plant and the other for agriculture.

The State Bank provided short-term credits only for projects involving mechanization of production or for expansion of the production of consumer goods, and the recipient must be able to pay back the costs from its earnings within one year.

In the original conception, the State Bank was to be in charge of foreign transactions in addition to domestic production and sales activities, even though the foreign banking institutions inherited from the former regime, such as the Vneshtorg Bank in the Soviet Union, the Bank Handlowy in Warsaw, and the Zivnostenska Bank in Czechoslovakia did not cease operations; the functions of these latter institutions were merely reduced, principally to handling the foreign exchange business of the public at large. The foreign trade banks, both new and old, did not develop their activities in full measure until later, when foreign trade was expanded considerably.

The savings banks, which earlier had concentrated their activities almost exclusively on accumulating cash deposits of the private population or issuing state bonds, have risen in status. They have also begun to issue loans to private individuals.

4. The Reorganization of the Banking System

4.1. Reorganization and the Economic Reforms

After nearly thirty years of existence, the Soviet banking system — which had served as a model for the whole Eastern bloc —

was modified considerably as a direct consequence of the economic reforms. Originally conceived in uniform terms, the banking systems of the other Eastern countries also underwent a series of differentiations corresponding to the various paths along which their steering models were developed. The economic reform provides the framework within which these modifications took place. Where the reforms were confined mainly to organizational and technical improvements while leaving the centralized model itself basically intact, banking reforms also concentrated on purely organizational changes in the original structure. In other countries, where decentralization was initiated and certain decision-making powers were delegated to the micro level, changes in the banking system followed suit as an important component of these changes.

4.2. Organizational Improvement in the Traditional Steering Model

The Soviet Union, in particular, undertook some fundamental structural adjustments, in order to improve and unify the financing of investment projects, adjust the banking system to increased activities in foreign trade, and adapt to the increasing role of household savings. The decree of the Supreme Soviet of April 7, 1959, abolished three investment banks, and merged the specialized banks for long-term financing into a single investment bank. At the present time, only one investment bank, the Stroibank (Construction Bank) is in operation; it has taken over the functions of the Prombank (Industry Bank) and a number of other discontinued banks, and concentrates mainly on financing industrial investment projects. The State Bank has assumed the functions of the former Agricultural Bank.

This reorganization must not be seen as a purely technical and organizational measure, however. To a great extent it was made necessary by the increased use of long-term credits to finance investment projects: between 1965 and 1974, the volume of short-term credits almost doubled, while long-term credits granted mainly for investment projects grew by sixfold.[14] The increasing part played by credit in investment financing, as well as the increasing role of the bank in controlling the technical efficiency of investment projects, dictated the unification of financing, credit, and control in a single investment bank.

In the early sixties, the Soviet Union made some further refinements in its credit system. In connection with the expansion of foreign trade relations, on January 1, 1962, all clearing operations and all credit activities of foreign trade organizations were placed in the hands of the Vneshtorgbank (Foreign Trade Bank). This bank, organized in 1922, was limited to noncommercial foreign exchange operations. It functions now as a joint stock bank, with the State Bank as the principal shareholder. The State Bank, however, continues to act as the guardian of the state monopoly over foreign exchange, plans and controls foreign exchange transactions, accepts foreign credits, and controls the payments balance, which includes supervision of the activities of the Vneshtorgbank.

Expansion of the activities of the Foreign Trade Bank was a direct consequence of the intensification of foreign trade and the increasingly active role played by the Soviet Union on the major world money markets, especially the Eurodollar market. Many Soviet bank branches have been opened in the West, and those that were already in operation — that is, the Moscow Narodny Bank and the Banque Commerciale pour l'Europe du Nord — have expanded their activities considerably. Moreover, many of the largest of the world's banks have set up branches in the East (their activities will be described in Chapter 6). On January 1, 1964, the Soviet savings banks, which formerly had been under the Ministry of Finance, and whose net inflow was considered as budgetary resources, were transferred to the jurisdiction of the State Bank, to better meet the needs created by expanding ties between the savings banks and the central state money issuing and credit institutions. The deposits of the population in savings banks, which become one of the sources of bank funds, have grown considerably in volume from 18.7 billion rubles in 1965 to 103.0 billion rubles in 1974[15]; at the same time, savings banks have begun to function as lending institutions for the public, although consumer credit is still in its infancy in the Soviet Union, and in fact decreased from 0.8 billion rubles in 1965 to 0.5 billion rubles in 1976.[16]

The reformed banking system of the Soviet Union functions within the framework of the centralized steering mechanism of the Soviet economy. As in other Eastern countries, it is more an "adjuster" rather than a "steerer" of the economy, to borrow Garvy's terminology.

The banking system of Romania, which remains a control component of the central steering system of the economy, evolved in the same direction. Romania made a few organizational adjustments, aimed mainly at expanding the existing banking system. On March 1, 1968, the old Agricultural Bank resumed activities, and on July 1, 1968, the Foreign Trade Bank began operation. The functions of the banking system in Romania are adapted for the most part to a centralized system.

4.3. Structural Reforms in the Other Eastern Countries

Poland and Hungary undertook extensive reforms of their banking systems in conjunction with new credit policies under their decentralized steering models. Originally, Czechoslovakia tried some far-reaching reforms; the reforms in Bulgaria and the German Democratic Republic were even more radical, but suffered some strong setbacks. The reform of the banking system accorded with the decentralization (actual or intended) of enterprise decision-making, which gave a more important role to profit in determining the overall index of economic performance, and permitted a greater share of earnings to remain in the hands of the enterprises, which use them increasingly to finance their own investment projects on an independent basis. The enterprises obtained the right to create a development fund from a portion of their earnings to finance the expansion of current and fixed assets. In light of the progressive integration of the enterprise funds and the growing influence of the micro level on how these funds are to be raised and utilized, the traditional separation of the banking system into institutions financing production and institutions financing investment projects is becoming less and less suited to the new tasks.

Another important factor contributing to the reorganization of the banking system was the growing conviction that budget subsidies, which did not have to be paid back, were not conducive to timely and wise management of capital investment projects, and that the interests of efficient investment activity would be better served if bank credits were repayable as this would encourage prompt completion of projects.

The strict separation of enterprise funds and their financing and supervision by different banking institutions was untenable under the new steering conditions. It was felt that the individual enterprises, which gradually had assumed all the responsibilities of management, would be better served by a bank that could finance, clear, and control all its production and investment activities together.

Czechoslovakia was the first to merge the Investment Bank with the State Bank. On January 1, 1959, the two banks were combined. From that time onward the Statni Banka Ceskoslovenska provided loans and financed both production and investments. Poland took the same step, on January 1, 1971, and was followed later by Hungary, where, pursuant to a government resolution of June 3, 1971, the National Bank was as of 1972 to take over the financing of investment projects either that enterprises had financed themselves within the powers delegated to them or for which they had taken out bank credits. At the same time, a Development Bank was established to finance investment projects that had been funded wholly or partly by budget funds or development bonds as specified in government decisions.

It is interesting that although the same structural transformation was carried out, its impact was by no means the same in each country. Czechoslovakia, which took this step earlier than Poland and Hungary, had in large measure abolished the preconditions for the measure — that is, decentralization of economic control. Hungary, which reorganized its banking apparatus much later than the other Eastern nations, has gone the farthest toward using the organized banking system for the decentralization of decision making.

4.4. New Developments in the Polish Banking System

A government resolution of June 27, 1975, in Poland abolished the Cooperative Savings and Loan Bank (Spoldzielnia Oszczęd-nościowa Poizyczkowa, SOP) and the Agricultural Bank, and in their place established the Bank for the Food Industries, which also assumed some of the powers of the National Bank; in addition, a new Cooperative Bank under greater state influence was created. At the same time, the savings bank (Polska Kasa Oszczędności, PKO) system was absorbed by the National Bank.

The reason for the liquidation of the SOP was its growing role in state affairs and the growing proportion of state funds in its financial resources.[17] The new institution is a central Cooperative Bank that has subordinate branch cooperatives throughout the country, representing a total of 3.5 million members. Henceforth, however, its function was to be supervising observance of "the centrally administered guidelines of state monetary and credit policies."[18] The managers of the cooperative bank branches were now to be recommended by the board to the president of the National Bank for appointment, rather than being elected by the board of the Cooperative Bank itself.

The same resolution subordinated the savings offices to the National Bank, since even more than in the Soviet Union, they had been gradually transformed from a savings institution into a savings and credit institution. Credits for the population increased from 23.6 billion zlotys in 1970 to 35.9 billion zlotys in 1976,[19] and though consumer credits amount to no more than 13.0 percent of savings deposits (276.2 billion zlotys at the end of 1976),[20] the principal reason for the measure was still to place entire control of money and credit activities in the hands of the State Bank.

The bank law passed by the Polish parliament in June 1975 created three main departments in the banking system: (a) the Polish National Bank (Narodowy Bank Polski, NBP), which functions as the central note-issuing, credit, savings, settlements, and clearing and foreign exchange institution of the state; (b) the Bank for the Foods Industry (Bank Gospodarki Zynościowej, BGZ), which in addition to its main functions of handling business for agriculture and the foods industry, also must supervise the activities of the cooperative banks, whose functions have been considerably reduced; and (c) the Bank for Foreign Trade (Bank Handlowy, Warsawie), which handles foreign trade activities and foreign credits, and the Trust Bank (Polska Kasa Opieki), which handles foreign exchange transactions for the public.

The bank law also stipulates that the National Bank should coordinate the overall state credit policy, cash circulation, savings policy, clearing procedures, and foreign exchange policy, and in addition provide most of the credits and financing for the economy as a whole.[21]

In the three countries mentioned above, where radical reforms of the banking system were carried out, this measure was efficient only insofar as the decentralized decision-making background remained in force. Only Hungary can assert that its reformed banking system conforms with its decentralized steering model; much less so, Poland and Czechoslovakia, where enterprises can use no more than 10 to 20 percent of their profits for development purposes. The banking reforms were not very successful in such countries as Bulgaria or the German Democratic Republic, where the market type of banking that was imitated came into conflict from the beginning with the centralized planning and management of the economy.

4.5. Attempts to Establish a Market-Type of Banking System

In a number of the Eastern countries, the economic reform that gave enterprises more of a say in their own development and in the use of their own funds precipitated a lively discussion over whether the banking system should be allowed to develop into an independent economic entity whose activities, like those of other economic entities, were oriented toward profits. The advocates of such development envisioned a genuine partnership between economic entities independently managing their own activities and the profit-oriented bank with which they did business. The partnership was supposed to stimulate the establishment of businesslike, mutually beneficial relations between enterprises and banks.

Credit activities were to become a matter between two independent partners enjoying the same status: the bank, which was to be promoted to the status of a firm in Schumpeter's sense, and the enterprise, which henceforth would be allowed to engage in entrepreneurial functions by virtue of the powers granted to it. The central authorities were to be relieved of their everyday responsibilities and restrict themselves to laying down guidelines for and planning the general course of development.

The State Bank was to serve as the bank of banks and concentrate on the planning and coordination of money circulation and credit policy as well as the refinancing of commerce banks. Direct activities such as lending, clearing, and foreign exchange transactions were to be delegated to the commerce banks, to be organized by branch of industry.

These ideas were actually implemented, however, not in the most decentralized economies but in the German Democratic Republic and later in Bulgaria, where the enterprise had only a small voice in decision-making, and where an effective partnership between the large industrial and trade trusts, and the commerce banks was contemplated.

East German economists such as P. Frenzel[22] and W. Bahl[23] held that responsibility for the financial proceeds of the banking system should be borne by each branch and not by the system as a whole, and that each branch should be empowered to make independent decisions.

The Bulgarians had already gone so far as to envision a self-sufficient banking system similar to that in a free market economy, in which the note-issuing bank would continue to look after the money and credit policies of the state, but lending and clearing activities would be relegated to the commercial banks. The State Bank was to influence the commerical banks through market-type instruments such as minimum requirements for reserves to be kept on deposit with the State Bank and appropriate interest rates for the refinancing of credits.[24]

These concepts were totally rejected in the other Eastern countries. For example, former Polish bank president L. Siemiatkowski observed that "for economic self-accounting to have its full effect in the banking system, a money and capital market must exist and money and capital must be put to use according to the rules of this market ... but this could become a reality only if the entire economic model were reorganized from the ground up."[25]

The German Democratic Republic reorganized its banking system on January 1, 1968, followed by Bulgaria on April 1, 1969.

The note-issuing bank and the Investment Bank of the German Democratic Republic were replaced by the State Bank and the Industry and Trade Bank, with the State Bank at the top. The latter was to be the note-issuing bank and put money into circulation, coordinate credit policy, and refinance the business of the other banks. It did not have its own network of branches, however. The Industry and Trade Bank carried out its activities through its fourteen regional boards and local branches, which also financed all investment projects. The commercial banks, established in early 1968, were supplemented in October of the same year by a Bank for Agriculture and the Food Industry.

Refinancing procedures built into the new banking system and a differentiated interest rate structure were to be integrated into the financing system and profit system of the overall economy.

Bulgaria's banking system underwent similar development. Between April 1, 1969, and 1972, Bulgaria's National Bank functioned as a central bank over the entire national banking system — that is, it was a bank of banks. The Industry and Trade Bank and the Agricultural Bank took care of credit and clearing transactions as well as the financing of investment projects.

Later developments, however, proved right the opponents of market-type banking in a planned economy. It soon became obvious that in a planned economy where there is no natural interplay between supply and demand for credits or between credits and the interest rate, and where all indicators must be regulated administratively, planned, and set centrally, a market-type banking system makes no economic sense. There was no apparent way to reconcile the refinancing and interest mechanisms and interest rates with the binding target figures of the economic plan. The market-type interplay and the impulses it was hoped this would give to economic efficiency were effectively blocked by a planned and stable interest rate and a ceiling on refinancing.

Neither the German Democratic Republic nor Bulgaria was willing to carry decentralization of economic decision-making powers further in order to create the preconditions for a functioning and effective market-type banking system; both countries preferred to revert to the traditional banking concept of the planned economies, Bulgaria was first on July 1, 1971, followed somewhat later by the German Democratic Republic on July 1, 1974.

The present banking system of the GDR consists of the following institutions. First, there is the State Bank, which now plans credits and coordinates credit policy and, as it did before the reforms, also grants credits through its branches and functions as a settlement and clearing institution for commodity trade. In addition to the State Bank as a note-issuing bank, the following banks serve particular branches of industry: the Bank for Agriculture and the Foodstuffs Industry; the Credit Cooperatives for the crafts and agriculture (their chairman is now appointed by the prime minister instead of being elected, as formerly); the Foreign Trade Bank, which clears foreign trade transactions, gives and procures credits abroad, and processes credits to the foreign trade organizations; and the savings banks, which are subordinated to the State Bank as in Poland and the Soviet Union.

The government resolution of January 1, 1971, converted Bulgaria from an economy with certain market features back into a centralized steered system in which market mechanisms were applied only narrowly. The banking system was restructured into a traditional control institution of the planned economy. The Bulgarian National Bank stands at the top of the banking system; it grants short-term credits for current assets and long-term credits for capital investment projects, and man-

ages the circulation of money. In addition to the state bank,
there are also the Foreign Trade Bank and the savings banks.
The savings banks grant short-term consumer credits in addition to long-term credits for private home building.

The banking systems of the Eastern countries are now much
more differentiated than they were during the first period of
existence of the Eastern bloc. The Soviet banking model as its
steering system is no longer a decisive example for all. But
the principles of a planned economy and the imperatives of state
ownership of the means of production remain determinative.

Deviations from the traditional model are not too great, however; the banking system shows common features in all the
Eastern countries. It remains an instrument of the state, a
controlling institution which delivers the necessary money for
enterprises and households, and functions in accordance with
the limited role of money, credit, and prices in the planned
economies.

The idea that terms of credit can influence the economy
foundered. The economy adapted banking activities to its actual performance much more than banking activities were able
to adjust the performance of the enterprises to the indicators
of the central economic plan.

5. Bank Resources

Bank resources consist of the following major components:

a) the monies of the nationalized sector of the economy and
the cooperatives, which are owned partly by central institutions
(state budget, insurance organizations, etc.) and partly by industrial factories or foreign trade enterprises;

b) money of private individuals, for example, cash and savings deposits.

The structure of banking resources is illustrated by the following statistics for Poland and Hungary. It is similar in the
other Eastern countries, although no figures have been published. The item "banks" also includes foreign credits and
bonds that are not counted separately from the total sum. Only

Money, Banking, and Credit

Structure of Bank Resources in Poland and Hungary at the end of 1974

	Poland		Hungary	
	Million zlotys	%	Million forints	%
Own funds	27,712	2.6	16,807*	6.1
Reserve funds	—	—	696	0.2
Deposits, etc.				
Banks,	401,152	37.4	95,538	34.7
including savings banks	269,200	25.0		
Enterprises				
Time deposits	161,111	15.0	50,742	18.5
Sight deposits	162,484	15.1	49,120	17.9
Budget funds	196,062	18.3	13,993	5.1
Bank notes and coins	117,151	10.9	34,609	12.6
Other	7,082	0.7	13,468	4.9
Total	1,072,754	100.0	274,973	100.0

Source: Information Bulletin, Narodowy Bank Polski, 1975, p. 35; Handelsblatt, August 29-30, 1975, p. 10.

*Hungarian banks' own funds are made up of founding capital: 300,000 shares worth 20,000 forints each = 6 billion forints and profits of 10.807 million forints.

Hungary mentions specifically three foreign bonds included under this item: one for $25 million (1971, due in 1981) with a forint value of 584.25 million (calculated at the 1975 official exchange rate of 1 dollar = 23.37 forints), one $50 million bond (1972, due in 1987) = 1168.5 million forints, and one $40 million bond (1974, worth 934.8 million forints and due in 1982). In addition to these, the Hungarian State Bank has other long-term obligations in hard currencies with an original maturity of eight years or more totaling $310 million at the end of 1974, mainly in the form of syndicate credits. [26]

The item "banks" for Poland contains 269.2 billion zlotys in savings deposits of the population at large and of small enterprises. The remainder is made up of the deposits of the other banks and foreign credits that are not planned separately.

A comparison of the above figures for the structure of bank resources shows clearly that the percentage of own funds and money deposits of enterprises is larger in Hungary than in

Poland, while the percentage of state budget funds is smaller. In connection with the economic reform, Hungary increased the own funds of enterprises and decreased budget subsidies.

6. The Credit-Creating Functions of Bank Resources

It is regarded as self-evident in the planned economies, as in any other economy, that the asset and liabilities columns of a bank balance sheet must be equal. The causal relationship between resources and credit activity is interpreted differently, however. The view is widespread that the accumulation of monetary resources is a precondition for lending. Traditional methods for credit planning provide a credible argument in this respect. Not only the volume of credits made available to the economy within a given period, but also the degree to which it is covered by money deposits, is planned. The notion that accumulated money is the source of credit activity is even more prevalent in the East than in the West. Credit goes to Albert Hahn and Joseph Schumpeter for dealing a considerable blow to the long prevailing view that monetary resources create credit.

Two sources for the notion of the creative function of monetary resources can be identified: planning methods themselves, and the attitude of planners toward their job, which they regard as a creative activity. Both lending and raising funds are viewed as creative, growth-promoting activities. Both activities mutually influence one another, and both are rooted in economic processes. [27]

It should be stressed that opinions differ considerably, however, as to the causal relationship between resources and the credits of a banking system. Leading banking specialists and economists maintain the view that accumulation of monetary resources remains a precondition for credit operations. Former chief planner of the Soviet State Bank, N. Barkovskii, declared the notion that credit resources are created by the lending process itself to be "theoretically unconvincing and dangerous in practice," since "such a view diverts attention from adequate planning and from the creation of funds the economy urgently needs." Barkovskii feels that if the view that "credits are self-serving" were ever to gain a foothold, it would undermine the "law of money circulation."[28]

Soviet expert V. Zaidenvarg shares this view. In his opinion, the task of planning and the regulation of circulation is to adjust monetary circulation to economic needs,[29] even within the various territories of the country. Every ruble, according to Zaidenvarg, should be an active ruble. Soviet experts M. Iampol'-skii[30] and A. Melkov[31] take a somewhat more tempered view.

The economic process and lending transactions show clearly, however, that monetary resources in the banks are not a prerequisite for lending. A bank branch is bound to credit limits and lending regulations, but it is by no means limited in its activities by a shortage of funds. A lending bank tries to keep the volume of credits as low as possible within the given limits so as not to create excess buying power, but it does this by carefully examining the projects for which a loan is requested and the finances of the enterprise asking for the loan. No attempt is made to correlate the size of a loan with the amount of funds that must be raised. Additional credits put more money into circulation, but excess money cannot be a source of excess credits in a planned economy, and deficient monetary resources are no grounds for withholding a loan that fulfills all the legal requirements. Existing monetary deposits are no yardstick for lending.

In Poland, for example, individual savings represent about 36 percent of bank resources, and for the most part owe their existence to a deficient supply of consumer goods; they cannot be used as a basis for credit in either the consumer goods industry or heavy industry, however, for the consumer market is kept almost totally separate from the production market, and in a planned economy money is not an anonymous buying power and hence can exercise no independent functions of its own.

Lending has a basis even when it is brought about by factors operating against the economic process. It is usually based on stocks of goods, whose turnover and inventory play determining roles in the planning of credit and later in allocations. Temporarily idle enterprise monies cannot be a determining factor in lending, however, nor can the idle savings of the public, which is unable to find enough goods to buy.

Credits can be granted in accordance or at variance with the plan, as a result of economic factors that may themselves concur or conflict with the plan. The quantity of money available or created by a loan are neither a basis nor a precondition for lending; indeed, too large a quantity indicates economic miscalculations. [32]

Only central banking authorities are concerned with maintaining a balance between resources and credits; local bank branches, which are the direct agents in credit transactions, do not coordinate these credits with their own resources, nor with the central resources of the state. Every attempt to induce the micro level to plan its own resources has failed. [33] Then again, planning of a balance between resources and credits at the micro level would be unsound since the need for credit does not necessarily only arise where monetary resources are available for it.

In a planned economy, what is important are the credits issued by bank branches on the basis of enterprise activities, not the volume set by the planning department of the state bank for the debit side of the credit plan in order to achieve a balance. The loans and monetary deposits they create produce a working balance in the banking system and serve as the basis for the next credit plan.

Hahn has examined in detail the causal relationship between bank resources and credits. His conclusion — that "lending is first and foremost the other side of deposit formation," that "every credit injected into the economy generates a deposit and hence the means to cover it" [34] — is more applicable to a planned economy than to a market economy. In a planned economy, there are no capital and money markets. Credits are planned and granted not on the basis of accumulated monies, which have an anonymous buying power, but on the basis of the need for money in current production and sales, which the state bank must satisfy in order to stop an endless chain of insolvent state-owned enterprises.

7. Banking Mechanisms

These instruments do not at all resemble the usual instruments for conducting business. They have evolved in accordance
with the principal that, in a planned economy, a bank is not an
enterprise which strives for a profit in its activities. Its task
is to furnish the economy with the money it needs within the
limits set by a planned economy and in keeping with its lending
rules. In the process, it must check the performance and efficiency of enterprises and help to eliminate flaws. There is no
direct parameter of the usual kind to measure a bank's efficiency, nor are any unequivocal criteria available for describing
the efficiency of the banking system. Maximization of profits
cannot be used, since profits may result from immoderate interest proceeds. Moreover, paid interest expands especially
when immoderate and overdue credits are utilized, since interest rates are much higher for these than for ordinary credits.
Expansion of lending activity is no criterion for the efficiency
of bank activity either, since it is a natural consequence of the
expansion of production; it is also caused by excessive stockpiling — a serious problem for the planned economies, which
are plagued with chronic shortages — or by payments difficulties due to inordinate production costs and a shortage of own
funds. Flaws in the economy as a whole can hardly be viewed
as advantages for the state bank. Above-average monetary resources, a large volume of money in circulation, or inordinate
savings deposits and cash assets of the enterprises or state
budget reserves are even less positive aspects of bank activity.
Excessive private savings of individuals and enterprises are
first and foremost a consequence of supply problems, and state
budget reserves result not only from overfulfillment of the budget income but also from delays in major state capital investment projects.

The banks in the Eastern countries always have a problem
when they are called upon to furnish indices for competition in
order to reward above-average performance. Minimalization
of overdue credits and overdue obligations between enterprises

has been the criterion traditionally used. But in the planned economies, there are no indices that cannot be doctored. Despite an endless list of rules and regulations governing lending procedures, overdue credits can be transformed into normal credits and overdue suppliers' claims can be covered by payments credits, which are being used more and more by the banks.

The attempt to introduce automatic economic mechanisms (Bulgaria and the German Democratic Republic took the most radical step in this direction when they endowed their banking systems with market features) ended in failure. It is impossible to define a bank's relation to the economy on the basis of the profit principle when everything is owned by the state. The ordinary business operations aspired to very quickly degenerated into traditional administrative mechanisms based on the mandatory limits and interest rates set by the authorities, and reduced the business system, so laboriously constructed, into nothing.

8. The Plans of the State (National) Bank

The banking apparatus steers the total monetary circulation of the state and has developed planning and steering methods for both cash and cashless circulation. Both money flows — notes and cash, and money in account — begin and end with the bank. The returns of retail enterprises and intakes of the savings banks, as well as other cash flows, come back into the central bank and are converted into deposit money. Only a portion goes toward expanding the holdings of private households, and corresponds to the amount of extra cash issued. In the planned economies as well, credit is the best instrument for expanding the money supply and skimming off excess money through repayments.

The credit plan of the central bank sets the contours for its overall activities as the central issuing institution.[35] Cash circulation, which is much more separated from general circulation than in a market economy, is also steered through the cash plan and the plan balance of money income and expenditures of the population.

Money, Banking, and Credit

The credit plan determines how much money the economy needs for current production (short-term credits) and investment projects that are to be financed by bank credits rather than budget subsidies (long-term credits).

Only the central bank compiles a full credit plan with liabilities (resources) and assets (credits) columns. Regional branches (in the Soviet Union, republic branch banks) determine credit needs only for the economy of the local district, and do not have to determine the passive side of the credit plan. All attempts to compile a complete plan at the local level have failed.

Credit planning is based on the credit applications of the different branches of the economy, which are presented either directly to the central bank (if of central importance) or to regional offices for review and processing.

The bank's control function begins with the planning procedure itself, as the vice-president of the Polish National Bank defined it: "A local bank is the executor of the state's economic policy with regard to stockpiles and can oppose any attempt to present excess stocks as security for obtaining credit."[36]

The credit plan of the USSR State Bank (which has its counterpart in all the other Eastern countries) looks as follows[37]:

Credit resources	Use of resources
Bank funds	Short-term credits (itemized)
Monetary funds of the state budget	Credits for stocks, broken down by
Money deposits of enterprises and	branch of the economy
organizations involved in production	Long-term credits (state of debt at end
Money for capital investment projects	of planning period)
Money of credit institutions (Investment Bank and Foreign Trade Bank)	Price difference (refers mainly to foreign trade)
Savings of population	Deductions from bank earnings
Money in circulation	Cash holdings of State Bank and other
Profits of State Bank	assets
Other resources	
Total	Total

The balance sheet for the State Bank's current activities looks similar. It should be stressed that the monthly balance

104

sheet of the Soviet State Bank is published on the tenth day of the following month, which makes possible a quick response to any deviations from the plan target.

The planning periods vary from country to country. In the Soviet Union, quarter-year and one-year plans for short-term credits and plan forecasts for five-year periods are compiled; in Bulgaria, a one-year plan with breakdown by quarters is drawn up; in the German Democratic Republic and Czechoslovakia, one-year and five-year plans are compiled; Poland has annual plans; and Romania has quarter-year plans. The Hungarian reform of 1968 abandoned binding credit plans. The government merely sets the guidelines of credit policy, and these are then adjusted each year to current goals. [38]

As is evident from the above, the credit plan includes cash circulation. This is money that is not included in bank holdings. Holdings of money that has been issued but not put into or retired from circulation are recorded on the assets side of the plan. The cash plan is compiled to steer the money in circulation, with detailed breakdown into income (proceeds from trade organizations and service agencies, income tax, postal and savings banks proceeds, etc.) and expenditures (wages and salaries, payments for the purchase of agricultural products, payments for the post and savings banks, etc.). The credit and cash plans are synchronized by maintaining an identical net result for the amount of money that must be added to and retired from circulation. [39]

9. Rules of Lending

With no money market, credits are injected into the economy by means of the allocation norms of the central plan; the state bank sets limits and guideline figures for the allocations. These norms are becoming less and less binding, however. To facilitate bank supervision, credit limits are set for specific items, such as raw materials, unfinished products, and finished products. But, even when bank controls were strict, not all credits were limited; for example, credits for the purchase of grain or other agricultural products were intended to be expanded, not contracted. In other cases, too, when breakdown by individual enterprise and item was extremely laborious, control guideline figures rather than limits (for example, for clearing credits or trade credits) were set for an entire branch of industry rather than for individual enterprises. A local bank could exceed these figures, but if it did so, it had to notify its head office.

Banking practices, which have become increasingly refined and more varied, have done much to eliminate credit limits. Turnover credits come into increasingly greater use in heavy industry. In this case, supplies as well as wages and salaries are paid out of a credit account and the credits are paid back from enterprise earnings. Credit limits would not be useful here, since turnover cannot be regulated exactly. In the Soviet Union, where credit limits have a long tradition, limited credits make up no more than 40 percent of the total credits granted for inventories and only 30 percent of the entire volume of credit for the economy as a whole.[40] Even in areas where limits are maintained, the management of regional offices has the power to restructure credit limits with the agreement of the economic branch concerned.

Credits for inventories are subject to rigid limits in Romania. The share of limited credits in total credits for industrial enterprises amounts to 60 percent. [41]

The 1968 Hungarian reform put an end to the limitation of credits. "Credit relations between banks and enterprises are concretely manifested within the framework described by the economic plan and the guidelines of credit policy in the form of credit and loan contracts"[42] concluded between a local bank and an enterprise.

10. Credit as a Stopgap Measure

Regardless of how strong an attempt is made to restrict credits, it is an inescapable fact that credits must always be resorted to when hitches, such as excessive costs, shortage of profits, losses and excessive stockpiles, or all of these together, give rise to payments difficulties. Credits are granted to avoid an endless chain of mutual obligations, even where this is regarded as unsound, or when an enterprise is unable to present any prescribed item as security for credit.

The State Bank cannot influence the activity of enterprises because of the way it operates itself. However, the economic process can force banks to come up with the required means of payment, especially if one considers that insolvency is more detrimental to banks than to enterprises. The state of overdue credits and suppliers' demands are the decisive factors determining bonuses for bank employees. It is therefore wrong to think that the credit plan and the way credits are allocated play the decisive role in shaping credit activities; credits are the most difficult of all indices to regulate with planned targets. They depend less on the banks and more on economic performance. Even the strictest bank controls are unable to counteract economic difficulties, which must be covered by additional credits in order to avoid other obligations.

When credit limitations are abolished or reduced, it appears that, rather than the banking system creating order in the economy, the economy creates chaos in the monetary system — even in a centrally steered economy.

A similar turn of events is obvious in cash circulation. In the first period of development of a planned economy, the net issue balance of the cash plan (expanding or contracting the money supply) was made binding on local branches by the government. Local banks were not permitted to make any expenditures in excess of earnings and the established cash limit without the approval of the higher bank office, even when this meant payments delays. Later, this command management of the money supply was relaxed considerably — even in the Soviet Union, where the net issue balance is still a state directive. Republic branch banks are authorized to allow excesses over the limits, but these must later be paid back from excess income.

11. Bank Controls

The credit reform of 1930-32 in the Soviet Union abolished

Money, Banking, and Credit

automatic lending without consideration of enterprise performance. Lending conditions were established and their observance was supervised. Every credit had to be earmarked and tied to a specific component of current assets. There was a vast number of different kinds of credit since a credit was set for every inventory item, in addition to clearing credits, credits for mechanization, and so on. Every credit had to be evidenced in a separate bank account. Before the 1956 credit reform, there were sixteen different kinds of credits in Poland and just as many in the other Eastern countries. Securing of a credit with a specific component of current assets was checked two or three times monthly on the basis of current enterprise statistics and later on the basis of balance sheet figures. Regardless of the repayment period allowed, a stock reduction in the item for which the credit was given forced early repayment. This practice is still followed today for earmarked credits.

A bank must ensure careful supervision of the economic activities of enterprises associated with it. Enterprise reports are analyzed, and clearing procedures for payments to the supplier and the state budget are supervised. When deviations from the planned target occur, Party authorities or superior bodies are notified.

A Soviet government ordinance of August 21, 1954, institutionalized the control functions of the Soviet banking system and introduced a certain order into things. This ordinance remained in force for bank-enterprise relations in the Soviet Union and some other Eastern countries for two decades.

Bank-enterprise relations differed depending on enterprise performance. Enterprises were classified as good or poor in performance according to formalized criteria for evaluation. Costs, profits and losses, own funds, and solvency were the major indices.

Bank controls were relaxed considerably for prospering enterprises, but rigidified for those that performed poorly. The former could usually obtain credits for twenty days to cover due supplier claims or pay salaries and wages without having to present any supporting documents.

The Banking System

A poorly performing enterprise that was unable to make its payments to the bank and to suppliers on time could expect no further loans and could anticipate a possible sanction placing unpaid deliveries in the bank's safekeeping, with the enterprise having no right to their use. In especially serious cases, when an enterprise could present no adequate proof that improvement was forthcoming, it could be declared insolvent, and the authorities would then require a restorative program.

Soon after the above regulations came into force, it was realized that the intended improvement in enterprise activities could not be achieved through the guiding hands of the banks. The deficiencies leading to deterioration of bank-enterprise relations did not always lie with the enterprise; in fact, these problems were often — indeed, usually — due to factors that were totally independent. Under these conditions, blocking loans could only complicate rather than improve the situation.

In some Eastern countries — Poland and Hungary, for example — the institutionalized classification of enterprises into those performing poorly and those performing well was abolished. Instead of a total stop on credits, they continued to be granted on special conditions — for example, with higher than average interest rates — in order to help an enterprise combat its difficulties and exercise supervision over its efforts to extricate itself from its difficulties.

The Soviet banking system was also obliged to concede that harsh treatment of poorly performing enterprises — the refusal of credits, in particular — did not improve the situation. Government Resolution 594 of August 22, 1973, represented an effort to adjust the August 1954 regulations. The essence of this arrangement was that banks would no longer refuse credits to an enterprise that had fallen into difficulties but would grant credits only on special terms. An enterprise had to commit itself to make up its arrears within the time agreed upon with the lending bank in order to ensure repayment of the loan. Credits are granted to replenish an enterprise's own funds depleted as a result of reduced profits or losses, and to finance excess stockpiles. [43]

An enterprise in payments difficulties was no longer declared insolvent, and hence shipments were no longer stopped or continued only against promissory note payment.

Thus, in the Soviet Union it is generally held to be better for a bank to finance measures to compensate for losses or increase profits than to break off relations with enterprises operating at a loss. In the other Eastern countries, however, it is viewed as better to refuse credits than to grant them in especially serious cases.

In a resolution of January 30, 1976, the Polish government empowered banks to chose between granting credits under more stringent terms or limiting or refusing further credits to firms in economic difficulties.[44]

The decision was made to employ the banking system more to prevent enterprises from exceeding the funds set aside for salaries and wages. The banks were henceforth empowered to intervene directly; their function was no longer restricted merely to informing higher authorities about enterprise excesses, with the demand that the latter be punished appropriately. When enterprises deviate from the established balance between growth in productivity and growth in wages, banks are empowered to stop bonus payments to the enterprise administration.[45]

In Hungary, credits are refused when payments difficulties are due to poor performance. A bank vice-president has declared: "No credits are granted for products that are difficult or impossible to get rid of, or for excess stocks."[46] The German Democratic Republic and Czechoslovakia are also trying to effect a reduction in excessive stockpiles by refusing credits.

12. Interest Policy

In an effort to diminish the administrative supervisory functions of banks and to enlarge the set of ordinary economic banking instruments, more and more emphasis is placed on the manipulation of bank interest rates. In the original concept of credit policy, interest rates were designed mainly to cover the costs of bank activities; they were not the price of credit. Hence, interest rates were extremely low: 1-2 percent annually, or 3 percent for overdue credits. Interest was not the price of money, nor is it today — even in Hungary, with its far-reaching reforms. There is no money or capital market to make this possible, that is, where the interplay between supply and demand could create an equilibrium interest.

The purely computational function of interest as a financing source for bank costs has been gradually abandoned, however, for two reasons: when a tax was instituted on factory assets, a considerable discrepancy arose between the 5-6 percent tax rate and the 2 percent interest rate for credits. Interest was supposed to gradually replace the relaxed administrative supervisory functions. Although it was still not the price of money, it had become more of a manipulatory instrument of the banks. As a result, the interest rate was increased across the board and a graduated system was worked out for different objects of credit. Interest rates for unplanned and overdue credits were increased, in particular. While in the Soviet Union the interest rates for clearing credits, planned stocks, and capital investment credits were 1, 2, and 2 percent, respectively, the rate for nonseasonal commodity stockpiles was increased to 6 percent and that for overdue credits 8 percent. The actual interest rate levied in 1974 (2.9 percent)[47] was much higher than that in 1968 (1.9 percent), but it was still relatively small.

The use of interest as an instrument of credit policy for influencing enterprise behavior is even more pronounced in Poland than in the Soviet Union. Polish banks are authorized to raise the interest rate 2-4 percent per annum if an enterprise departs from regulations.[48] The average interest actually levied increased from 1.8 percent in 1972 to 5.2 percent in 1975 for capital investment credits, and from 2.9 to 6.2 percent for current assets credits. Punitive interest brought the Polish National Bank 293 million zlotys in 1973, 386 million zlotys in 1974, and 375 million zlotys in the first half of 1975.[49]

In Romania, government Resolution 234 of December 23, 1974, established a graduated interest rate schedule as of January 1, 1975. The rate set for planned credits ranged from 0.5 percent (for example, for factory kitchens) to 5 percent (for industrial plant). The rate for overcoming payments difficulties caused by economic problems (special credits) was 4-7 percent, while the rate for overdue credits ran to 12 percent.[50]

Hungary's interest rate policy differs from that of the other Eastern countries in that it is used as an accounting parameter by economic enterprises to enable them to choose more intelligently between the use of their own funds and of credits. The Hungarian National Bank is more inclined to use bank credits to bridge short-term payments difficulties in production and turnover. Therefore, as a rule credits must be paid off in 90 days. If payment is delayed beyond the set term, the interest rate for each succeeding 90-day period is raised by 1 percent, up to a ceiling of 10 percent.[51] A Hungarian enterprise can also transform its clearing monies into bank deposits and obtain an interest rate of 3-7 percent depending on the term of commitment.

In a planned economy, interest is no more than an accounting parameter of banks. It has become respectable not, however, as the market price of money but as an instrument of banks for influencing their relations with enterprises. A bank may lower or raise the interest rate depending on what is to be financed. A bank branch is much less tied to a centrally set interest rate than formerly. Within limits, banks may differentiate interest rates to compel enterprises to tender a service in return. A differentiated, more elastic interest rate has made the banking mechanisms in the planned economies more efficient.

NOTES

1. K. Marx, Critique of the Gotha Program, 1891, quoted in Socialist Economics: Selected Readings, ed. by Alec Nove and D. M. Nuti, Penguin, 1972.
2. V. I. Lenin, Collected Works (Russian edition), Vol. 26, Moscow, 1960, p. 106.
3. G. Garvy, Money, Financial Flows, and Credit in the Soviet Union, Cambridge, Mass., 1977, p. 20.
4. O. Bauer, "Der Weg zum sozialismus," Vienna, 1919, p. 26, quoted from L. von Mises (1920), "Economic Calculations in the Socialist Commonwealth,"

112

The Banking System

in Socialist Economics, p. 85.

5. Lenin, Collected Works, Vol. 34, p. 37.

6. Z. Atlas, Sotsialisticheskaia denezhnaia sistema [The Socialist Monetary System], Moscow, 1969, p. 138.

7. Ibid., p. 139.

8. Ibid., p. 132.

9. George Garvy says: "The role of monetary flows is to implement the planners' intentions and not to evoke responses." In "Banking, Money, and Credit in Eastern Europe," NATO colloquium, Brussels, January 1973, p. 62.

10. Atlas, op. cit., p. 280.

11. The Eastern banking system has been more successful than the Western one in centralizing clearing. As Schumpeter noted: "Even in the countries with the most developed banking organizations, in England and the USA, about 10-20 percent of transactions still take place outside the banks." Das Wesen des Geldes, Vandenhoeck and Ruprecht, 1970, p. 149.

12. See Finansy i kredit SSSR [Financing and Credit in the USSR], Moscow, 1972, pp. 270-271 (collection).

13. "If, on the other hand, [a firm] sells the note to a bank, the commodity credit is eliminated and economically the situation produced is similar to that which would have occurred if the transaction had been financed from the outset by a bank credit to the purchaser." Schumpeter, op. cit., p. 149.

14. Narodnoe khoziaistvo, 1975, p. 760.

15. Narodnoe khoziaistvo, 1977, p. 516.

16. Ibid., p. 656.

17. The Polish Party newspaper, Trybuna ludu, justifies this policy as follows: "The savings and credit societies for a long time have had considerable state funds, took part in the purchase of agricultural products, performed services for state organizations, and quite recently even began to finance the social budget" (July 2, 1975).

18. See Życie gospodarcze, April 28, 1975.

19. Bank i kredyt, 12/1975, p. 370.

20. Rocznik statystyczny, 1977, pp. 420, 421.

21. See W. Bien, "Zmiany w systemie bankowym" [Changes in the Banking System], Bank i kredyt, 7-8/1975, p. 238.

22. Wiadomości NBP [Reports of the Polish National Bank], 3/1968.

23. Deutsche Finanzwirtschaft, 12/1967.

24. See C. Uzunova, "Principles of Short-term Credit under the New System," Finansi i kredit (Sofia), 4/1968, p. 28.

25. L. Siemiątkowski, "Reforma bankowości" [Reform of the Credit System], Gospodarka planowa (Warsaw), 1/1969, p. 8.

26. See Handelsblatt, August 29-30, 1975, p. 10.

27. Soviet finance expert M. Atlas says: "The circulation of money in Soviet enterprises reflects an increase in production and profits and creates the conditions for later expansion of credit transactions." See "O meste i roli kredita v sisteme ekonomicheskikh otnoshenii sotsializma" [The Role of Credit in

Money, Banking, and Credit

Socialist Economic Relations], Den'gi i kredit, 12/1975, p. 87.

28. Quoted in Professor V. Zaidenvarg, "Kreditnyi protsess kak tselostnaia sistema" [The Credit Process as an Integral System], Den'gi i kredit, 12/1975, p. 40.

29. Ibid., p. 37.

30. M. Iampolskii, Resursy kratkosrochnogo kredita [Resources of Short-term Credits], Moscow, 1974, p. 50.

31. A. Melkov, Kreditnye resursy gosudarstvennogo banka SSSR [Credit Resources of the Soviet State Banks], 1969, p. 130.

32. The epigraph Albert Hahn put in his book Economic Theory of Bank Credit (Tübingen, 1930) is even more true for a planned than for a market economy: "A bank is not an institution for receiving and lending money, but an institution for producing credit" (cited in Macleod, Theory of Credit, p. 594).

33. See V. Solov'ev, "Organizatsiia kreditnogo planirovaniia i problemy ego sovershenstvovaniia" [Organization of Credit Planning and Problems of Its Improvement], Den'gi i kredit, 10/1975, p. 25.

34. Hahn, op. cit., Preface, pp. 4 and 25.

35. The credit plan is the backbone of credit control and makes possible ongoing supervision of economic activity, says the vice-manager of the planning division of the Soviet state bank. Solov'ev, op. cit., p. 22.

36. Jan Wasenczuk, "Umacniamy oddziaływanie za pomocą kreditu," [We Are Reinforcing the Effect by Means of Credit], Bank i kredyt, 4/1976, p. 118.

37. See V. Solov'ev, op. cit., p. 24.

38. See Gy. Tallós, "Bedingungen der Kreditgewährung in der VR Ungarn," West-Ost Journal, 6/1975, p. 27.

39. Soviet expert Solov'ev notes: "The short-term credit plan reflects the amount of money issues and is tied directly to the steering of the amount of money in circulation." Op. cit., p. 23.

40. See W. Jaworski, Bank i kredyt w europejskich krajach socjalistycznych [Banks and Credit in the European Socialist Nations], Warsaw, 1971, p. 272.

41. Ibid., p. 295.

42. Tallós, op. cit., p. 27.

43. N. Barkovskii, "Kreditnyi mekhanizm i ego ispol'zovanie" [The Credit Mechanism and Its Use], Den'gi i kredit, 9/1975.

44. See W. Bien, "O wyzsza jakość pracy NBP" [Bank Activities and Their Improvement], Bank i kredyt, 3/1976.

45. Ibid.

46. Tallós, op. cit., p. 27.

47. See M. Atlas, "Kredit w sisteme ekonomicheskikh otnoshenii razvitogo sotsializma" [Credit in the System of Economic Relations of Developed Socialism], Den'gi i kredit, 10/1974, p. 69.

48. See Wasenczuk, op. cit., p. 119.

49. Bien, op. cit., p. 71.

50. Buletinul oficial, 166, December 26, 1974.

51. See Economic Bulletin of the National Bank of Hungary, May 1969.

Chapter 5

THE CREDIT POLICIES
OF THE PLANNED ECONOMIES

1. Credit Policy and Steering Models

As with the banking system, the development of credit policy has reflected the evolution of the economy as a whole. Money and credit policies are important steering instruments in a planned economy; at the same time, they reflect how efficiently it functions. Credit policy has varied over time, but two basic models can be distinguished, with the dividing line between them lying somewhere in the fifties. The major credit reform of 1930-32 established the major contours of the first. This was the period during which the Soviet economy was definitively transformed into a centrally administered system after two brief transitional phases — War Communism and the NEP.

2. The Programmatic Credit Reform

The USSR government resolution of December 5, 1929, "On the Reorganization of the Principles of Management of Soviet Industry," laid the groundwork for the credit reform. The reorganized management strictly centralized control of supply, production, and distribution of the final product. The government resolution of January 30, 1930, on credit reform, which established the State Bank as a central monetary and clearing institution for the state-run economy, was designed to provide an adequate credit system for the centralized steering of the economy.

During the two years between the first two stages of the reform, the basic concept of lending and credit underwent a radical change — a fact that underscores the difficulties encountered
by the centralized planned economy as it tried to introduce
credit relations into an economy based on state ownership of the
means of production.

It was only natural that an attempt should be made to centralize lending as well by eliminating all credit activity not initiated
by the banks. The state bank was the only institution authorized
to lend money to economic enterprises; it coordinated all monetary flows, cleared accounts between enterprises, and put money
into circulation. Centralization of decision making was supposed
to make it possible to centralize the planning of money flows, to
supervise a uniform system of lending regulations, and to coordinate the credit plan with the economic plan of the state.

The guidelines laid down at that time, which established
credit policy as a steering instrument of a planned economy are
still in force today to the extent that the planned economies have
kept the system intact. At any rate, Dr. Gy Tallós, vice-president of the Hungarian National Bank — which has perhaps gone
further than any other Eastern bank in adapting its credit policy
to the changing times — believes that this is so: "The principal
terms of lending that derive from the nature of a socialist
planned economy are a matter of principle and have remained
basically unchanged."[1]

3. From Automatism to Rigorous Lending Rules

Considerable changes have taken place, however, in the regulations governing lending, in the way credits are used by the
borrower, and in relations between banks and enterprises. The
latest developments in the area of credit in the Eastern countries seem to be more in line with the original conception than
with later ideas of the 1930-32 credit reform: credit policy is
tending toward looser lending terms, as in the first stage of the
reform, rather than toward the tighter lending policy that
marked the second stage. In 1930, credits were extended auto-

matically via the borrower's current account; no security was required. In any event, this was the policy when money was required. This loose policy was blamed for the galloping inflation of the First Five-Year Plan, when consumer goods prices rose by 250 percent.[2] In 1930 credit volume doubled, and the amount of money in circulation increased by 52 percent. The cause was not the easy credit terms, however, but the rapid growth in heavy industry and the defense industry, at the same time that agriculture and the consumer goods industry were being neglected.

A radical turnabout was made from extremely lax to rigorous lending policies, and in 1931 the credit system was saddled with the same cumbersome executive and administrative apparatus as the rest of the economy. The foundations on which this rigorous credit system was built remained unchanged, however; that is, it still served a planned economy in which all monetary funds — state budget funds, the monetary resources of the banks, and those of the enterprises — were all state property. The credit system had to be accommodated to the inescapable fact that the function of credit was first and foremost to put needed means of payment into circulation, whether in accordance with official regulations or not. It took a year to make the transition from an automatic to a rigorous credit system. The return to automatic mechanisms, especially in relations with prospering enterprises, dragged over twenty years and was marked by several setbacks.

The second stage of the credit reform of 1930-31 had a lasting effect on the credit system in the planned economies, for it established a sharp division between the use of budget funds and the use of borrowed money. Since there was no market to establish such a dividing line naturally,[3] it was drawn on the basis of convention. According to a government resolution of July 23, 1931, the state budget was to cover a fixed need for financial resources by providing enterprises with a fund of their own. Credit was not intended automatically to replace deficient current funds, however, but to finance seasonal pileups of inventory, clearing documents on the way from supplier to buyer, a fixed percentage of goods turnover in the domestic trade, and temporary short-term enterprise needs. The credit reform also laid down rules for the lending and use of credits that would allow the state bank to influence operating costs and stockpiles.

4. Five Commandments of Credit Policy

Five principles for credit policy were set down:

a) In contrast to budget subsidies, credits were to be paid back. Therefore they were used to finance only projects or items such as seasonal and similar needs, for which repayment would be possible after accumulated stockpiles were depleted or expenditures covered.

b) The repayment period was to be set in accordance with the planned turnover of enterprise stocks and was to be no longer than one year for short-term credits.

c) Special stress was placed on earmarked credits, particularly during the first phase of development. To facilitate bank control, credits were tied to specific items in the working assets, such as raw materials, finished products, and so forth, rather than being injected into the economy as an anonymous purchasing power. The upper credit limit was to be set by the central banking and economic authorities.

d) In accordance with the third principle, a credit had to be secured with some portion of working assets within the time limit. If such security was not provided, the credit fell due immediately, regardless of the term of payment agreed upon when the loan was granted.

e) Credits were specified in the State Bank's credit plan, as a part of the overall economic plan. The intention here was to keep the allocation of credit in line with material values.

The basic principles of credit policy laid down in the beginning of the thirties remained in force for more than twenty-five years in the Soviet Union and a decade in the people's democracies. As time passed, however, they became more and more cumbersome — even more so than the steering system as a whole. Countless procedural rules and regulations made the credit system, which tended to be inscrutable anyway, a source of total

118

despair for both borrower and lender. The borrower, that is, the enterprise, and its success or failure were lost behind the mass of different kinds of credit — at the high point of centralized control, there were fifteen to twenty different types of credit, all registered in special accounts and under bank controls. For the bank, the enterprise as an economic entity was lost from view, and only one component of its circulating assets, which were supposed to be brought under control by the lending and repayment terms, remaining accessible for consideration. These terms could at times be hard, but the fact still remained that credit relations were between economic entities under the same ownership. Since credit relations between enterprises were prohibited, and since the state budget financed the rigidly regulated enterprise funds only within certain limits which could not be transgressed, bank credits were the only means to bridge any payments gaps. Faced with the alternative of either initiating an endless chain of interenterprise obligations and commitments of economic units to the state budget and to their staffs, or granting a loan that could take care of all obligations with a single sweep, banks would usually opt for the latter, even when they could count on a reprimand from higher-echelon banking authorities at the next inspection. But a shrewd credit inspector could always find some loophole in the tangle of rules and regulations that would enable him to legitimate any loan with which he might be confronted. Moreover, he had an interest in doing so as well, for overdue payments — not the size of a loan — were the crucial criterion for evaluating bank performance.

In time, however, authorities came to realize that even the hardest lending terms could not prevent hitches and discrepancies in planning and plan fulfillment, and that credit had to finance them. The hope that credit could bring in the missing proceeds through the rigid mechanisms it set in force gradually faded. If an enterprise could evade the commands of the state plan and state authorities, it could also evade bank controls, especially since banks had much weaker executive powers than the other instrumentalities of the state.

The credit system of the planned economies, with its restrictive and mostly administrative regulations, proved to be less effective in influencing the economic process than were discount interest and open market policy, and other instruments of market economies.

Thus, there was a gradual return to the more liberal concept of credit that marked the first stage of the 1930-31 reform; no one wanted openly to admit retreat — failures then were blamed on the enemies of the people, as was the wont at the time — but there could be no denial that some mistake had been made.

5. Redefinition of the Limits of Credit

A radical reform of the credit system would require reorganization of the economic model as a whole and could be no more successful nor innovative than an overall reform. The economic reforms have shown the extent to which a planned economy can and wants to use credit as a steering instrument. Long years of both separate and joint experience by the CMEA nations have made it possible to define the limits of credit as a special instrument of the planned economies better than could have been possible in the initial period and accordingly to adapt lending policies to the modest means of control available.

The long years of experience, however, have also shown the untenability of manipulating lending terms in the effort to develop bank credits into an instrument of control that would permit the detection of every hitch or miscalculation in the operations of an enterprise, and its guidance back onto the road toward the planned target.

Still, credits have proven themselves a flexible instrument. The money needed by economic development may not always be injected into the economy as prescribed by the plan, but it is still done more efficiently and economically than would be the case if the state budget did not allocate enterprise funds on the basis of minimal needs, as it is done normally, but covered all payments needs arising in the course of enterprise activities with nonrepayable budget subsidies.

Credit Policies

The planned economies seem to be still caught up in the pre-classical theory of credit. They continue to believe that existing money resources create the basis for lending, rather than that credit creates money.[4] Some also hold that when money is allotted as a clearing and payments medium, credit also injects capital into the economy.[5] This was the view of the preclassical economist MacLeod. The classical economists, on the other hand, believed that "no matter how many credits or how much new money is raised, no new capital is created in the economic sense, since making money does not mean making commodities."[6]

The notion of the capital-creating function of credit in a planned economy did not arise by accident. The most important of the five lending commandments — that credit must fit in with the plan — means that credit is tied directly to the desired, and hence planned, creation of value. A credit that was not in line with the plan could be granted only in a very special, strictly regulated case. Thus the capital-forming function of credit does not derive from its basic function. As the means of financing the planned economic process, its function is to promote the fulfillment of economic tasks and prevent deviations from the plan target. A neutral credit — that is, one that did not create capital — would violate the principles according to which the society operated, as well as its steering mechanisms. Credit can only create capital by design if lending follows desired and established principles, which it does not always do. Theory may not always have kept pace with practical experience, but practice itself has long since abandoned theory. Bank activities are shaped not by the learned disputes of credit theoreticians — these are disregarded in the East just as much as they are in the West — but by the laws of economic activity, which are growing ever more complicated and are not always immediately obvious. For a long time now, credits have been granted for purposes that would have to be regarded as a violation of the spirit as well as the letter of the economic plan — for stocks that have been hoarded in excess of plan allotments to the detriment of other economic entities, or for replenishment of an enterprise's own funds that have been depleted by unforeseen losses.

121

6. The Relaxation of Credit Terms

Long years of practical experience diverging from officially approved principles have been tacitly recognized by government dispositions, the most recent and most explicit of which can be found in the government resolution of the Soviet Union dated August 22, 1973, "Measures to Improve Credit and Clearing Practices in the Economy." N. Barkovskii, Soviet expert on credit planning, commented on the newly approved but long practiced credit policy as follows: "Banks complement their economic influence on enterprises that fail to meet quantity and quality plan targets with de facto credit assistance, which is also extended to enterprises operating at a loss."[7] The regulation represents a considerable step forward over government Resolution 1789 of August 21, 1954, which provided looser lending terms for prospering enterprises only, while poorly performing enterprises or those operating at a loss were faced with extremely stiff terms.

Credits that, in opposition to the plan target, replenish an enterprise's own funds depleted by losses do not create new capital; they only replace it. This is also the case when credits are granted for stocks that are hoarded in inordinate quantities to the detriment of the overall economy. The credit that puts the required additional money into circulation in such cases eases payments difficulties but does not create desired capital nor value.

Over the course of time, other lending commandments were also abandoned — in particular, the narrow restrictions placed on the use of credits by the major credit reform of 1930-32. The restriction of credits to seasonal and similar temporary pileups and expenditures very soon came into conflict with the ambitious intentions of the State Bank, which wanted to expand bank controls to a maximum by putting credit on a solid and stable foundation. But the uses of credit could no longer be expanded with the laborious lump-sum lending procedures. The amount of work required was totally out of proportion to its effectiveness, and a bank branch did not have the facilities to control transformation of the item for which a loan was granted from one component of the working assets to another.

The traditional distinction between sources of financing — that is, budget funds for minimal and standing enterprise stocks, credits for seasonal and other transitory needs, and lump-sum and earmarked credits — was also gradually abandoned.

It is becoming more and more the practice to grant credits in terms of a percentage of an enterprise's working assets; for example, this is done in the Soviet Union for heavy industry, internal trade, and purchasing stations for agricultural products, and in Poland and Bulgaria for all economic entities. A net change took place in lending practices as well as in the basic concept of credit, which was transformed from a source for financing transitory needs into a budget-like component of an enterprise's working assets. According to this conception, credits may be granted for all materials and expenditures for labor — in other words, wages — and not merely for a single component of the working assets. Total input is covered in a credit account, rather than a credit being deposited in a special account for each item.

Abandonment of the basic principle of traditional credit policy by which the credit could be applied to working assets is of much greater significance. Formerly, working assets were financed by bank credits, and capital investment projects by state budget subsidies. The importance of the change lay in the fact that a strict line was no longer drawn between investment activities and production activities, and the notion that an enterprise had to feed its entire profits into the state budget for reapportionment rather than to use a portion for investment projects of its own was abandoned.

The economic reforms, which widened the decision-making powers of individual enterprises, also granted them certain powers — which varied from place to place — to invest on their own and to finance these investments out of their development funds or with bank credits. In some Eastern countries, financing by means of bank credits was also extended to investment projects that ministries for the different branches of industry

could undertake on their own initiative. The extension of credits to finance capital investment projects abolished another basic principle of traditional credit policy — namely, that bank
credits had to be short-term — for capital investment credits
often run up to fifteen years.

The changes in credit policy described above depict tendencies that are present in all the planned economies. Nevertheless, there is as yet no such thing as a unified credit policy for
the Eastern bloc; its forms are as varied as those of the steering system itself.

7. Diversity Within the System

Central planning and central administration are regarded as
the natural steering systems for an economy based on state
ownership. Neither before the revolution nor today, however,
have unambiguous definitions been given of the scope of the
binding plan target figures, which are supposed to steer economic growth, or the mechanisms that are to utilize them to
achieve the plan targets. During the Sturm und Drang period
of the first years after the revolution, money was regarded as
a vestige from capitalism and hence an evil to be abolished.
Indeed, at the time, it was not impossible to believe that radical
change had already occurred. The complete depreciation of
money caused by the galloping inflation perforce gave birth to
a barter economy. But this was hardly a situation out of which
modern industrial society could emerge to transform the vast
agrarian expanses of the Russian empire. To create a modern
industrial society, more was needed than the commands of the
planning authorities and administrative steering instruments.
It was not realized until later that an efficient economy could
be built up only if every job done not only was carried out effectively, but moreover was recognized as having been done well
and rewarded accordingly. And for this, a working monetary
system and money relations were necessary.

The material exigencies of the war and postwar period put
money relations at the top of the agenda. But the attempt to

make a moneyless economy a natural and necessary goal, as the
Eighth Party Congress tried in 1919, failed because it violated
the inexorable laws of economic development. A moneyless
economy is still postulated for the vague epoch of the future
communist society — as, for example, in the formulation of Soviet professor M. Atlas: "Under Communism, commodity and
money relations, and all the categories of value, credit included,
will die away"[8]; but for the concrete near future, the guidelines of the Twenty-fourth and Twenty-fifth Party Congresses
are more realistic. They specify an effective expansion of instruments such as independent cost accounting, prices, profits,
credits, bonuses, and so on. It is now realized that an administered economy which rejects an effective monetary and credit
system has a dim future; that one cannot plan and command
everything; and that recommendations, however reasonable they
may be, cannot always be implemented. The belief in the om-
nipotency of the plan, of its ability to bring order into a planned
economy, has been thoroughly shaken, as has the belief in the
ability of a credit plan and cash plan and their instrumentalities
to bring order into monetary and credit relations.

Every CMEA country, as a matter of practice, has tried to
accommodate traditional economic categories to the limited
means for assimilating them in a planned economy. The Soviet
steering system and its credit policy, which were the rule in the
entire Eastern bloc until the mid-fifties, are no longer considered models for imitation. The search for more effective steering mechanisms has given rise to a more diversified steering
concept. Efficiency is conceivable only if a steering system is
adapted to the realities of the times and to existing economic
structures. The variety of solutions that have appeared shows
clearly that diversity, not uniformity, in steering systems
stands the best chance of promoting economic performance.

In none of the CMEA nations, however, has the steering system been changed radically enough to allow creation of the conditions for a qualitatively new credit system. The material
constraints imposed by the fact that the state completely owns
both the means of production and the banks continue to deter-

mine the basic principles of credit policy. Even the broad decentralization of decision making that has given certain enterprises and banks a measure of independence in this respect is
not enough to create a functional money and capital market in
the planned economies. Therefore, when the term "socialist
market" is employed in Hungary, it defines the content no better than the term "social market" as used in the West. [9]

Hungary's present steering model is distinctly different from
the Soviet model of the thirties, which set the groundwork for
traditional credit policy; it differs as well from the Soviet
steering model of today. Indeed, each Eastern nation exhibits
certain peculiarities of its own that have had considerable influence on credit policy. It might be useful, therefore, to discuss briefly how credit policy has taken shape in each of the
CMEA nations.

8. The Modified Credit Policy of the Soviet Union

The reform project announced at the Twenty-fifth Party Congress represents the third attempt to make the Soviet model
more effective and bring it in tune with new developments, although in essence it is only a continuation of the economic reform introduced by the Party leadership under Brezhnev with
the October 2, 1965, resolution of the Central Committee. The
great economic reform started by Khruschchev in 1957, which replaced vertical control over the various industries with 107 regional administrative bodies (Sovnarkhozes), was abandoned by
the new leadership because regional administrations were tending toward autarky and coming into conflict with the general interests of the state.

The October 1965 resolution restored the economic ministry
and strengthened the powers of the planning committees. The
planning procedure itself, however, was considerably simplified. The mass of binding plan target figures were reduced to
eight in number, and those retained were made more responsive
to the needs of development. The volume of goods sold has
now replaced gross output as the most important parameter.

Credit Policies

Enterprise earnings are now a more important plan indicator, although they are planned in relation to plant assets, not to production costs as before. The reform also attempted to reorganize administration, whose pillars are the industrial associations, which have been given more decision-making powers as in Bulgaria, the German Democratic Republic, and Poland. In addition, long-term programs for the development of technology, science, and society as a whole are designed to give the overall plan a broader perspective.

The reformed Soviet system, however, is not qualitatively new, nor is it a mixed system that tries to reconcile the traditional mechanisms of planning and administration with market mechanisms. The main import of the reform is elimination of the petty and ineffective control of the central authorities over each individual enterprise, and better adaptation of market categories, appropriately modified, to the conditions of a planned economy.

Enterprise earnings, calculated as a percentage of assets, are oriented more toward a market concept than cost-induced earnings. However, they still remain an index, a target, an item calculated into prices, and they are to be attained and reapportioned under planned conditions of operation. Because of the distorted price structure, which is shielded from world prices, profits do not adequately express efficiency, nor can they be used as an apportionment factor to influence enterprise activity. Though a larger portion of earnings is now left in the hands of the enterprise for its own purposes (in 1965 the state budget took 71 percent of total earnings; in 1970, 61 percent; and in 1974, only 57 percent), the state still decides on its use. Soviet industry turned over 30 percent of its earnings to the state budget as residual sums and used only 13 percent for enterprise investments.[10]

Soviet state enterprises have not been decentralized enough to allow them to be integrated by a market type of money relations. They are still an organic part of a state cartel. Therefore credit is not an alien category opposed to the enterprise through its interest rates, which depend on supply and demand.

It is still an instrument of the state and an integral part of state administrative steering. Thus, the chief emphasis in the reform of credit policy, as in the reform of the administrative system as a whole, was on debureaucratization and simplification of procedures rather than on any basic change in principles. The scope of credits and of lending terms is still determined by the central authorities, although credit agreements between a bank branch and an enterprise may modify certain details in the lending terms. Real credits extended to the economy differ considerably in scope from what is anticipated by the credit plan.

Investment projects now are financed more with bank credits than formerly, but decision making is still largely centralized. In the Soviet Union, decentralized investment projects started at the initiative of enterprises comprise no more than 10 to 20 percent of the total plant, and availability of money is not an indispensable requirement for undertaking capital investments.[11] The central authorities must approve centralized investment projects even when they are financed by bank credits. The prerequisites for a loan are that accrued earnings must be paid back within a term of five years, and that the project to be financed with credits must be integrated into the state capital investment plan.

The share of credits in the total financing funds of the centralized investment projects of Soviet industrial enterprises increased from 4.2 percent in 1970 to 7.2 percent in 1973, but it is still low. The share of credits taken out by enterprise management for mechanizing production (506 million rubles in 1974) and for expanding the production of consumer goods (1,639 million rubles) is no more than 2.2 percent of total investments (93.8 billion rubles in 1974).[12]

In the Soviet Union, the credit financing of capital investment projects is not a result of the decentralization of decision making but a measure taken to prevent shoddy work: in 1974, the construction time for projects averaged 5.4 years as contrasted with the normative period of 3 years, and in 1973, 73 percent of construction projects were turned over to the enterprises only after considerable delays.[13]

Credit Policies

Interest rates in the Soviet Union (0.5 percent for credits for centralized investment projects and 1.5 percent for overdue credits) have little to do with market interest rates. They bear no rational relation to profit rates, which comprised 17.7 percent of enterprise funds in 1974,[14] and are much lower than the interest rates for credits for working assets. A construction enterprise receives a bonus for early completion of a project; if the construction time is shortened by six months, the interest is halved; if it is completed less than six months early, the interest is reduced by 25 percent.

The economic reform focused on improving the technical and organizational aspects of the steering model, but credit policy in the area of working assets was affected as well. A number of erroneous notions were abandoned, and the realization was reached that not much can be achieved through rigorous credit terms. This conclusion was reflected in an August 1973 government resolution which provided for credit assistance to every enterprise, even those that performed poorly; this resolution superseded the August 1954 resolution, with its severe sanctions on poorly performing enterprises.

The credit system, which is still unable to pursue interests of its own, remains a dependent entity: "The parameters describing credit efficiency are commensurable with parameters characterizing overall efficiency, such as profits, sales, and the earnings of enterprise funds."[15] Soviet credit planner Barkovskii has pointed out that the credit mechanism is only one instrument of state control, albeit an important one.[16]

The Soviet reform eliminated the administrative constraints of the banks on poorly performing enterprises and relaxed credit policy in general. Centralized control over every individual component of current assets was abandoned; instead, central authorities henceforth were to determine only the total sum of enterprise resources — how they are to be broken down is the affair of the enterprise itself. The controlling bank, however, may still question the enterprise's apportionment if it finds that the normative component is set too low to justify large credits. With this arrangement, the traditional linkage between the centrally planned component of current assets and a centrally (State Bank) assigned credit limit lost the control function for which it was originally intended. The limitation of credits for individual items in an enterprise's working assets and their placement in special accounts was gradually abandoned; where it was maintained, it lost the influence it was supposed to have because of the maneuverability given to regional banking boards and because of the increased practice of granting payments credits without requiring any ties to commodity stocks.

Turnover credits are being used more and more; in this type of credit, the total costs of materials and wages are paid for regularly out of a credit account and the loan is later paid back from enterprise earnings. In such a case, credit is only another form of homogeneous state funds, different from budget money. Turnover credits are useful, however, because they provide a means of ongoing supervision by the controlling bank over the production and sales activities of an enterprise, and because they can be used when needed, without the tapping of budget funds, which must be earmarked and tied up over a long term.

The credit reform also influenced the structure of credits already outstanding. When investment credits were expanded, the share of long-term credit in the total sum of credits available to the economy as a whole ($74 billion in 1965, and $228 billion in 1976) increased from 9.9 percent in 1965 to 21.9 percent in 1976.[17]

Shifts in the structure of financing sources were also evident, as the following table shows. Structural changes in financing resources are apparent in all branches of the economy. The share of an enterprise's own funds has decreased everywhere, while the proportion of credits has increased except in the construction industry and internal trade organizations. The share of creditors has risen considerably, from 11.5 to 20.4 percent of the total funds — especially in construction, where it grew from 21.7 percent to 56.4 percent. In the latter case, the increase was due to the growing practice of granting client advances to the contractor, as well as delayed completion of construction projects; the share of incomplete construction and installation projects in the current assets of the construction industry in-

Credit Policies

(in percent)

Type of financing	Total economy		Industry		State agricultural enterprises		Construction		Trade	
	1965	1974	1965	1974	1965	1974	1965	1974	1965	1974
Enterprises' own funds	38.3	28.0	45.7	35.4	50.7	40.3	53.6	22.4	27.7	25.7
Bank credits	47.1	45.0	42.6	45.4	35.0	40.0	21.2	16.7	62.0	60.5
Creditors	11.5	20.4	8.6	10.5	5.5	6.6	21.7	56.4	9.6	12.0
Others	3.1	6.6	3.1	8.7	8.8	13.1	3.5	4.5	0.7	1.8
Total	100.0	100.0	100.0	100.0	100.0	100.0	100.0	100.0	100.0	100.0

Source: Narodnoe khoziaistvo, pp. 746, 747.

creased from 8.3 percent in 1965 to 65.4 percent in 1974,[18] with the result that creditors could not be paid off within the stipulated time.

The share of agriculture in the total sum of credits granted almost doubled from 13.0 to 24.7 percent[19] in connection with the promotional efforts undertaken by the Soviet government to increase the low level of productivity in agriculture. The share of the public in the credit sum is relatively low, decreasing from 1.0 to 0.3 percent of the credit sum over 1965 to 1974, and from 4.3 to 0.7 percent[20] in proportion to rapidly growing savings deposits (18,727 million rubles in 1965 and 78,905 million rubles in 1974). The new Soviet credit policy fit into the reformed centralized economy; planning and administration were decentralized to some extent, but their basic principles were retained. Credit policy consisted more of technical and organizational refinements than structural modifications in the system.

The only CMEA country that introduced qualitative changes in both credit policy and the steering system was Hungary, which will be discussed in the next section.

9. Hungary's Economic and Credit Reforms

9.1. The Reformed Steering Model

The Hungarian steering model that came into force on Janu-

131

ary 1, 1968, is more decentralized than other steering systems in the CMEA. More than in any other Eastern country, central planning is limited to a few profiling indicators, and economic mechanisms are given broad play. The new system, referred to as a socialist market, is based on the following principles.

The economic plan, which is compiled for one, five, and fifteen years, specifies only the major directions — that is, growth rate, factors promoting technological progress, and the most important mechanisms for fulfilling the plan. Economic ministries now control economic policy and steer plan fulfillment; they no longer maintain ongoing control of and supervision over enterprises under their jurisdiction. Their staff therefore has been reduced by 30 percent, that is, about 2,000 persons.[21] Enterprises are managed independently and may be authorized to conduct business abroad on their own. The management has full decision-making powers for enterprise affairs and carries full responsibility; however, it is stressed that the enterprise remains dependent on the state as the collective owner of the means of production.

Instead of administrative commands, there are now economic mechanisms: in particular, a mixed price system with free, limited, and fixed prices (such a system is a good indicator for allocation and performance and hence is adjusted to world market prices); a modified investment policy that authorizes enterprises to decide on some of their own investment projects; and a credit policy that places greater importance on the credit contract between the bank and the enterprise.

9.2. The Principal Trends of Credit Policy

In Hungary's reformed system, the binding parameters of a credit plan are not indispensable. Credit regulations and terms are set for a five-year period and issued in the form of guidelines to bank branches. They are incorporated into the five-year plan and adjusted every year to the current objectives of economic policy. Mandatory limits for annual and quarterly plans have been abolished for credits for working assets. Relations between borrower and bank are set down by agreement within the framework provided by the economic plan and the State Bank guidelines.

Solvency is a prerequisite for any loan. An enterprise is regarded as solvent if it "operates at a profit, sells its products on a regular basis, meets its payments commitments within the specified periods, and ensures that its credits are properly covered." [22] The bank checks the soundness of the borrower and the soundness of the project for which a loan is requested, and receives a legal right of lien on the total assets of the potential borrower to the amount of the loan. A credit extension is refused if money is needed because products have been difficult to sell or excessive stockpiles are on hand.

Payments operations and settlements function differently in Hungary than in the Soviet Union or some of the other Eastern countries. An enterprise itself selects how clearing is to be effected, but the purchaser is obligated to pay a bill within 30 days after shipment. In 1975, most payments were in the form of bank transfers (78.4 percent); collection on demand of the supplier accounted for only 13.5 percent. (In the Soviet Union, this proportion is reversed: 27.5 percent and 63.8 percent.) Bank investigations in October 1975, however, showed that only 78.6 percent of all claims were paid within the allotted 30-day period. [23] The supplier is authorized to demand a bank guaranty for a purchaser who is not regular in his payments or to obtain a court order for the payment of outstanding bills. In the latter case, a bank credit may be requested.

9.3. Capital Project Loans

In Hungary the way capital projects are financed depends much more on the degree of decision-making autonomy enjoyed by an economic entity than it does in the Soviet Union. The enterprise development fund, bank credits, and, in special cases, budget subsidies as well are used as sources of financing for enterprise capital investment projects. The composition of financing sources is set by the five-year plan and the guidelines

133

for credit policy, although the aim of extending investment loans on the basis of competition, giving the choice to the most profitable projects, remained unfulfilled in 1971-75 because of a contraction in enterprise willingness to invest. Up to 85 percent of the projects submitted for loans received credits supported by the Council of Ministers and industrial ministries. In these instances, the bank simply acted as executor of the commands of the central authorities. In other cases, however, banks must follow the stipulations of the authorities within a credit line of 15 percent instead of choosing the most profitable projects by competition.

In 1974, the share of enterprises' own funds in the financing of enterprise capital investment projects totaled 54 percent, that of bank credits 24 percent, and that of budget and other funds 22 percent.[24] In 1976, the State Bank was given broad powers to promote through credits capital investment projects that would help to expand the production of export goods: 55 percent of capital investment credits were granted in quota form by central authorities and the rest was to be granted to enterprises that committed themselves to expanding exports to hard currency areas, on the condition that credits be paid back in convertible currency within two to three years. Credits are granted for a period of up to twelve years and bear a 6 percent interest per annum.

Priority projects started by the government are financed by budget subsidies or budget loans, which are granted by the Hungarian Development Bank and refinanced by the State Bank. The percentage is set in accordance with the profitability norm.

The way capital investments are financed reflects the operating principles of the current steering model more than any other aspect of finance policy; but it, too, is very much dependent on the economic situation. If the latter deteriorates, the decision-making powers of the enterprises are curbed and rigorous terms are adopted for allocating material goods and financial resources.

9.4. Credits for Current Needs

Reforms of the steering model also affected credit policy for current needs. Hungarian authorities abandoned the practice of setting limits for the working assets of enterprises. An enterprise itself determines the volume of current money it needs on the basis of planned growth in production. The financing of growth in stocks, like the financing of capital investments, is viewed as the financing of enterprise development funds, formed from a portion of enterprise earnings. While this fund is being accumulated, bank credits supply the necessary financing funds, which are later paid back from the development fund. The term of this loan is usually three years, but eight-year middle-term credits are also currently being given.

An enterprise can also receive short-term loans:

— for seasonal stocks and expenditures, at a 9 percent interest rate;

— for temporary, unspecified needs, a scaled interest rate of 9 to 13 percent, depending on the term;

— for financing (under guarantee from the Ministry of Finance) of the depletion of an enterprise's own funds caused by losses, with a one-year repayment period and an interest rate of 6 percent;

— as renovation credit extended to enterprises to carry out a renovation program worked out under the supervision of a special committee of the Ministry of Finance, the industrial ministry, and the bank.

A bank may refuse a credit extension if it finds irregularities in economic activity. The appropriate ministry is informed of the reasons for the refusal: in 1973 and 1974, the Hungarian State Bank refused credit applications or extended a lower sum than requested in 8 percent and 9 percent of the cases, respectively. The Hungarian State Bank also tries to influence enterprise activity — its stocks, in particular — by applying a scaled interest rate.[25] In 1976, the interest rate was raised from 8 percent to 9 percent for middle-term credits and from 9 percent to 13 percent for short-term credits to extract a greater share of enterprise profits by means of the interest rate. In 1974, the share of accumulated interest in economic profits was only 7.9 percent.

135

Hungary's interest rate system is also more flexible than that of the other Eastern countries. Interest rates are set on the basis of the costs of domestic sources and the interest borne by credits obtained abroad (money deposits bear 3 to 8 percent interest depending on the term of commitment — 180 days to 2 years, respectively). The relatively high interest rate on credits has an impact on enterprise costs; since there is no obligation to accept a credit, its cost is calculated and the credit is not accepted if it is more advantageous to use the development fund to finance enterprise needs. There is also a clear trend toward self-financing. In 1974 in Hungary, the share of credits in enterprise funds was lowest (middle-term credits, 8.0 percent; long-term credits, 8.4 percent); the share of unutilized profits, obligations, and other sources was largest (50.4 percent); and the share of enterprises' own funds was 33.2 percent.[26]

Hungary, which has the most highly decentralized economy in the CMEA, opted against attempting to create a market economy banking system, as had been tried and failed in Bulgaria and the German Democratic Republic. Efforts were concentrated on creating a modern credit system to fit the needs of decentralized decision making in the framework of a planned economy. The tense economic situation meant that not all projects were going to be successful.

10. Poland's Contradictory Credit Policy

10.1. From Reform to "Reform"

As in Czechoslovakia, Bulgaria, and the German Democratic Republic, whose development has moved along extremely contradictory lines, Polish credit policy has met with many setbacks. It was the first CMEA country (in the mid-fifties) to institute a radical reform of the traditional steering system. The planning commission was transformed from a superministry that planned and watched over every detail of economic activity into a body that concentrated on development plans and tried out progressive steering methods. The enterprise was converted from a mere executor of the state plan into a self-financing en-

Credit Policies

tity able to operate without state subsidies. Prices became per-
formance-oriented yardsticks and allocation factors, and monetary relations were to be the integrating factor for the widely
decentralized economic units. The self-management boards,
with their specified functions, were to be the vehicles for participation in enterprise affairs.

These commendable aspirations to reform were doomed to
failure, however. The Gomulka regime returned after a time
to traditional management methods and traditional steering
models. Subsequent reform projects in 1964 and 1968 were no
more successful. The Party and government leadership that
came to power at the end of 1970 contemplated a more modest
reform of the steering model; under this system, the pillars of
economic management were to be the large firms (wielkie or-
ganizacje gospodarcze), which were granted limited decision-
making powers in investment projects, foreign trade, and wage
policy in a preset relation to labor productivity. At the beginning of 1976, 110 major firms constituting 65 percent of industrial production were involved in the reform projects.

10.2. Brakes on the Credit Reform

Credit policy followed the same ups and downs as the economic reform. Not much is left of the radical projects of the
reformers. An independent credit policy might be necessary as
a steering instrument in a decentralized system, but in a centralized system it is dispensable. Some measures have been
undertaken, however, to make traditional credit policy more efficient and streamlined within the existing framework. For example, the inordinate number of different kinds of credit, which
at the heyday of the centralized economy totaled no less than
sixteen, has been progressively decreased; the strict separation
between capital investment funds and circulating funds has been
abolished; and a more active interest policy has been instituted.

10.3. The Financing and Administering of
Capital Investment Projects

This change in credit policy entailed a fusion (in early 1970)

137

Money, Banking, and Credit

of the Investment Bank and the National Bank, and the gradual replacement of budget subsidies as a means of financing capital investment projects by credits from the National Bank and from the development fund, formed from an enterprise's own earnings. The share of capital investment loans in Poland's total credit volume increased from 12.4 percent in 1965 to 34.1 percent in 1970 and 45.4 percent in 1974.[27] In 1975, credits accounted for 54.1 percent of the financing of capital investment projects; enterprises' own funds for 29.0 percent; and budget subsidies for only 16.9 percent.[28]

Capital investment loans and their interest are paid back out of the profits and depreciation funds of the functioning or newly built enterprise. The term of payment is usually not more than five years. The differentiated interest rate scale is intended as a steering instrument. Overdue credits are burdened with a 12 percent interest rate. The actual average interest rate increased from 1.8 percent in 1972 to 2.9 percent in 1973 and 5.2 percent in 1974 and 1975.[29] In Poland, however, the switch to financing capital investment projects out of an enterprise's own funds and credits was much less a consequence of decentralization than in Hungary and instead was a measure designed to promote the economical and swift implementation of decisions made at the macro level.

Since the volume of capital investment projects increased by 89 percent during the five-year period of 1971-75, instead of 45 percent as planned; and since delays in project completion led to a higher wage bill (every zloty of capital investment increased the wage bill of the economy by 50 groszy)[30] without creating a commensurate supply, even more stress was laid on bank control of investment activities than before the reform. The Polish prime minister Jaroszewicz announced this government policy to the plenary session of the Party Central Committee in January 1976: "We shall oppose any attempt to initiate capital investments beyond those planned and punish the principals accordingly."[31]

The National Bank is the supervisory agent which sees to it that investment policy is carried out. It checks the soundness

of every project and supervises its completion in accordance
with the plan. But the National Bank cannot control enterprise
willingness to invest nor force completion of a construction
project on time. In 1975, credits extended for capital investment projects increased by 14.5 percent, but repayments were
8.5 percent less than specified in the plan target. [32]

The experience of Poland shows clearly that the switch to
credit financing of capital investment projects in the place of
nonrepayable budget subsidies is useful only when decentralization of decision making is carried out at the same time. Financing investment projects with credits that have been designed
only as a control instrument yields little effect. The hope that
this kind of financing would promote prompt and economical
completion of projects was not fulfilled.

10.4. Expansion of Credits for Working Assets

Poland was the first CMEA nation to abandon the package-
type apportionment of credits and instead tie credits to individual components of working assets. It was unable, however, to
establish a form of lending that gave credit a content corresponding to this concept. Polish credit policy is directed toward the expansion of credit relations, which will also be diversified enough to serve as an instrument for effective control of
economic performance.

The use of credits has been clearly defined. Credits finance
a specific portion of working assets, with the exact share set
centrally. As a rule, planned stocks are financed 60 percent
from enterprises' own funds and 40 percent from bank credits.
Bank credits are not very different from budget subsidies in
this respect, since they are a permanent source of financing
that need never be repaid.

Enterprises also receive repayable credits: for example,
credits for claims on purchasers, special credits to replenish
their own funds, and payments credits to bridge temporary liquidity shortages. Credit policy is integrated into the state's
economic policy; the credit plan is a component of the state

plan and is coordinated with state preferences.

Two limits are placed on such credits:

a) a limit on the basic credit line, which can be raised only if unforeseen circumstances occur, such as greater sales than foreseen, price changes, and so on;

b) a limit for temporary needs; this limit may be raised at any time on the petition of the borrower.

Lending policy varies. The basic credit, which bears a normal interest rate, is adjusted as closely as possible to normal needs and used as a control instrument of state activities; stopgap credits, on the other hand, which bear a higher interest rate, are not restricted, on the assumption that it would be unwarranted to limit credits bearing a high interest rate if withdrawal of credit is not to be used as a punishment.[33]

The Polish National Bank, the "guardian of the state's economic policy with regard to stocks,"[34] tries to influence lending policy by varying credit terms — for example, by applying punitive interest rates that may be raised by as much as 4 percentage points in case of deviations from the plan target.

The Polish interest rate system, which is meant as a state steering instrument, works as follows when hitches occur. Instead of the relatively cheap basic credit, the expensive stopgap credit is applied. If there are no legal grounds for a loan, both types of credits must be replaced by an overdue credit bearing a 7-12 percent interest rate. Complete refusal of a credit would necessarily delay the meeting of suppliers' claims, with the result that penalties would be paid and relations between suppliers and their clients would deteriorate. The increasing costs of credit and overdue payments to suppliers, as well as concern for good relations with the bank and with suppliers, will force an enterprise in payments difficulties to take corrective measures to cover the delayed obligations.

After many experiences and experiments, Poland has adopted the Soviet policy of bank controls, with some modifications and with somewhat different lending policies: a well-functioning enterprise can always count on a credit at moderate interest rates; poorly performing enterprises must expect a relatively expen-

Credit Policies

sive credit and in limited cases even refusal.

Considerable importance is placed on the expansion of credit relations. This process is promoted, however, through administrative regulations: through the existing pressure to finance enterprise needs with a centrally set share of credits, on the one hand, and through measures that cut off occasional financial sources to eliminate influence on the payments situation of an enterprise, on the other. In 1975, for example, a radical cleanup of enterprise funds was carried out, and a large part of development and promotion funds was removed from circulating assets and deposited in a special account.[35]

In Poland, credits for working assets are increasing at a greater rate than the national product — by 15.1 percent in 1973 (GNP + 11.4 percent), 19.7 percent in 1974 (+ 10.5 percent), and 27.9 percent in 1975 (+ 8.1 percent) — as a consequence of the rapidly rising stockpiles and delayed payments of suppliers' claims. In 1975, stocks increased by another 13.5 percent, and by as much as 20 percent in the construction industry as a result of nonfulfillment of construction plans and inadequate supplies of construction materials.[36]

Enterprise stockpiles are loaded down with finished products, which increased by 19 percent in volume in 1975, indicating sales difficulties due to discrepancies in the supply and demand structure.

Credits constitute roughly the same share of financial resources as in the Soviet Union: the proportion of enterprises' own funds is lower than in the Soviet Union, but other resources (development and promotion funds) are higher.

Sources of Financing of Circulating Assets in Poland

	1973	1974	1975
Enterprises' own funds	24.4	22.3	19.0
Credits	40.1	39.6	40.3
Obligations	20.6	21.9	22.6
Others	14.9	16.2	18.1
Total	100.0	100.0	100.0

Source: T. Klinger, "Kredyty przedsiebiorstw uspołecznionych 1975," Bank i kredyt, 7/1976, p. 254.

As is evident from the table, the share of enterprises' own funds has decreased; the share of credits is close to the officially set figure of 40 percent. The share of the development and other funds shows a steady increase, although measures have been taken to eliminate their influence on enterprise finances.

The way in which financing sources have developed, and especially the decrease in the share of enterprises' own funds, does not accord with the aims of the central authorities, who are trying to get enterprises more interested in accumulating their own funds. This effort has not succeeded, nor has it been possible to bring overdue suppliers' claims under control (the share of claims in the working assets of the economy had risen to 32.2 percent at the end of 1975, as compared with 26.0 percent at the beginning of the year, and overdue claims had increased threefold). Spot checks in the third quarter of 1975 showed that 17 percent of claims were not presented in time for collection and 15 percent were paid with a delay.[37]

Poland's monetary and credit policy has not achieved its goal of counteracting excessive stockpiling through stepped-up bank controls. The instrumentalities employed — punitive interest rates for unplanned credits to cover unplanned stocks (the average interest rate for credits for working assets increased from 2.9 percent in 1972 to 3.6 percent in 1973, 5.6 percent in 1974, and 6.2 percent in 1975)[38] — proved to be of no help in stopping the mismanagement of stocks. Restrictions on loans which made up only 0.7 percent of the total debt in 1975, were almost completely abandoned since they could have no further effect.

Efforts to prevent an inordinate inflow of cash by restrictive money policy proved just as ineffective: the gross national product increased by 62 percent in the 1971-75 five-year period, but circulation of cash rose by 139 percent and savings deposits increased by 154 percent.[39]

Polish credit policy could progress no further than the steering system as a whole. Lump-sum allotments of credits for a portion of working assets with a scaled interest policy, including punitive interest rates for unplanned credits, becomes no more efficient, however. The rapid growth of credits and money in

142

circulation in recent years reflects the inflationary tendencies triggered by the government with the drastic price rises of June 1976. The public's rejection of the price increases, which the government was temporarily forced to accept, shows clearly that Poland's economic difficulties cannot be overcome without a radical change in the steering system and the basic principles of credit policy.

11. Setback in Czechoslovakia

All the components of the Polish reform project of 1956-57 were present in the short-lived political spring of Czechoslovakia: far-reaching modifications were projected in property relations, with state ownership to be retained only in the principal branches of industry, in the banking system, and in transport, while consumer goods were to be produced by staff-owned cooperative or private firms under state supervision.

The status of the enterprise within the economy was defined more clearly than in Poland. The enterprise was to be a completely independent firm operating on normal business principles with joint management by the factory board, the factory council as co-owner of the enterprise, and the trade unions.

The reorganized monetary and credit system was supposed to integrate the broadly decentralized economic units, and competition was supposed to select the most efficient capital investment projects; only projects with the highest profit rates, sure sales, and more favorable repayment possibilities than other projects were to have access to bank credits.

Enterprises were to be given the choice of putting unearmarked monies into either interest-bearing deposits or bank bonds; interenterprise relations, which the programatic credit reform of 1930-32 had abolished, were once again to be permitted. A more effective interest policy that could serve as an allocation factor was supposed to replace the administrative instruments of the banking system; convertibility and real exchange rates of the Czech koruna were even contemplated to create a link between domestic and foreign prices.

143

Money, Banking, and Credit

Most important in the reformed credit system was the decentralization of decision making for bank branches, which were to finance enterprise undertakings without being tied to binding target figures.

Political developments, however, brought things once again back into the traditional channels.

Leopold Ler, former deputy and now finance minister of Czechoslovakia, had the following to say about the flaws of the reform: "The reform overestimated the role of the state budget and the role of credit. Credits were to adjust incomes, make up for flaws in the steering system, and serve as a currency regulator in the control of inflation. The budget and credit were overburdened with steering responsibilities for the state plan that they could not fulfill in a socialist economy." [40]

In the steering model in force in Czechoslovakia today, enterprises control only 1-2 percent of their investment projects. Bank credits constitute 40-60 percent of the financing of decentralized investment projects, but — as in Poland — banks act only as the state's supervisory agent and not as the partner of an independent enterprise that is able to make decisions itself within the powers granted it.

The federal or republic government, or the appropriate ministry — not the enterprise — makes investment decisions. Bank credits finance projects if their efficiency is sufficient to guarantee repayment in eight years. In this case, credits are not a prerequisite for the project but a control instrument of the state to promote prompt and economical fulfillment of decisions taken centrally.

Banks make liberal use of punitive interest rates, which may be raised to 50 percent if the course of a project deviates from the plan target. The bank can also refuse credits and demand repayment before the specified term. Credits are extended for rationalization processes on favorable terms, with a repayment period of three years and an interest rate of 4 percent per annum. Credits for centralized capital investment projects, on the other hand, bear 6-8.5 percent interest.

Competitions to select the most effective capital investment

project, which were to have played an important role in the reform, are given no place in the present system, in which such
decisions are made centrally.

Lending practices for credits for working assets have most
conspicuously moved away from the concept of a modernized
credit system. The reformers proposed to finance the entire
sum of additional assets needed with bank credits. The share
of credits in the financing resources of the Czech economy increased from 51.5 percent in 1967 to 65.3 percent the next year,
but it dropped to 43.9 percent in 1969 and to 38.5 percent in 1974.[41]

A considerable portion of the credits for financing working
assets (34.2 percent or 54.2 billion koruny), however, is only
formally different from budget subsidies, since they are granted
to make up for temporary shortages in an enterprise's own
funds and are paid back only when the borrower has some non-
earmarked funds.

Banks try to influence enterprise activity by varying lending
terms for credits for working assets, and limitation of credits
on particular portions of working assets has been reinstituted.
Applications for additional credits must always show the reason for a deviation from the plan target; payments credits are
granted for three to six months on the condition that the enterprise commits itself to measures that will restore its soundness.

Prospering enterprises, trade organizations, and purchasing
units for agricultural products get their credits from a current
account without any special difficulties. Credits obtained in this
way made up 67 percent of the total volume in 1974.[42]

Czechoslovakia is striving for a stable economic policy and
is trying to curb inflationary trends. But credits are growing
at a greater rate than the national product, although not as in-
tensively as in Poland. The national product increased by 4.9
percent in 1971 and 5.3 percent in 1975, but credits grew by
11.0 percent and 10.4 percent. Credits to the public expanded
much more slowly (2.1 billion koruny in 1971 and 2.3 billion
koruny in 1975) in comparison with the increase in savings deposits (10.3 billion koruny in 1971 and 8.5 billion koruny in 1975).[43]

Credit policy, restricted again to a controlling function, cannot ensure equilibrium nor promote economic efficiency. Czechoslovakia, which supplied the most advanced technology and knowhow in the first postwar years, must now import its efficiency-promoting factors.

12. The East German Attempt to Introduce
    a Market Economy Credit System

The German Democratic Republic tried to introduce a market economy credit system into its centralized economy on January 1, 1968; Bulgaria made a similar attempt on April 1, 1969, after some major changes were made in the steering model. In January 1963, the Sixth Party Congress of the Sozialistischen Einheitspartei Deutschlands (SED) decided to introduce the New Economic System; its main objective was to achieve optimal synchronization of the central state plan with indirect steering management of economic units by means of economic levers. Industrial associations (Vereinigung Volkseigener Betriebe) and enterprises were given some independent decision-making powers, most notably in the use of earnings and the setting of wages.

In the reorganized banking system, the State Bank was given the function of a bank of banks, and a new set of financial assistance regulations, bearing some market features, was worked out.

The whole system functioned, however, only until the first economic difficulties occurred. The Fourteenth Congress of the SED Central Committee in December 1970 considerably curtailed the powers of industrial associations and enterprises and restored those of the central authorities. The new banking system lost its rationale under the new conditions, and in 1972 its powers were reduced.[44] On July 1, 1974, the German Democratic Republic returned to a traditional credit system.

The present credit policy is more rigorous than before the 1968 reform. Credits are now granted on the basis of limits agreed upon between the economic ministry and the State Bank for particular items in current assets (raw materials, unfinished products, finished products). The share of credit in the financing of enterprise assets is regulated by two indicators, set by the central authorities:

a) the ratio between the growth in enterprise assets and the growth in production, set at 0.8 percent for industry as a whole in 1975;

b) the share of an enterprise's own funds in the financing of current assets (46 percent in 1975).

Usually, bank credits are given only for planned stocks. In special cases, unplanned and excess stocks are financed with bank credits. A graduated scale of interest rates is intended to help control enterprise stocks and keep them within plan limits. Credits for planned stocks carry an interest of 5 percent, while an interest of 8 percent may be placed on stocks in excess of the plan. Banks are also empowered to grant credits at the favorable interest rate of 1.8 percent if the plan target is exceeded.

Decisions on capital investment projects are centralized in the German Democratic Republic. Only 1-2 percent of total plant is built at the decision of enterprises. Credit is a source of funds for financing capital investment projects as in Poland, although to much less a degree. In 1974, the finance structure of East German capital projects appeared as follows: [45]

Self-financing (earnings and amortization funds)	38.4%
Bank credits	26.8
State budget subsidies	18.3
Money from the industrial associations	16.5
Total	100.0

As in many other Eastern nations, the GDR State Bank determines its credit relations with economic units on the basis of their earnings: for prospering enterprises (63 percent of the total), a limit is set on average indebtedness; any unused funds below the set limit may be borrowed during the next period; for less prosperous firms (26 percent), a maximum limit is set in addition to the average indebtedness; for poorly performing enterprises, only the limit for maximum indebtedness applies. [46]

The German Democratic Republic has abandoned a market-oriented credit policy and expanded the administrative functions of the banking system. Bank branches must supervise lending and, in addition, assess plan drafts, participate in the discussion of possible plan projects, collaborate with other state control agencies and enterprise boards, and report to higher authorities on how activities are proceeding.

13. Bulgaria's Short-lived Experiment with Market Economy Credit Policy

The April 1, 1969, economic reform in Bulgaria was even less suited to assimilating a market credit system than was that in the German Democratic Republic. A reform of the centralized economy was announced in July 1968, but was not ready for introduction until early 1969 — at a time when the events in Czechoslovakia were bound to have an influence on Bulgaria. Hence, the reform did not make any deepgoing structural changes in the traditional steering model and was restricted to organizational features. The administration of industry was streamlined by reducing the number of industrial associations from 120 to 64. But decentralized decision-making powers were given to the associations, not to the enterprises. Within the powers allotted to them, industrial associations decide on supplies, sales, financing, and so on.

Central planners still decide on the general direction of economic development, on production and distribution, and on capital projects. A market economy banking system had no chance for success under these conditions, and the experiment was soon dropped in 1972.

Under these conditions, the return to a traditional credit policy was correct; it was more in keeping with Bulgaria's steering model than the credit policy introduced in 1969. The credit system is now used more as an instrument of control than before the reform.

Bank credits are now granted for capital investment projects, although decisions are still more or less centralized. A graduated interest rate system is used to encourage prompt completion of investment projects.

Credit practice is different from that in other Eastern countries; two kinds of credits are used to finance every investment

Credit Policies

project:

a) credits to cover the services of the construction enterprise and the value of the equipment used;

b) credits for the completed project.

The first type of credit is provided for the duration of the planned construction time and carries an interest of 2 percent per annum. If there is a delay in the start of operations, the interest rate is raised to 6-8 percent, levied on the builder or the client or both together, depending on the decision of the planning commission, which is authorized to determine who is to blame for the delay.

Credits for completed projects, granted after the start of enterprise operations, cannot exceed 15 years. The actual period of repayment is determined by the efficiency of the project. The interest rate is 4-6 percent depending on the term of repayment. Overdue credits carry an interest of 8 percent.

The Bulgarian National Bank grants credits for quick-return mechanization projects that are to be paid back from the enterprise's development fund. In this case as well, the interest rate depends on the term of repayment: 2 percent for credits up to two years, 4 percent for those up to six years, and 6 percent for longer periods.

Lending practices to cover working assets are the same as in the other Eastern countries: an agreement between a bank and an enterprise determines the source of the financing funds, that is, what portion is to come from the enterprise's own funds and what portion is to come from credits. As a rule, a credit covers the difference between the quantity of enterprise stocks projected for the end of the planning period and current own funds on hand or to be accrued. The share of credits must not exceed 50 percent of the total stockpiles.

A credit limit is determined by the National Bank's credit plan and is allocated to individual enterprises by the industrial association with the approval of the central bank. Only payments and clearing credits are not limited. Credits for working assets are usually granted for one year. Unsalable finished products and excess goods and stocks on hand for longer than one year cannot be financed by credits.

The credit policy just described is better suited to Bulgaria's economy than the market-type system in operation between 1969 and 1971, for which the prerequisites had not been created in the steering model.

14. The Subordination of Romania's Credit Policy to the Centrally Managed Economy

Romania has not tried any notable experiments either in overall management of the economy or in credit policy. Decisions are still made by the central political and economic authorities, and credit policy is also centralized in accordance with the aim of controlling economic activities.

The state handles capital investment projects, which are financed from the state budget. Credits are used only as a stopgap measure when planned financing funds are not sufficient to finance investment projects specified in the state plan. Credit is therefore a technical device paid back out of budget subsidies.

Credits bear 2-4 percent interest depending on the terms of repayment. Punitive interest rates are levied if construction or repair is not finished within the stipulated time: a surcharge of 2 percent if there is a delay in putting a project into operation, and of 6 percent if machinery and equipment no longer needed are not freed within six months.

Banks also grant credits for modernization, but the amount must not exceed 5 million lei for each project. The repayment period is up to four years, and the interest rate is 1 percent.

Credits for capital projects and current assets are limited by the central authorities. Credits for working assets follow the traditional patterns. Short-term credits are provided for seasonal and other perishable stocks and for suppliers' claims on the buyer. In some cases, stopgap credits are provided to finance planned growth of working assets for a period lasting until the planned resources are procured.

Prospering enterprises have the advantage of being able to exceed the specified credit limit by as much as 15 days. They can also obtain 90-day credits to bridge temporary payments difficulties provided the lacking liquid assets are not already owed elsewhere.

Romania's centralized economy sets narrow limits on credit policy, which is used mainly as a control instrument of plan fulfillment. It is therefore noteworthy that Romania, which has the most centralized steering system, is the first CMEA country to become a member of the Bretton Woods institute.

15. Summary

The centrally managed economy was unable to find a proper way to extend credit to state-owned enterprises. A credit transaction in the real sense of the term is a category of the market economy. Where banks and the means of production are state property, no real demarcation can exist between banking credit and budget resources. The line drawn by the programmatic credit reform of 1930-32 has lost its economic impetus. Credit enters the economy more and more in the form of a percentage of own funds of the enterprise, and thus the difference between credit and budget resources consists mainly in the way by which each enters into turnover. Credit can be carried on more easily and withdrawn from circulation more easily. But the idea that the method of credit extension could influence economic performance is very far from the reality. Credit is extended more automatically than in the first period of the Soviet credit system.

The highly centralized steering system with its attendant monetary and credit policies proved to be incapable of bringing about efficient economic performance. Economic reforms were undertaken which introduced considerable variations in a steering system that had been more or less uniform until the mid-fifties. The most radical of these — the reforms in Poland in 1956-57 and in Czechoslovakia in 1967-68 — foundered, mainly for political reasons.

The reforms contemplated in monetary and credit policy were limited by the existing steering model, which remained basically unchanged.

Money, Banking, and Credit

The credit system underwent extensive debureaucratization, and overambitious plans to institute pervasive control of economic activity by means of rigorous lending policies were later adapted to realities. Prospering enterprises now have no limits on the credit they may obtain, and drastic sanctions were abandoned even for poorly performing enterprises.

Instead of administrative instruments, a graduated interest scale and punitive interest rates are applied if a credit is used to finance unplanned stocks. But even when exercising this function, interest rate is not a regulator of the amount of money available. There is no capital or money market in the East where an adjustable interest rate could act to bring supply into line with demand.

The hope that a variegated credit policy would prevent the hoarding of excess stocks has faded. Excess stocks and chronic supply problems are the chief evils of a planned economy.

Switching over from nonrepayable budget subsidies to bank credits to finance capital investment projects, while keeping decision-making powers in the hands of the central authorities, proved ineffective in combating the second evil — namely, unsatisfactory investment performance.

However hard the lending terms, they are unable to counteract hitches in planning and plan fulfillment. Bank credits must be used to finance them.

Except in Hungary, the economic reforms have been limited to organizational improvements. Large enterprises are being built and have been delegated certain powers and responsibilities in utilizing earnings, setting wages, and defining the occupational structure. Credit policy, which became quite differentiated in the sixties, is now beginning to show certain common features once more.

Credit is being used more and more often to finance a portion of current assets, and in this function differs little from budget subsidies.

Credit systems in the planned economies can advance no further than other aspects of the steering model.

Credit Policies

NOTES

1. Dr. Gy. Tallós, "Bedingungen der Kreditgewährung in der VR Ungarn," West-Ost Journal, 6/1975, p. 27.
2. See I. Konnik, Den'gi v period stroitel'stva kommunisticheskogo obshchestva [Money in the Period of Construction of a Communist Society], Moscow, 1966, p. 148.
3. G. Garvy says: "The history of banking in Eastern Europe abounds with examples illustrating that the two types of financing have the same ultimate source and that any existing arrangements are rooted more in accounting convenience than in matters of substance." In Money, Banking and Credit in Eastern Europe, Federal Reserve Bank of New York, 1966, p. 72; Soviet credit expert Ikonnikov has a similar opinion: "There is no permanent fixed demarcation between self-financing funds and funds obtained through credits." In Finansy i kredit SSSR, Moscow, 1972, p. 85.
4. Soviet banking expert Mitelman has the following to say: "Banking credit seems to be a reapportionment of money by the state through its concentration in credit institutions and distribution in repayable form to the enterprises." In Finansy i kredit SSSR, p. 297.
5. W. Jaworski, Banki i kredyt v krajach socjalistycznych [Banks and Credit in the Socialist Countries], Warsaw, 1971, p. 149.
6. See A. Hahn, Volkswirtschaftliche Theorie des Bankkredites, 3rd ed., Tübingen, 1930, p. 129.
7. N. Barkovskii, "Kreditnyi mekhanizm i ego ispol'zovanie" [The Credit Mechanism and Its Use], Den'gi i kredit, 10/1975, p. 31.
8. M. Atlas, "O meste i roli kredita v sisteme ekonomicheskikh otnoshenii sotsializma" [The Role of Credit in Socialist Economic Relations], Den'gi i kredit, 12/1975, p. 89.
9. See J. Friss, Principal Features of the New System of Planning, Economic Control and Management in Hungary, Budapest, 1969, p. 12.
10. Narodnoe khoziaistvo SSSR, 1974, p. 740.
11. This is the opinion of Polish credit specialist Jaworski, op. cit., p. 342.
12. See D. Molakov and I. Uvarov, "Finansovye i kreditnye problemy v kapital'nom stroitel'stve" [Finance and Credit Problems in Capital Investment Projects], Den'gi i kredit, 12/1974, p. 48; Narodnoe khoziaistvo, pp. 520 and 762.
13. Ibid., p. 47.
14. Narodnoe khoziaistvo SSSR, p. 742.
15. This is the opinion of Soviet authors N. Valenzeva and I. Mamonov, "The Credit Mechanism as a Factor in the Profitable Utilization of Bank Funds," Den'gi i kredit, 2/1975, p. 46.
16. "Bank controls and their credit mechanism are a degenerate form of economic and, in some cases, purely administrative control. They are only one part of state economic controls, albeit an important one." N. Barkovskii, in Den'gi i kredit, 9/1975, p. 29.
17. Narodnoe khoziaistvo SSSR, p. 760.

Money, Banking, and Credit

18. Ibid., p. 750.

19. Ibid., pp. 760 and 761.

20. Ibid., p. 607.

21. Details on the Hungarian economic reform can be found in Reform of the Economic Mechanism in Hungary, edited by Istvan Friss, Budapest, 1969.

22. Tallós, op. cit., p. 27.

23. See W. Jaworski, "Zmiany v węgierskim systemie kredytowym" [Changes in the Hungarian Credit System], Bank i kredyt, 6/1976, p. 224.

24. Ibid., p. 226.

25. These efforts apparently were no more successful than in the other Eastern countries, however: stocks increased by 18.5 billion forints in 1973 and by 35 billion forints in 1974 (see ibid., p. 225).

26. Ibid., p. 224.

27. Rocznik statystyczny, 1975, p. 509.

28. T. Klinger, "Kredyty przedsiębiorstw uspołecznionych 1975" [Credit of State-owned Enterprises], Bank i kredyt, 7/1976, p. 255.

29. Ibid., p. 256.

30. See W. Bien, "O wyższą jakość pracy Narodowego Banku Polskiego" [For a More Efficient Polish National Bank], Bank i kredyt, 3/1976, p. 71.

31. Quoted in ibid., p. 73.

32. See Klinger, op. cit., p. 255.

33. See Jan Wasenczuk, "Umacniany oddziaływanie za pomocą kredytu" [The Influence of Credit Is Increased], Bank i kredyt, 4/1976.

34. The vice-president of the Polish National Bank describes bank prerogatives in this way. Ibid., p. 118.

35. See Klinger, op. cit., p. 253.

36. Rocznik statystyczny, 1975, pp. 67 and 509; and Trybuna ludu, January 22, 1976.

37. See Klinger, op. cit., p. 255.

38. Ibid.

39. See Edward Wieczorek, "Zasoby pieniężne ludności" [Monetary Resources of the Public], Bank i kredyt, 5/1976, p. 166.

40. L. Ler, "30 let budovani socialistickych financi v CSSR" [Thirty Years of Development of Socialist Financing in the CSSR], Finance a úvěr, 5/1975, p. 297.

41. Statistická ročenka, 1975, p. 199.

42. Ibid., p. 198.

43. See S. Potac, "Menovy vyvoj a menovy plan na rok 1976" [The Development of Currency and the Currency Plan for 1976], Finance a úvěr, 2/1976, p. 79.

44. See Gesetzblatt der DDR, 4/1972.

45. See W. Jaworski, "O niektorych nowych rozwiązaniach w systemie kredytowym i rozliczeniach bezgotówkowych NRD" [On Some of the New Policies in the Credit and Clearing System in the GDR], Bank i kredyt, 5/1976, p. 193.

46. Ibid.

Chapter 6

MONEY, CREDIT, AND
PRICES IN FOREIGN TRADE

I. THE BACKGROUND: FOREIGN TRADE
WITHOUT A FUNCTIONING MONEY

1. The Changing Concept of Foreign Trade

The recent period has shown more clearly than ever before
where the Eastern European economies and their steering systems are heading. The planned economies are gradually developing into industrial societies, with all the attendant advantages
and disadvantages. Many ideas have been abandoned, above all
the unrealistic notion of building an autarkic economy. The advantages of the international division of labor have been recognized. The Western share in the total trade of the Eastern nations has increased considerably, since the Western nations
have also adopted a policy of expanding trade with Eastern Europe.
The planned economies are endeavoring to adapt the management of foreign trade to new needs. Have they been successful?
Are there any discernible signs that the Eastern market and its
steering mechanisms are beginning to be integrated into the
world market? In what follows we shall try to answer these
questions.

Internal money and credit relations have been subordinated
to the functioning of a planned economy, monetary and credit
systems cut off from the outside world, and an autonomous
price structure created — and in many instances these have
functioned successfully; but the system of control over foreign

trade created in an earlier period has shown itself to be poorly suited for active involvement in world trade, and even less suited for effective accounting.

When the Soviet government established its monopoly over foreign trade and foreign exchange with the nationalization decree of April 22, 1918, its objective was not to develop trade but to build a self-sufficient economy with as few ties to the outside world as possible. Though we may sympathize to some degree with such an objective when we consider that, at the time, the Soviet Union had to deal with foreign intervention and economic blockade, over the long term such a position has clearly reduced foreign trade to a system of pure and undesirable makeshift and stopgap operations.

For many years after the 1918 nationalization decree, the Soviet economy bore the stamp of the old objective of achieving economic independence from the outside world. This is quite apparent, for instance, in the 1930 resolution of the Sixteenth Party Congress to review the planned target of the machine-building industry with the aim of "freeing industry and the economy as a whole from its dependence on other countries."[1]

The Soviet Union maintained economic relations with the West during the period between the world wars, but these ties were developed only sporadically and came to an almost complete halt just before World War II. During the entire period between the wars, Soviet foreign trade never once achieved its 1913 volume (10,090 million rubles at the 1950 exchange rate). During the first two years after the revolution, foreign trade declined to 395 million rubles and 11 million rubles, respectively; it rose to 804 million rubles again in 1921, reached a peak in 1930 at 7,302 million rubles, and declined rapidly thereafter, until in 1939 total Soviet foreign trade amounted to only 1,207 million rubles.[2] Soviet industrial production was eight times larger in 1940 than in 1913, while the volume of foreign trade was only one-fourth the 1913 level.

2. Variations in Foreign Trade Policy in the Planned Economies

The Soviet Union as well as the other Eastern nations have

come a long way from the situation prevailing during the first years of existence of the Soviet state. Most have developed into modern industrial societies with their sights now set on attaining the level of technology reached in the Western industrial nations. This requires active participation in international foreign trade, however, and views on the function of foreign trade in a planned economy, as well as the attendant institutions and steering mechanisms, have undergone notable changes.

Although it is true that the basic system of foreign trade management has been molded by factors inherent to a planned economy, the instrumentalities of trade have varied in different stages of development in accordance with the needs of the moment. The decentralized model in use in some Eastern countries has exerted a significant influence on the management of foreign trade.[3] The extent of economic reform has not been the same in all countries, however.

The foreign trade management system has progressed further in Hungary than in the other Eastern countries. In the 1968 reform, the state foreign trade enterprise — which had been under the Ministry of Foreign Trade — was deprived of its monopoly status. Authority to engage in foreign trade was extended to major firms (in 1970, 111 firms accounted for 23 percent of exports and 11 percent of imports) and to foreign trade companies, which served as agents for manufacturing firms and engaged in foreign trade transactions on a commission basis.

Some of the other Eastern countries that have decentralized decision making less than Hungary have undertaken similar measures: foreign trade has been transferred either to the large firms or to specialized trading enterprises set up under the ministry in charge of the respective branch of production. In these cases, the major aim of foreign trade reform was to mend the flaws arising in management and accounting when the production enterprises were divested of any responsibility for foreign trade and its efficiency; accordingly, the reform was more technical and organizational in nature and was not directed at a restructuring of the entire system. Institutional reforms generally paralleled those in Hungary, but the changes introduced in the organizational structure have not gone very far toward decentralizing foreign trade competence.

In Poland, the major machine-building enterprises were given authority to engage in foreign trade, and about 60 percent of the specialized trading companies have been placed under the ministries for the various industries.

In Czechoslovakia, production enterprises were brought into foreign trade either by investing them with the competency to deal directly with the foreign partner (there are now about 50 firms engaging in foreign trade) or by affiliating them with joint stock companies in which foreign trade enterprises, industrial associations, and banks also participate. The planning authorities and the foreign trade ministry still retain steering functions, however.

In Bulgaria, the German Democratic Republic, and Romania, the organizational structure of foreign trade management has tended to return to its original forms. Indeed, in Romania the reform of March 19, 1971, established even stricter planning and control of foreign trade — mainly as a consequence of the growing debt to the West, which rigid state controls are supposed to reduce.

With the goal of expanding its involvement in foreign markets, Romania has founded mixed companies with the participation of foreign capital. There were twenty-one such companies at the beginning of 1977 — sixteen in Europe, three in Asia, one in North America, and one in Africa. In nineteen of them, Romanian capital comprises 50 percent of the total; the other two are wholly Romanian owned. The companies are engaged primarily in the sale of machinery, automobiles, agricultural products, and so on, although they also carry out some import and financing transactions. In this area more than anywhere else, foreign trade is the business of the state, that is, the collective enterprise "Romania."

In the Soviet Union, the organizational and command structure of foreign trade has remained unchanged; about 50 specialized trading organizations, all under the Ministry of Foreign Trade, conduct all the business of the state foreign trade monopoly. But foreign trade still plays a relatively minor role in the USSR,

comprising only 5 percent of the national product. The situation
is different in the other Eastern countries, however. Before
World War II their trade with the Soviet Union represented only 1.5
percent of their total trade; but after the war they had to restructure their economies to fit the needs of the Soviet Union
and, in addition, adopted the Soviet steering model, although it
scarcely suited their situation.[4]

In all the Eastern countries, including Hungary — where now
the reformed organizational structure functions as a component
of the "socialist market"[5] — the foreign trade steering system
continues to be but an outgrowth of the planned economy. Foreign trade functions here in a vastly different way than in a
market economy. Primary stress is given to imports in order
to supply the economy with goods that cannot be produced do-
mestically. Exports are not structured with competition in
mind, and do not constitute an independent sphere of activity of
an enterprise in its quest for new markets; their one and only
function is to raise foreign exchange to pay for imports. It has
been this aspect of foreign trade policy, more than any other,
that has left a telling mark on East-West trade: the backward
export structure cannot keep pace with imports, and large trade
deficits are the result.

Since the system called for the isolation of foreign trade from
the domestic economy and its accounting system, comparative
cost advantage was initially rejected as a meaningful concept
in the planned economies; when it finally acquired respectabil-
ity, there were no adequate accounting instruments available.
In the planned economies, foreign trade — like monetary relations — remained in the hands of the state.

3. Inconvertibility — a Part of the System

The state, which controls foreign trade through its central
authorities, also controls all foreign clearing and credit business through the state banking and financial apparatus.[6] The
reforms did not affect the state's monopoly over foreign exchange, which has features all its own that are quite different

from any form of foreign exchange control found in the market economies. Control measures are not merely temporary steps applied in emergency cases to ease foreign exchange shortages; the state has total and permanent control over the inflow and outflow of foreign exchange. In some cases, large concerns are allowed to retain a share of their foreign exchange proceeds to pay for imports, but the basic situation remains unchanged: the state still decides how much independence an enterprise will have in this respect, and broadens or contracts the powers of individual enterprises depending on the balance of payments.[7]

The original reason for the foreign trade monopoly was to shield production enterprises from fluctuations in world prices, exchange rates, and the business cycle. In the traditional model, foreign trade enterprises sold goods intended for export for domestic currency at domestic prices. But however desirable isolation from the outside world might have been from the viewpoint of maintaining stable conditions for plan fulfillment, it was hardly conducive to creating a competitive and efficient foreign trade.

Enterprises were protected from price and exchange rate fluctuations, but the economy as a whole was not.[8] The higher world prices had to be paid, and fluctuations in the exchange rate affected foreign exchange holdings, liabilities, and commitments. The individual enterprise, shielded from the impact of this problem, is not constrained to seek alternative ways out of the situation.

The monopoly over foreign exchange institutionalized the isolation of the domestic monetary system from foreign trade; it reduced the national currency to an internal currency and the collective accounting unit of the CMEA — the transferable ruble — to the internal CMEA currency. There are no feedback mechanisms between world prices, exchange rates, and domestic prices. Exchange rates, shut off from International Monetary Fund (IMF) regulations and the world market, cannot function as they normally would; they are used only for internal clearing purposes and are set arbitrarily by the state without being recognized by the world market.

The nonconvertible currencies of the planned economies cannot be used for business transactions, nor can they serve as a basis for developing effective credit relations. In dealings with the hard-currency countries, the planned economies are borrowers, not lenders, while in the CMEA area credit is used exclusively as a pure technical instrument for accomplishing IBEC settlements.

Barter is thus the intrinsic form of exchange, and from their very beginnings the planned economies have aimed for a bilateral balance of deliveries, regardless of what form of settlement was used — for example, multilateral clearing in intra-CMEA trade, bilateral clearing with the developing countries, or in U.S. dollars or partner's currencies in trade with the Western industrial countries. The only way the planned economies could plug into the world market was through bilateral clearing, since the conditions for convertibility did not exist. It is no coincidence that the most prominent Soviet experts, such as Frey, Smirnov, and Slobin, have proclaimed bilateral clearing to be the type of settlement procedure most suited to a planned economy.

The negative consequences of bilateral clearing — that "foreign trade is perforce limited in its scope and structure to countries with the least interest in or fewest possibilities for trade"[9] — affect all who engage in bilateral trade, regardless of the reasons or the economic system.

The Eastern bloc employed a uniform settlement system based on bilateral clearing in intra-CMEA trade and in trade with the West only until the end of the fifties, that is, only during the period when the industrial nations had not yet restored the convertibility of their currencies. The restrictions this system placed on foreign trade came gradually to affect its scope and profitability. Ways and means were devised to get around these limitations. In intra-CMEA trade an internal, self-contained, multilateral settlement system was evolved by way of trilateral and multilateral agreements, and in trade with the West switch and transit transactions developed into a payments system using foreign exchange.

161

4. The Clearing Ruble and Transferable Ruble

With their foreign trade based on commodity quotas and their
unit of currency limited to domestic currency, the planned economies were forced to adopt bilateral clearing. Though they tried to
make a virtue of necessity, reality demanded that ways be found
to eliminate the limitations the system had imposed.

At first, trilateral and multilateral agreements were concluded only sporadically and remained a marginal phenomena;
trade continued to be predominantly bilateral. The agreement
concluded by resolution of the Eighth Session of the CMEA
June 20, 1957, "On Multilateral Clearing among the CMEA Member Nations," did not go much further, although the institutions
established did help to improve the flow of trade. (In contrast
to bilateral clearing, limits were set to indebtedness — 3 percent of exports to other Eastern countries — and only 25 percent of the limit was to be interest free; the rest was to carry
an interest of 2 to 3 percent.)

The experiment showed beyond doubt that institutional measures would be completely ineffectual as long as foreign trade
continued to rely on bilaterally balanced delivery quotas, and
there remained a general unwillingness to prepare the way for
currency convertibility. Efforts continued to be directed toward
refining clearing procedures rather than changing the foreign
trade system, and thus were bound to fail.

An agreement on multilateral settlements in transferable
rubles and the founding of the International Bank for Economic
Cooperation (IBEC) was signed on October 22, 1963, and eight
years later the second CMEA bank, the International Investment
Bank (IIB) was established.

5. The Fiat Money of the International CMEA Banks

The transferable ruble is the common unit of currency for
both international CMEA banks. Their activity therefore depends on the functionability of this unit or, as George Garvy put
it, on its "moneyness." But has this collective CMEA currency

162

been able to fulfill the functions of money better than national currencies? Any answer to this question must take into account the fact that the exchange of goods quotas in intra-CMEA trade differs in no essential respects from the way goods are apportioned at the domestic level, where an order to distribute seems to be more important than the money a bank must supply when needed.

Money has even less a universal purchasing power in intra-CMEA trade than it does in domestic production. The transferable ruble is merely a clearing instrument for prearranged goods quotas that are delivered regardless of whether the purchaser has the money to pay for them or not. Money is not a condition for deliveries, for the IBEC provides it even more automatically than does the domestic banking system. Money is merely a makeshift means of bridging the gap between mutual deliveries, which should be balanced but sometimes cannot be. In the given case, the country with the deficit receives a stopgap credit to pay the country with the surplus. The loan is not given to obtain the goods, but to pay for goods that were delivered in accordance with the prearranged quotas as part of multilateral clearing activities.

The collective CMEA monetary unit did not evolve as part of the process of expanding the monetary functions of the national currencies, nor does it represent the culmination of this process. Its creation had nothing to do with internal monetary relations. In the conditions under which the transferable ruble functions, no translation mechanism exists either between the transferable ruble and the national currencies, or between the international price structure and the prices within CMEA trade.

The signatories of the October 1963 agreement had different aims in mind. Some — most notably the Soviet Union — wanted a better clearing system but preferred that the foreign trade system remain basically unchanged, while others — first of all, Poland — wanted to create a clearing system that would transform bilateral trade into multilateral trade. Article 1 of the agreement was formulated in accordance with the wishes of those who advocated multilateral foreign trade. It required multilateral rather than bilateral balancing of mutual deliveries among the signatories, as did the Comprehensive Program of 1971. In practice, however, the bilateralists had their way.

The IBEC's fifteen years of activity could be regarded as successful only by those who wanted a multilateral clearing house for bilateral trade. IBEC clearing procedures are unquestionably better than bilateral clearing. The multilateralists, who conceived of the IBEC as an effective international bank rather than a clearinghouse, were defeated; no reliable source estimates the share of multilateral trade in total intra-CMEA trade at more than 2 or 3 percent.[10]

"The IBEC is tailored to fit any type of trade," observed Hungarian bank director T. Bacskai in his talk in Vienna on January 27, 1977. But multilateral settlements are feasible only if trade is also multilateral.[11] The 1971 Comprehensive Program proved unable to reconcile the conflicting goals of the partner states. On the one hand, it established bilateral exchange of goods on the basis of bilaterally agreed quantity and value quotas for the next fifteen or twenty years; while, on the other, it recommended that "economic and organizational measures be taken to strengthen the common currency, the transferable ruble, enough for it fully to fulfill the basic functions of an international socialist currency among CMEA nations (as a measure of value, a means of payment, and a medium of accumulation) so that in the future it may play a role in world trade as well...."[12] Bilateral clearing, however, is incapable of creating the conditions for developing a currency that performs a full range of monetary functions.

6. The Limited Functions of a Clearing Currency

The transferable ruble does perform all the usual functions of money, but only to the extent that conditions for a functional currency already exist within the IBEC clearing system. The "moneyness" of any money involves three major functions: a measure of value, a means of payment, and a reserve medium. The transferable ruble performs these functions if existing foreign trade relations make this possible.

Prices in intra-CMEA trade are expressed in transferable rubles, although they are based on neither price nor value relations inside the CMEA, but on adjusted world prices. The transferable ruble functions merely as a conversion coefficient; it is not a value-creating factor keyed to the price basis of the sphere in which it operates. It translates foreign prices for use in areas where domestic prices are not considered an adequate price basis for the socialist market. This translation function has nothing to do with the function of money as a measure of value.[13]

The unsuccessful attempt of the Ninth Council Session in 1958 to create an independent price basis founded on intra-CMEA value relations deprived the transferable ruble of any possibility of functioning as a measure of value and condemned it to this translation function. At the 1967 Budapest conference the concept of an "own price basis" founded on internal cost relations was buried once and for all as a theoretically and practically insoluble problem. If from time to time it still appears in various articles, it expresses only the futuristic dreams of the author. The Comprehensive Program established current practice as the price-forming basis for 15 to 20 years.

The attempt to make the transferable ruble a measure of value failed because it is impossible to make money function through mere arithmetic. The function of money is a category of the market; it is the product of a market, with all its value-creating conditions, and can exist only in a market. The planned economies, whose economic relations are based on quota exchanges, are unable to create the market functions of money; moreover, they are also unable to create a money with functions peculiar to their own structures. They have therefore relied on categories that evolved in alien or even antagonistic production and exchange relations.

The transferable ruble has also failed to develop into a means of payment. The necessary conditions for this are even less present in intra-CMEA trade than in the production sphere of the member nations. The transferable ruble is a clearing unit for the exchange of preset quotas, but on the socialist market it is not a universal medium with which one can purchase anything one chooses. It has no intrinsic value, but merely follows the planned goods exchange.

The imperfections of the transferable ruble show up especially clearly in the credit relations of the CMEA banks. In the IBEC, credit is not a creative value that can promote the exports of one party by expanding the import possibilities of another; rather, it is a technical stopgap instrument used to maintain an uninterrupted flow of trade. The International Investment Bank has been even less able to create the preconditions necessary for making loans for capital investments within the limited monetary system of the CMEA. The clearing unit of the IBEC has been unable to develop any properties that would have allowed its use as a currency for middle-term and long-term credits. The gap between dream and concrete possibility was even more painfully apparent here than in the case of the IBEC. The IBEC could at least function as a clearing institution, but the investment bank could not even serve as an effective credit institution. For it to do so, an effective money with a universal purchasing power of its own was needed.

Loans for capital investments, granted in transferable rubles, are therefore merely the monetary expression of prearranged goods credits. Every loan must be preceded by a goods guarantee, agreed upon beforehand by the bank, the supplier, and the borrower. The prediction made when the bank began operations that capital investment loans granted in clearing units would create lending difficulties, has thus proved to be well founded.[14]

At the end of 1977, the volume of credits was 1,857.5 million transferable rubles; of this amount, only 427.6 million came from the bank's own funds; the rest was raised on the international money market.

The collective currency of the CMEA, which has developed into neither a measure of value nor a means of payment, was even less suited as a reserve currency. Both CMEA banks have a statutory capital, but the attempt to pay it in and activate it in the amount declared foundered because of the limited money properties of the currency.

After two years of operation, both the IBEC (declared capital, 304.4 million transferable rubles) and the IIB (1,068.3 million transferable rubles) have given up trying to pull in the rest of the capital stock; 60 million transferable rubles were paid into the IBEC in 1964 and 1965, and that was the level at the end of 1977. Only payments in foreign exchange continued, up to a sum of 60 million transferable rubles ($81.0 million). The amount of capital stock paid into the IIB in the first two years (374 million transferable rubles) also remained unchanged through 1977; 30 percent of this total was in convertible currencies.

The IBEC has limited its operations in transferable rubles to clearing within the CMEA and hence can get along without capital; for the investment bank, however, capital is the only means whereby it can exist if it disregards the facilities of the international market.

Nor is the deposit activity of the IBEC a demonstration that the transferable ruble can function as a reserve currency. The accumulation of monetary reserves is not the result of deliberate policy on the part of the bank's members, but an unavoidable and undesired consequence of the clearing system. A bank member accumulates money not because it wishes to save it for a project put off to some time in the future, or because it wishes to collect the interest on the idle money, but because it had not received planned deliveries at the specified time. It can buy nothing with the accumulated money than what had previously been agreed upon, and only from the source specified in the plan.[15]

It is also wrong to suppose that the transferable ruble functions as a reserve currency because the funds accumulated through the IBEC are a prerequisite for lending.[16] This view belongs more to preclassical thinking than to the notion prevalent in the Eastern nations that bank deposits are credit sources for the lending activities of national banks. Lending is an automatic process in the IBEC; the bank advances credit to a member with payments difficulties and deposits the money in the account of the creditor.

The interest system of the IBEC also functions differently

from an ordinary interest mechanism. There is no money market in the CMEA on which the interest rate can function to keep supply and demand in equilibrium.

The interest rates for deposits as of January 1, 1977, was 1.5 percent in current accounts, 2.5 percent with three months' notice, 3.5 percent with six months' notice, 3.75 percent with twelve months' notice, and 4 percent for more than one year. These rates, however, are not the price of money but a recompense for delays in deliveries. The IBEC borrower, who has caused the delay, in effect pays a delay penalty, graded according to the duration of the loan: for clearing credits (2 percent of the volume of commodity turnover), the first half is at 2 percent and the second half at 3 percent; for time credits (after the limit has been reached), the rate is 3.25 percent for up to six months, 3.5 percent for up to one year, 4 percent for up to two years, and 5 percent for up to three years.

The CMEA banks, which have not been able to develop an effective credit system from their own resources because of the lack of convertible currencies and capital markets, are forced to obtain loans from Western markets to finance the industrialization and modernization of existing plant.

7. The Effectiveness of Credits of the CMEA Banks

The limited "moneyness" of the collective CMEA currency

	1971		1972		1973		1974		1977	
Volume of business	Billion TR	Share in %	Billion TR	Share in %	Billion TR	Share in %	Billion TR	Share in %	Billion TR	Share in %
In transferable rubles	39.3	62.5	43.3	61.4	47.4	57.2	52.6	47.5	94.7	54.5
In convertible currency	23.6	37.5	27.2	38.6	35.5	42.8	58.2	52.5	79.2	45.5
Total	62.9	100.0	70.5	100.0	82.9	100.0	110.8	100.0	173.9	100.0

Source: IBEC records.

has prevented the IBEC from developing into an effective credit institution. From its very beginning, therefore, it has been active on the international money markets, where it raises short-term money and middle-term credits which it then passes on to its members and, to a limited extent, to third countries. Its foreign exchange capital, which is equivalent to 60 million transferable rubles, also serves as a source of credit funds.

The volume of business conducted in convertible currencies and in transferable rubles is roughly the same, although the content of the transactions differs. The table on page 168 shows the volume of such business from 1971 through 1977. Indeed, as can be seen from the table, in 1974 the share of transactions in foreign exchange in the total volume of transactions was even greater than the proportion of transactions in rubles. The share of outstanding credits in foreign exchange has also grown considerably: $60 million of the IBEC capital stock paid in has been given out in loans.

The IBEC has become increasingly active on the Eurodollar market; in May 1974 it obtained three syndicate credits there totaling $100 million with a seven-year term of payment, and in 1975 obtained a $60 million credit with a five-year repayment period.

	1971		1972		1973		1974		1977	
	Million TR	Share in %	Million TR	Share in %	Million TR	Share in %	Million TR	Share in %	Million TR	Share in %
Loans outstanding at year's end										
In transferable rubles	626	84.4	798	73.9	1,291	79.2	1,277	74.2	1,494	75.0
In convertible currency	116	15.6	282	26.1	339	20.8	445	25.8	499	25.0
Total	742	100.0	1,080	100.0	1,630	100.0	1,722	100.0	1,993	100.0

Source: IBEC records.

The IBEC's activities in convertible currencies help to stimulate East-West trade, in that they ease the payments difficulties
of IBEC's member nations through its deposit activities and finance
major transactions with the West by offering middle-term foreign exchange credits.

The IBEC also participates in international syndicates that
have provided credits to a few third countries (for two Algerian
banks and one African bank).

The IIB is much more active than the IBEC in seeking credits
on international markets, since its capital stock, in transferable
rubles, can be used only to pay for a preset list of goods valid
only for a particular borrower. The foreign exchange quota —
30 percent of total capital, which at year's end 1977 constituted
$112 million — is generally reclaimed immediately by the
members in the form of credits. There is thus no source except the world market from which the IIB can obtain funds that
it can then lend to its members. In 1977, it increased the sum
of loans granted from 1,157.4 million to 1,857.5 million transferable rubles, without having to augment its basic capital stock.
It borrowed $70 million on the Euromarket in May 1975, and
another $350 million in October, both with a five-year term of
payment and a surcharge over the LIBOR (six-month London
interbank offered rate) of 1.25 percent in the first case and
1.5 percent in the second case. In 1976 and 1977 the IIB borrowed $1,200 million on Western markets.

Its failure to raise working capital stock in nonconvertible
currency has forced the IIB to concentrate on financing high-
priority CMEA projects, such as the Orenburg gas pipeline,
whose total cost is estimated at 2.4 billion transferable rubles.
The authoritative Soviet economic periodical Ekonomicheskaia
gazeta describes the mode of financing this project as follows:
"The IIB will give a loan in foreign exchange to the parties to
the Orenburg pipeline agreement, to pay for the pipe, machinery, and equipment supplied by the Western countries; other
costs of materials and wages will be financed from the participants' own sources."[17] The financing is to the Soviet Union's
advantage. The credit is to be paid off with the gas delivered

by the new pipeline. In this case, the IIB is only a middleman for the credits obtained in the West. To finance the Orenburg pipeline, it obtained a $600 million credit with a six-year repayment period on the world market in July 1976. In 1974 the IIB obtained for the same purpose $600 million.

Since the collective CMEA currency is not convertible, business activities in transferable rubles and in convertible currency proceed in parallel, with no organic relation between them in any area. The banks keep their books in transferable rubles, however, and transactions in foreign exchange are recalculated in transferable rubles at the official exchange rate, which is the same as the rate for the Soviet ruble.

Article 2 of the October 1963 agreement recommends an investigation of the possibilities for making the transferable ruble convertible for gold and the freely convertible currencies, although nothing concrete has come of this so far. There has been no lack of studies of this problem, but concrete conditions have remained the same as when the IBEC began its activities fifteen years ago.

The resolution of September 1, 1973, to make the transferable ruble partly convertible (in which all member nations except Cuba, Romania, and Mongolia participated), has produced nothing of a concrete nature either. The experience gained in this way was to have served as a basis for extending the resolution to all IBEC members and raising the exchange share,[18] but as of the end of 1977 the agreement still remained without effect.

For years efforts have been going on in vain to extend clearing in transferable rubles to third countries. As of the end of 1977, agreements to this effect had been made only between the USSR, Czechoslovakia, and Morocco, and between Iraq, Finland, and a few of the IBEC countries, but none of these has attained any notable scope. Applications from Peru, Colombia, Panama, and Costa Rica to deliver bananas to the Eastern countries for transferable rubles, which they could then use to purchase machinery, have been put off to some unspecified time in the future. The IBEC was unsuccessful in its efforts to extend the transferable ruble to clearing transactions with the developing countries, but the Forty-third Session of the bank council did adopt a resolution in October 1976 to tender a proposal to Western industrial nations that they do their business with IBEC members in transferable rubles. Credits with an interest rate of only 1.5 percent per annum would be offered to members to finance temporary negative balances, while sight deposits were to bear 1 percent interest.[19] Members are also authorized to pay back IBEC ruble loans in hard currencies, but may not exchange their ruble deposits for hard currencies.

As long as there is no firm basis for an exchange rate between the transferable ruble and the convertible currencies, equivalent exchange is impossible. A realistic exchange rate can be established, however, only if it is anchored to an adequate price basis. We will discuss the present price basis in intra-CMEA trade in the following section.

8. The Capitalist Price Basis of Socialist Foreign Trade

It is no exaggeration to say that since 1958 — in other words, since the Ninth Session of the CMEA, which discussed it — the price problem has become the most pressing item on the CMEA's agenda. Even then, the CMEA's experience in the three preceding phases of price formation had not been especially inspiring. These phases were the following:

a) during 1945-50, with few exceptions, current world market prices were used in trade among the Eastern countries;

b) during 1951-53, frozen 1950 prices were used as the CMEA price basis;

c) during 1954-57, frozen 1950 prices were adjusted to the new situation on the Eastern market by means of bilateral agreements.

In none of these phases were internal prices employed as a viable price basis for intra-CMEA trade. In the light of developments since 1975, the period of 1950-53 is of special interest, since though prices rose as a result of the Korean War (for raw materials in particular), prices in CMEA trade were kept stable until the war's end. The price explosion that be-

gan in 1973, however, has carried intra-CMEA prices along
with it.

The Ninth Session of the CMEA in 1958 determined to put an
end to the abnormal situation in which the national prices of the
CMEA had no influence on intra-CMEA trade, and the way was
prepared for establishing a price basis that rested on internal
value relations. Until the preparatory investigations were completed, the average world market prices, corrected for cyclic
and speculative fluctuations, were to serve as a price basis for
intra-CMEA trade. As of yet, however, alien world market
prices, not the intrinsic price basis postulated by the Ninth
CMEA Session, constitute the price basis of internal CMEA
trade; after numerous studies and investigations, any hope of
introducing such an intrinsic price basis was abandoned.

The Ninth Session of the CMEA was convinced that the primary objective of shielding the prices of CMEA trade from cyclic and speculative fluctuations could be achieved only if, instead of current prices, average prices over a five-year period
were used as the price basis for the next five-year period; for
1965-70, average prices for 1960-64 were used to set prices in
intra-CMEA trade, and for 1971-75, average prices for 1965-69
were used.

The 1965-69 average price schedule was abandoned one year
earlier than agreed upon, however. In the aftermath of the
abrupt rise in oil prices, the Seventieth Session of the CMEA
executive committee in January 1975 decided to make a partial
accommodation to the price rise in 1975, and henceforth to employ the five-year average price basis for one-year periods
rather than over a five-year span.

9. Difficulties Caused by Alien Value Relations

World market prices are the price basis for the Eastern bloc,
although the Eastern nations accounted for only 8.7 percent of
total world trade in 1975. Domestic prices in the Eastern countries have no influence whatsoever on the formation of this
price basis, although they account for one-third of total indus-

trial production in the world.

Experts in the East are well aware of the contradiction in maintaining such a price basis, as is evident from the resolution to create an own price basis; still, there has been no lack of attempts to justify this paradoxical situation.[20]

Such rationalizations are no more than vain attempts to make a virtue out of a vice, however, as had been tried before when bilateral clearing was hailed as the best clearing procedure for planned economies. The experts are not at all deceived, for it is they who are encharged with the task of coming up with a price basis, yet each time find themselves faced with an insoluble problem. Viable criteria for valuation exist only for raw materials and fuels; for finished products, and especially machinery, one must rely on one's sixth sense because of the "high dynamics of quantitative criteria for finished products and equipment, for which the sheer range of products covers literally hundreds of thousands of type sizes and models,"[21] and the final decision depends on the partner's negotiating capacity. The committee (seated in Varna, Bulgaria) encharged with working out the price basis for 1956-70 included 35.6 percent of the machinery sold in the CMEA countries in its investigations,[22] and later surveys extended this scope no further. No one ever believed that total identity had been found between the goods sold in the CMEA and those sold on the world market. There was no other way out, however; the alien value and price relations had to be accepted, for the automatic price structures of the CMEA member nations could neither be linked through exchange rates nor evolve some form of interplay. The planned economies eliminated the possibility for such a self-regulating mechanism when they divorced foreign trade accounting from production accounting, reduced the national currencies to domestic currencies, and threw up a barrier between exchange rates and fluctuations on the money market.[23]

The only possible practical solution, which was to accept adjusted foreign price relations as a price basis for the socialist market,[24] leaves the transferable ruble with no value-creating functions. It is not a measure of value, but a common denominator for the foreign value relations transposed from a foreign market to the CMEA.

The CMEA price problem can be solved only by modernizing the domestic monetary systems and intra-CMEA monetary relations, and a prerequisite for this is decentralization of economic steering.

10. Structural Changes in the Terms of Trade

The guidelines for price formation laid down by the Ninth CMEA Session in 1958 make a point of stressing that accepted value relations of the capitalist market can be used in intra-CMEA trade only if they first are freed of cyclic, speculative, and para-economic influences. This condition was meant to shield the socialist market — which for reasons given above is unable to develop its own value relations — from the negative effects of the foreign market, and better adapt foreign price relations to the needs of the socialist community.

These protective measures were not something stumbled upon at random; in the early fifties the Eastern bloc was confronted by inflation as a result of the Korean War, and at that time it was decided to freeze prices at the 1950 level to protect the small Eastern countries from heavy losses.

But the price explosion in 1973 did not spare the Eastern countries. Nevertheless, in 1974 it seemed likely that the price basis established according to the average prices for 1965-69 would not run out until 1975, as agreed, and that the average prices for 1970-74 would form the price basis for the next five-year period. Although the price of oil increased fourfold in 1973, the average prices for 1965-69 were still in effect in the CMEA in 1974. The Seventieth Session of the CMEA Executive Committee in January 1975 altered the guidelines for price formation and made some important changes in the internal terms of trade favorable to countries that export raw materials and fuels.

The Soviet Union, which reaped the benefits of this decision, advanced two trenchant arguments at the meeting, one procedural and the other substantive:

1) the programmatic regulations of the Ninth Council meeting permitted adjustments in existing prices if world prices underwent notable changes;

2) the Soviet Union had always considered the pre-1973 world market prices for raw materials and fuels adopted by the CMEA as unfair, and hence felt that prices should be set at a level that would allow a profit rate more in line with the domestic situation. The Soviet delegate, Ladygin, made this position quite explicit at the 1967 Budapest conference: "The producing countries, however, are entitled to propose a price that corresponds to their national efficiency norms." [25]

Soviet reasoning on this issue becomes clearer when one considers that more than 80 percent of Soviet energy reserves are in Siberia and the Far East, where only 21 percent of the total energy produced in the Soviet Union is consumed, while about 80 percent of the total energy is consumed in the European part of the country, which has only 8.5 percent of USSR energy reserves. The tapping of distant deposits has therefore been made a top-priority goal, especially since such reserves could help cover the needs of the other Eastern countries as well; nevertheless, capital costs and production costs are three times higher in the remote areas than in the European USSR.

Before the end of 1973, prices for raw materials and fuel in intra-CMEA trade were unfair for all producers, including the Soviet Union, regardless of production conditions. To free itself of the constraints of existing world prices, which formed the price basis for intra-bloc trade, the Soviet Union has always postulated an "intrinsic price basis." As mentioned, however, this price basis has remained purely hypothetical, so the Soviet Union had good reason to support the oil-exporting countries in their price hikes. The motives were not purely political: the Soviet Union wanted to raise its own prices as well.

Before the January 1975 price rises, the average price in intra-CMEA trade for one ton of oil was 18.1 rubles ($23.80), which was somewhat higher than the 1972 Kuwait price ($17.13). [26]

The Seventieth Session of the Executive Committee had found

a viable solution that, while enabling the USSR to double 1975 prices and follow with regular increases thereafter, still accorded with the resolutions of the Ninth Council Session.

The five-year average set by the Ninth Council Session was reduced to three years (1972-74), at least for calculating 1975 prices, which were to be in force for only one year instead of five.

The average price for one ton of crude oil was established at 32.80 transferable rubles ($43.75) in 1975, while the Kuwait price was $82.69. The CMEA price of crude was scheduled for a further increase of 8 percent in 1976 and 22 percent in 1977; a further increase of 20 percent followed in 1978.

The price of oil in intra-CMEA trade is still one-fourth lower than the world price, which is what the Soviet Union demands from third countries, and what the other Eastern countries must pay when they import oil from the Near East.

The Soviet Union was the beneficiary of this thorough price restructuring: its additional earnings from crude exported to the other Eastern countries (63.4 million tons) amounted to $1.3 billion in 1975 alone. This made for a considerable improvement in its trade balance in intra-CMEA trade: from 1971 through 1973, it had a negative balance of $2.1 billion, but in 1975 it showed a $737 million surplus.[27]

For commercial reasons alone, the Soviet Union was quite justified in raising its crude oil prices in trade with the other Eastern nations. But though the world price for oil before autumn 1973 may have been unfair, increasing it fourfold was no fairer. A sale price 80 times higher than production costs cannot be justified.[28]

The price skyrocketing made Kuwait the richest country in terms of income per inhabitant, among the forty nations with the highest gross national product: its per capita income was $11,365 — 62 percent higher than in the USA and almost five times higher than in the Soviet Union.[29]

The 1975 intra-CMEA oil price of $44 per ton was enough to cover even the highest transportation costs to the outlying territories (which ran about $9 per ton), ensure the average profit rate called for by the Soviet delegation to the Budapest conference, and at the same time bring in above-average earnings. Nevertheless, the intra-CMEA oil price is scheduled to reach world levels within the next two years and shift the terms of trade further in favor of the Soviet Union.

The Eastern European nations thus have every reason to claim that the programmatic stipulations of the Ninth Session of the CMEA are not being respected, since the influence of the monopolies, from which they were supposed to be shielded, had made an impact on the CMEA market.

They have other reasons as well to be dissatisfied with the price rises in intra-CMEA trade since 1975. The low pre-1975 prices for raw materials were used by the Soviet Union as an argument to induce the smaller nations to help tap the natural resources in outlying Soviet territories.[30] These countries not only must furnish credits from their own resources in the form of construction materials and labor (usually bearing an interest of no more than 2 percent per annum), they must also obtain loans on the world market through the IIB, as in the case of the Orenburg pipeline, to buy large pipe and other items in the West.

The Eastern nations participate on a considerable scale in the construction of large Soviet projects; for example, in Czechoslovakia, investment in Soviet projects amounts to 13 percent or 32 billion koruny in the projected growth of capital investments for 1976-80 over the preceding five-year period[31]; in the German Democratic Republic, such investments make up 3 percent, or 8 billion marks, of the capital project plan for the current five-year period for 1976-80[32]; and Bulgaria and Poland will have contributed credits of 610 million transferable rubles ($800 million)[33] and 500 million transferable rubles ($670 million)[34] to the Orenburg pipeline.

The switch from a five-year to a one-year price basis, however, represents a step forward. Price stability — which is what setting a five-year term for the price basis (computed from the average prices for the preceding five-year period) was intended to accomplish in the first place — considerably widened the disparity between the terms of trade on the Eastern market and those on the world market. The stress on stability

178

was buttressed further by the fact that a smaller number of commodity prices were to be reviewed in determining prices for 1971-75. For instance, Poland reviewed only 2 percent of export prices and 13 percent of import prices in trade with Bulgaria, 24 percent of exports and 13 percent of import prices in trade with the German Democratic Republic, and 34 percent of exports and 19 percent of imports in trade with Hungary. [35] "At the time they are determined, intra-CMEA trade prices are already 2.5 to 3.5 years behind the real prices on the world market." [36]

The gap continues to widen; at the end of 1970, the difference between CMEA and world market prices was 15 percent. Despite intra-CMEA price rises over 1971-74, which were 6 percent higher than increases in the previous five-year period, the discrepancy has continued to grow: by 15 percent in 1971, by 24 percent in 1972, by 52 percent in 1973, and by 116 percent in 1974. [37]

Updating the price basis at one-year intervals should reduce the discrepancy between prices in intra-CMEA trade and world market prices, and might even help set the stage for working out a viable system of exchange rates for the CMEA.

11. The Exchange Rate as an Accounting Instrument

In the planned economies, exchange rates do not conform to the generally accepted definition: namely, that they should express domestic prices in other currencies.

Since currencies are not convertible, they can neither be used in business transactions nor be traded on world money markets. Therefore they have no internationally recognized price. The official exchange rate is a unilaterally set price that has meaning only within the domestic economy, where it functions simply as an accounting instrument, not as a link between the internal and external price systems.

The exchange rate of the transferable ruble, the collective CMEA currency, does not function as does the price of an internationally accepted business currency; it is merely a conversion factor for translating world prices and Western credits into rubles.

Foreign trade balances can be exchanged neither into the national currencies of the CMEA nations nor into convertible currencies. Bilateral outstanding balances may be converted in transferable rubles only in noncommercial trade. In these cases, however, there are special rates that differ considerably from the officially established rates. A multiple exchange rate structure has developed which has made the calculation of trade and its earnings even more cumbersome.

The following different exchange rates are in force:

a) The official exchange rate is set on the basis of gold parity; since 1973, this rate has been regularly adjusted to fluctuations of the convertible currencies. Since it is cut off from the world market, it is unrealistic and is used only for planning and statistics, and, in some Eastern countries, for clearing between foreign trade organizations or between the banks and the Ministry of Finance.

b) In several Eastern countries, especially Poland and Czechoslovakia, special rates or coefficients are used for economic accounting and for clearing with banks; these rates are adjusted to the major trading areas (CMEA, Western countries, developing countries).

c) For noncommercial payments, surcharges to or deductions from the basic exchange rates were set at the Prague conference of February 8, 1963, and adjusted in 1975.

d) Special rates are set for Western tourists.

e) The transferable ruble exchange rate is established on the basis of gold parity (0.987412 grams fine gold) and has been adjusted every quarter since 1973.

f) Exchange rates between the transferable ruble and the national CMEA currencies were set by the CMEA committee for financial and monetary affairs in 1971-74, but never used.

g) Coefficients were established for exchange of outstanding balances of noncommercial payments in transferable rubles.

h) Conversion coefficients are set for joint ventures.

12. The Multiple Exchange Rates of the National Currencies

Though the exchange rates of the nonconvertible currencies are either too high or too low, they generate neither profits nor losses in foreign trade, since trading is not done in these currencies, and they are therefore neither bought nor sold for such purposes. A realistic exchange rate also has no special significance for accounting purposes in a situation where economic control is centralized and foreign trade is transacted at the macro level by "balancing out prices," as it is called; that is, the exchange rate serves no parametric function for economic policy.

In a decentralized steering model, however, where larger enterprises have been given the authority to engage in foreign trade and foreign trade accounting is integrated into production accounting, the exchange rate must be realistic. Enterprises with foreign dealings must have an economically sound exchange rate that will allow earnings to be calculated and incorporated properly into production accounting.

Since the mid-sixties, Poland, Czechoslovakia, and Hungary have used conversion factors that aim at providing a realistic picture of the purchasing power of the national currencies on the major world markets. These factors are calculated on the basis of the costs of procurement of foreign exchange with the national currency in intra-CMEA trade and in trade with the developing countries. It was found that the relationship of the national currency to the transferable ruble and to the U.S. dollar, when calculated in terms of purchasing power parity, is very different from the relation set in the official exchange rates: (1 transferable ruble = 1.11 U.S. dollars in 1971, 1.2 U.S. dollars in 1972, 1.34 U.S. dollars in 1973, 1.32 U.S. dollars in 1974, and 1.39 U.S. dollars in 1975). Hungary explicitly recognized this disparity on January 1, 1976, when it set the official exchange rate at 41 forints per dollar and 35 forints per transferable ruble.

A realistic exchange rate is used mostly when national cur-

181

Money, Banking, and Credit

rencies are actually bought and sold. This is the case in noncommercial relations among the CMEA countries, where mutual
exchanges are carried out, in tourist traffic with the Western
countries, or in unilateral exchange of foreign currency for the
national currency.

The exchange rates for noncommercial payments were set at
the Prague conference on February 8, 1963, on the basis of an
agreed market basket of goods and services; services that come
under the heading of noncommercial payments were also defined.

The Multiple Exchange Rate as of June 1, 1978

		Official rate per U.S. dollar	Tourist rate per U.S. dollar	Rate for noncommercial payments per ruble	Rate for noncommercial payments per transferable ruble
Bulgaria	Lev	0.91	1.365	0.88	2.02
GDR	Mark	2.10	2.10	3.20	7.36
Poland	Zloty	3.33	33.30	19.70	45.31
Romania	Leu	4.47	12.00	8.30	19.09
Czechoslovakia	Koruna	5.40	9.45	10.00	23.00
Hungary	Forint	37.83	18.915	14.75	33.92
USSR	Ruble	0.696	0.696	–	2.30

The tourist rate is equivalent to the official rate only in
the Soviet Union and the German Democratic Republic. In
Poland, the official rate (1 dollar = 3.32 zlotys) has lost all
foundation in reality. The tourist rate alone is ten times
higher, and a special rate (19.92 zlotys = 1 dollar) is used for
transactions between foreign trade enterprises and the banks.

The rate for noncommercial payments set in January 1963
on the basis of domestic prices was reviewed in 1975 and rose
from 15.30 to 19.70 zlotys per ruble, 0.78 to 0.88 leva per ruble,
9.65 to 10.00 koruny per ruble, 13.11 to 14.75 forints per ruble,
and 3.12 to 3.20 marks per ruble. The rate for the Romanian
leu remained the same.

The demand for foreign exchange is more or less satisfied

only in intra-CMEA relations and in this area no gray market has grown up. The situation is different in the case of tourist trade between East and West; here the disparity between demand and the state supply is considerable. A quite active gray market has therefore grown up in which Eastern currencies are sold at rates far below the official tourist rates. The following table gives the relation between the gray market rate (Vienna, February 21, 1977) and the official rates for Western tourists:

Forint	Koruna	Leu	Lev	Mark	Ruble	Zloty
1.2 : 1	2.30 : 1	3.47 : 1	2.02 : 1	3.39 : 1	2.34 : 1	3.00 : 1

These ratios derive from the supply and demand situation, not from purchasing power parity. The disparity is therefore smaller in Hungary, where the demand is better covered than in the other Eastern countries.

13. The Exchange Rate as a Conversion Factor

The transferable ruble exchange rate is not a price recognized on the world market. It is only a means for determining prices for intra-CMEA trade and a bookkeeping instrument in the international CMEA banks where it functions as a uniform accounting unit. Thus the exchange rate is not a connecting link among domestic prices of the member nations nor between world prices and prices in intra-CMEA trade. It is no more than a conversion factor for translating adjusted world prices into rubles.

The transferable ruble exchange rate is also used to translate deposits and credits obtained on the world market, as well as credits granted in convertible currencies, into ruble values. It is not a price factor and its magnitude is unimportant.[38]

The exchange rate between the transferable ruble and the national currencies, set in compliance with the Comprehensive Program of July 1971 by the CMEA Committee for Monetary and Financial Affairs, was a dead issue from the beginning, since there was no place it could be applied.[39]

There is only one area where the relation between the transferable ruble and the national currencies is indispensable, however. This is in noncommercial payments, where outstanding
balances are cleared in transferable rubles. Therefore it was
agreed at the Prague conference (February 1963) that outstanding balances in bilateral transactions should be translated into
Soviet rubles and then into transferable rubles, using a conversion factor of 3.4 (lowered to 2.3 in 1971). The transferable
ruble rate for noncommercial transactions (1 transferable ruble =
2.3 Soviet rubles) is much higher than the official rate (1 transferable ruble = 1 Soviet ruble = 1.35 dollars).

The lack of an economically realistic exchange rate has a
particularly negative impact on specialization projects in the
CMEA countries. It is difficult to calculate costs, determine
prices, and compute earnings, especially where the transfer of
profits is concerned. It was therefore agreed that the costs of
joint ventures should be divided into costs of materials and
costs of labor, and that separate conversion factors be used for
these two components of total expenditures. For the cost of
materials in both investment projects and production, the conversion factor is based on the relation between domestic prices
and the existing prices in intra-CMEA trade. Expenditures for
wages and allied expenses are converted using the rate for noncommercial payments.

How cumbersome these conversions can be is well illustrated
by the Polish-Hungarian joint venture Haldex, which uses 60
different conversion factors.

Exchange rates are only part of the monetary problem in the
planned economies, and accordingly can be dealt with only as
part of the entire complex of East-West relations.

II. SETTLEMENTS AND CREDIT RELATIONS
IN EAST-WEST TRADE

1. Influence of the Different Monetary Mechanisms

No other single aspect of East-West trade is so influenced by the inherent characteristics of the system as clearing and credit relations, and no other single aspect is more detrimental to smooth trade relations than the differences in the monetary systems.

In intra-bloc trade, the clearing and foreign trade models are equally good or equally poor for all; but in trade with the West the Eastern country, with its planned economy, underdeveloped monetary system, autonomous price structure, nonconvertible currency, and exchange rates with no function on the world market, is forced to deal with a partner that has all the trade and monetary instruments at its disposal and knows how to use them as well. The planned economies were unable to develop instruments for foreign trade that could compete on a par with the traditional market mechanisms. This became painfully apparent in their unsuccessful efforts to extend clearing in transferable rubles to third nations. The latest effort to arouse Western interest in this system, made by the Forty-third Session of the IBEC Council in October 1976, has so far received no response.

The planned economies will continue to be the weaker partner in East-West trade for reasons quite apart from those that have reduced their currencies to a domestic currency, and regardless of whether they find it necessary to insulate their prices and their currency to ensure plan fulfillment. Eastern bloc countries have been on an equal footing in trade only when clearing procedures have been equally poor for all — that is, during the first years after the war when bilateralism was the rule in world trade.

The effect of the different trade mechanisms in use in East-West trade first became apparent after Western Europe restored convertibility. Switch and transit transactions, which the Eastern nations were obliged to devise to reduce the growing outstanding balances in bilateral clearing, were too costly. There was a gradual movement into convertible currencies in clearing operations, but this was inadequate to drive forward trade, originally based on a bilateral equality between partners, to the higher stage of multilateral relations. Only the Western

nations could use their currencies, which were convertible;
the Eastern partners, which retained nonconvertibility, were
obliged to use a foreign currency as a payments medium or
continue to rely on squaring exports with imports.

This clash between the market and the plan and their instrumentalities did not prevent trade between East and West from
growing in the seventies, although it did have a considerable influence on the structure and balance of trade.

2. The Thirst for Imports and the Meager Range of Exportable Goods

With the embargo lifted, both sides were interested in expanding economic relations. Western firms wanted to get a
foothold in the alluring Eastern markets as fast as possible
and, as competition intensified, governments were prepared to
support the drive Eastward with monies to promote exports and
with credits at attractive interest rates. The principal factor
in the growth of East-West trade, however, has been the Eastern thirst for imports. With Western markets once again accessible, it was now possible to close the severe technological
gaps that had developed during the cold war with the latest
Western know-how without having to decentralize economic
control, which, though it had become an urgent need, might have
weakened the state's hold on the economy. The beckoning op-
portunities were all the more attractive since Western markets
were ready not only to provide advanced technology, but also to
grant credits on favorable terms, for example, by means of
budget-subsidized interest rates. The financial resources
offered in the West were indeed a crucial element in bridging
the widening gap between the need for imports and the chronically lagging supply of exportable goods. Accordingly, the
CMEA authorities hit upon the solution that not only might the
West have a hand in financing the latest industrialization phase,
it could also provide the means for repayment of outstanding
loans by sharing in the construction of plants producing exportable goods. [40]

The spectacular expansion of East-West trade in the seventies is due largely to Eastern imports and has been accompanied by a rapid growth in the trade deficit and in indebtedness, as the following table shows.

East-West Trade from 1970 to 1975*

	1970	1971	1972	1973	1974	1975	1971/75
Eastern exports to the West (million $)	6,681	7,369	8,729	12,958	18,571	19,428	73,736
Eastern imports from the West (million $)	7,643	8,272	11,025	16,395	23,219	31,010	97,564
Foreign trade deficit (million $)	962	903	2,296	3,437	4,648	11,582	23,828
Share of Western imports in total imports (in %)	25.3	25.3	26.8	30.9	35.0	35.0	
Share of Western exports in total exports (in %)	21.6	21.9	21.6	24.7	28.9	24.7	

Sources: Statistical yearbooks of the CMEA countries; volumes in transferable rubles were converted into dollars using the exchange rates of 1 transferable ruble = $1.11 through 1971, $1.21 in 1972, $1.34 in 1973, $1.32 in 1974, and $1.39 in 1975.

*Including Bulgaria, Czechoslovakia, the German Democratic Republic, Poland, Romania, Hungary, and the USSR in the East, and the OECD countries in the West.

During 1970-75, East-West trade more than doubled, although exports still clearly lag behind imports, with only 62.7 percent of imports covered in 1975. The foreign trade deficit has become chronic; in no year have the Eastern countries shown a surplus in trade with the West. Deficits have grown especially fast in the past three years — from $3.4 billion in 1973 to $4.6 billion in 1974 and $11.6 billion in the next two years. The deficits of the Soviet Union and Poland have been above average, and were about the same level for both countries for the five-year period 1971-75 ($6,971 million and $7,070 million, respectively). In 1975, Polish and Soviet exports were able to cover only 51.8 percent and 63.3 percent of imports, respectively.

It is remarkable that the planned economies, which have always tried to avoid discrepancies between income and expenditure (a balanced budget, a balance between household income and household spending, and bilaterally offset goods exchange in intra-bloc trade are stock principles for them) should accept large and growing deficits in trade with the West. One may reasonably ask, therefore, to what extent planned targets are responsible for the imbalance in trade with the West. The first drafts of the 1971-75 five-year plans reveal no evident connection. But the final versions show a much greater difference between actual imports from and exports to the West than had been intended. In Poland, for example, 4 percent was planned but the actual gap was 43 percent.

It would be wrong to blame the uncertainty on the world market for Eastern deficits, however. Although it is true that the recession throttled the expansion of Eastern exports in 1975, the extremely high import volume was due mainly to Soviet and Polish harvest failures and the feverish capital investment activity in Poland; an inadequate and poor-quality export structure, on the other hand, has been the principle reason for the chronic lag in Eastern exports.

A meager export structure seems to be rooted in the system; the planned economies have always regarded foreign trade as but one source of supply, and exports simply as a source of funds to pay for vital imports. Export has never been regarded as a profit-yielding venture and hence has never been structured competitively in accordance with world standards.

The factors the centrally controlled, planned economies set into motion were inadequate to ensure sufficient sales of finished products on the world market. Production enterprises have always operated on a seller's market and have never been forced to deal with the forces of the world market and its demands for quality and service, and therefore have never had to carry full responsibility for the returns from foreign trade; neither have they had to bear the impact of events on the world market nor been obliged to construct their activities on a competitive basis.

The isolation of the producers from the world market and of the national currencies from the world monetary system have reduced even the most powerful of the planned economies to the status of a developing country on the world market. Their currency is nonconvertible not only for inherent reasons, but also because of an insufficient ability to compete.

The structure of East-West trade does not adequately reflect the level of development in the East[41]; it resembles more the patterns of trade between industrial nations and the developing countries. The share of SITC commodity groups 5-8 (industrial products) in the exports of OECD countries to CMEA nations rose from 67.3 percent in 1965 to 82 percent in 1975, while imports of this commodity group from Eastern countries to OECD countries rose only from 33.7 percent to 36 percent. [42]

3. The Growing Mountain of Debt

The CMEA community does not have a functioning money market on which funds for financing trade or capital projects can be raised. The only credits existing in intra-bloc trade are the technical stopgap credits granted by the IBEC. Capital development loans are granted in commodity form. The establishment of the two CMEA banks did not increase the internal credit funds of the CMEA. Both banks have employed the world market to develop their credit activities. Eastern nations with intra-bloc trade surpluses cannot use them to cover the deficit with the West, since the transferable ruble, which is not very transferable even within the CMEA, cannot be converted into hard currencies. Trade deficits with the West have had to be covered by credits obtained on the world market, which more and more is being used as a source for funds to finance major investment projects.

East-West credit relations are expanding rapidly, but there are discernible differences from one country to another as to which world market facilities are preferred. The Soviet Union and Hungary favor bank-to-bank credits; Poland makes more use of syndicate credits than the other Eastern countries. In

the German Democratic Republic swing credits are becoming
more and more frequent since the Federal Republic admits this
type of credit in trade with East Germany; its limit (850 million
deutsche marks) is always overdrawn.

4. Types of Credit Relations

The Eastern countries employ every kind of credit available
on the world market. There are two major flows discernible
from the West:

a) short-term and middle-term credits for financing current
transactions and payments deficits;

b) middle-term and long-term credits to finance capital investment projects.

As is customary on the world market, short-term credits are
given to finance raw materials, consumer goods, chemicals,
and so on, usually with a repayment period of one year, but for
two years in trade with France and Great Britain.

This credit flow passes principally through the commercial
banks, with the normal payments instruments used in settlement. In contrast to intra-bloc trade, in which immediate payment on presentation of the appropriate documents is the only
form of settlement, in East-West trade letters of credit are
the preferred form.

Letters of credit often require a supplier's credit and are
tied to an acceptance credit of between 60 and 360 days. The
Western bank does not pay the exporter until the stipulated
term has lapsed. Even when payment is made on presentation
of a document, a supplier's credit of 30 to 45 days for Soviet
buyers and 30 days for buyers from the other Eastern countries
is given. The simplest, but also the riskiest, form of short-
term credits is payments into open accounts; in these cases
payment terms are between 30 and 360 days. This form is generally used in dealings with the Soviet Union. Czechoslovakia,
and Hungary, and less often the other Eastern countries, use
settlements in open accounts occasionally with Western firms.

As payments difficulties grow, Eastern nations are asking

for longer and longer repayments terms; for example, the German Democratic Republic now receives a 360-day repayment term for consumer goods, while before only 180 days were given. Credits are now being granted for smaller orders than formerly — even as low as $80,000 (Poland) or $200,000 (Romania).[43]

Suppliers' credits increasingly are being replaced by direct bank-to-bank credits; the former are still used with relative frequency only in Czechoslovakia ($600 million, or one-third of total credit volume at the end of 1975).[44]

Bank credits are usually procured on the Euromarket, where the Eastern nations also deposit their meager foreign exchange holdings, which in most cases are reserves from credits obtained on the world market.[45]

Since the Eastern nations keep secret their payments balances and their debt, the most authoritative source of information we have are the statistics of the Bank for International Settlements (BIS) on the assets and liabilities of Western banks in their relations with the Eastern nation.[46] The following table shows assets and liabilities for the years 1971-77.

(in millions of dollars)

	Deposits			Credits		
	Eastern Europe	USSR	Total	Eastern Europe	USSR	Total
1971	1,100	1,200	2,300	2,750	720	3,470
1972	1,600	1,800	3,400	3,470	1,760	5,230
1973	1,730	2,540	4,270	4,775	3,005	7,780
1974	2,420	3,535	5,955	8,807	3,778	12,585
1975	3,060	3,200	6,260	12,400	9,100	21,500
1977	3,289	4,496	7,785	21,406	11,502	32,908

Source: Bank for International Settlements, press reviews.
*The residual is not broken down into separate items in the IBS reports (December 1977: liabilities, $455 million; assets, $2,407 million; we have divided it up between the Soviet Union and the other Eastern nations on the basis of the percentage share in the total sum.

Between 1973 and mid-1976, credits received by the Eastern nations from the major Western industrial countries increased by more than threefold, while deposits increased by only 43.8

191

percent. The small foreign exchange holdings are interesting, though one must keep in mind that the statistics of the BIS do not give the total sum, and that some Eastern countries — most notably the Soviet Union — also have gold reserves of their own. Most of their foreign exchange holdings, however, are kept in the banks of the Western industrial nations, although the total sum ($7,785 million at the end of 1977) is not much higher than Italy's monetary reserves ($6,620 million at the end of 1976).[47]

5. Syndicate and Other Middle-Term Credits

In the last few years, the CMEA nations have been making increasing use of middle-term syndicate credits, in which the largest banks of Europe, Japan, and the United States and Soviet banks abroad, such as the Moscow Narodny Bank in London and the Banque Commerciale pour l'Europe du Nord (Eurobank), participate.

The share of CMEA countries in the total syndicate credits obtained on the world market increased from 3 percent in 1972 to 12 percent in 1974, but declined again during the first eight months of 1976. Poland heads the list of CMEA countries with $1.8 billion of credits. Since 1975, however, it has slackened

Syndicate Credits, 1972-76 (in millions of dollars)

	1972	1973	1974	1975	1976 (to Nov.)	Total
Bulgaria	40	115	160	125	240	680
GDR	35	15	12	280	235	577
Poland	20	370	509	475	385	1,759
Czechoslovakia	—	—	—	60	200	260
Hungary	70	90	150	250	150	710
Soviet Union	—	—	—	750	282	1,032
CMEA banks	140	50	100	480	600	1,370
Total	305	640	931	2,420	2,092	6,388

Source: Financial Market Trends, OECD, No. 14, XII, 1976.

its pace of borrowing. In 1974, Poland had eleven credits (highest sum, $100 million); in 1975, only five credits (largest, $240 million); and in 1976, again five (largest, $140 million) with a repayment term of five to eight years. Poland was also the most active CMEA borrower on the Euromarket, at $1.1 billion.

The Polish Bank Handlowy is the principal borrower, obtaining all-purpose loans. In some cases large concerns of their associations are the borrowers — as, for example, the mining association in September 1974 ($100 million with a repayment period of seven years) or the association for inorganic chemistry in June 1976 ($140 million for five years) and the shipping company one month later ($20 million, also for five years). [48]

In the last five years, Poland has taken earmarked loans to finance major projects that are to be paid back with the goods manufactured by these projects. At the initiative of the International Harvester Company, a group of American banks provided a loan of $240 million to finance the expansion of the Polish copper industry; in August 1974, a group of British banks put up a loan of $304 million to fund the expansion of the Polish tractor plant Ursus; Austrian banks gave a loan of $236 million to finance the expansion of the Jelcz automobile plant by the Austrian firm Steyr-Daimler-Puch. West German banks have also been quite active in financing Polish industrial projects: a one billion deutsche mark all-purpose loan was granted in 1975 and $234 million for the gasification of coal a year later.

The Soviet Union first turned to the Euromarket for syndicate loans in 1975. In three successive transactions, it borrowed $100 million (January 1975), $250 million (May), and $400 million (December); in July and August 1976, it took two more credits amounting to $282 million. All these loans were for five years.

Soviet interest in bilateral credit relations has also grown over the years; the USSR began to borrow from the West in the early sixties — first in Italy, where it received a loan of $100 million. Five years later, Italy granted a credit of $363 million to build the Togliatti automobile works. The Soviet Union has also concluded major credit agreements with the Federal

Republic of Germany — in particular, to finance Soviet gas pipelines (in two credit tranches of 1.2 billion deutsche marks each), for which the FRG supplied the pipe.

West Germany, France, and the United States have all provided major loans for financing the Kama truck works; other countries have advanced credit lines to finance current business (e.g., France, $1.5 billion; Great Britain, $1.0 billion; Japan, $1.5 billion; Canada, $0.5 billion).[49] So far, however, the Soviets have been unsuccessful in inducing Japan and the United States to provide credits for tapping the oil and gas deposits in Siberia and the Far East (the first tranche is supposed to be $8 billion). When the Export-Import Bank quota was set at $300 million for the next four years, American banks were compelled to cut back on their activities on the Soviet market, and Japan is unwilling to assume the entire risk herself, granting only $330 million in credit, of which only $100 million was to finance oil drilling in Sakhalin.

Since 1972, Bulgaria has been an active borrower of syndicate credits. Despite a growing indebtedness, Bulgaria took out three syndicate loans amounting to $160 million in 1974, five amounting to $125 million in 1975, and three totaling $240 million as of November 1976. Confidence in Bulgaria's credit worthiness remains, as evidenced by the hiking of a loan originally estimated at $75 million to $100 million.

The German Democratic Republic has likewise experienced no difficulties so far in obtaining credits on the Euromarket: in 1974, it had only one loan of $12 million, but in 1976 it had seven outstanding loans amounting to $280 million and in 1976 three credits amounting to $235 million.

Since July 1976, however, the German Democratic Republic has refrained from borrowing on the Euromarket in the hopes it will obtain better terms through suppliers' credits. As of the end of 1976, suppliers' credits to East Germany were estimated at 4.6 billion deutsche marks, including 2.6 billion deutsche marks in trade commitments between the two Germanys. This sum also includes an interest-free swing credit of 850 million deutsche marks.[50]

Money, Credit, and Prices in Foreign Trade

Hungary has made more use of the different kinds of credit than any other CMEA country. Bank-to-bank credits top the list. Between 1972 and 1976, Hungary obtained $710 million in middle-term credits, and in January 1977 another $150 million, with a repayment term of five to eight years on the Euromarket. Hungary leads the CMEA nations with seven bonds so far amounting to a total of $240 million, floated on the Euromarket with a term of six to eight years. The first was in May 1971 and the last in February 1976 — both for $25 million.

Thus far, Romania has not made use of syndicate credits. A member of the Bretton Woods agreement since 1972, Romania had obtained $540 million in credits as of the end of 1976 on favorable terms, and in January 1977 received another long-term credit in the amount of $130 million. Romania has been granted large loans by the German Democratic Republic, Great Britain, Japan, and the United States.

Czechoslovakia has been more restrained in its credit policy. During 1950-60, it received no more than $14 million in Western credits. It was at the bottom of the list of nations in the Berne Union at the end of 1970, with a credit volume of $155 million. Its first loan on the Euromarket was a syndicate credit of $60 million in November 1975; its next was in October 1976, when it received a $200 million credit.

The two CMEA banks have also been active as borrowers of syndicate loans on the Euromarket; in 1974, the IBEC had received three loans totaling $100 million, and in 1975, one loan of $75 million with a repayment period of five to seven years. The IBEC encountered difficulties in January 1977, however, when it sought a five-year credit of $200 million under the auspices of the Bank of America. The loan was blocked because a British expert felt there were some doubts as to its legal status — according to IBEC statutes, the IBEC's legal liability is limited to the CMEA.[51]

The IBEC for the most part has dealt in short-term money as a borrower on the Euromarket; it then passes these monies on to its members to help them bridge temporary payments difficulties. It must be judged as quite successful in this area when one considers that transactions in convertible currencies, which amounted to 63 billion transferable rubles ($85 billion) in 1975, were only 5.7 percent less than clearing and credit transactions in the collective clearing unit (transferable ruble) of the CMEA.

The International Investment Bank has also had to turn to the Euromarket to supplement short own credit funds, and as of the end of 1976 had obtained three loans amounting to $70 million, $350 million, and $600 million. In 1977 the IIB received an additional $600 million. The last was earmarked to finance the participation of the Eastern countries in the construction of the Orenburg pipeline. Basically, the CMEA banks act as agents for their members on the world market.

6. The Size of the Debt

Since no official statistics are available, estimates of indebtedness must rely on a few reference points such as foreign trade deficits, overall statistics of the Bank for International Settlements on obligations and commitments of the twelve major industrial nations, and statistics on credit agreements concluded with Eastern nations to finance major capital investment projects. One important index for estimating the size of the debt is lacking — namely, figures on invisible payments, whose importance has increased because of the growing debt service.

Estimates vary, but one thing is clear: the debt continues to grow, and prospects for reducing it are nil, at least until 1980, for those countries with the largest debts to the West. The following table shows indebtedness figures based on the statistics of the Chase Manhattan Bank and, for 1976, on current balances for East-West trade. The breakdown by individual country is only rough, because of the inadequate data available and because credits extended by the CMEA bank to individual countries are not known.

The debt has increased more rapidly in Poland and in the Soviet Union than in the other CMEA countries. These two countries together make up 60 percent of the total. If one bears in

196

Money, Credit, and Prices in Foreign Trade

Net Indebtedness of the CMEA Countries, 1974-77
(billions of dollars)

	1974	1975	1976	1977
Bulgaria	1.4	2.0	2.5	2.9
GDR	3.1	4.2	4.4	6.6
Poland	4.4	7.1	9.1	13.9
Romania	2.2	2.3	2.3	3.2
Czechoslovakia	0.7	1.2	1.5	1.9
Hungary	1.8	2.3	2.7	9.3
Soviet Union	2.4	8.4	11.4	16.3
CMEA banks	1.9	2.6	3.2	3.5
Total	17.9	30.1	37.1	52.6

Source: Financial Times, January 26, 1977; Chase World Information,
East-West Markets, May 29, 1978.

mind that both the Soviet Union and Poland possess considerable resources in fuel and raw materials, and that a portion of the Western credits has gone to tapping new deposits, it is not unreasonable that these two countries should account for such a large share of the total sum. The ratio of their debts to the West (0.8 : 1.0), however, is totally out of line with their relative economic strength. More than any other Eastern nation, Poland owes its rapid development to Western credits and to a greater volume of capital investments (132.6 percent higher in 1975 over 1970) than in the other countries.

Bulgaria, the German Democratic Republic, Romania, Czechoslovakia, and Hungary have concluded credit agreements amounting to $5.2 billion with the West and, as of the end of 1975, have used $3.5 billion of this sum.[52] The German Democratic Republic has the largest debt, and Czechoslovakia the smallest. One-fourth of the GDR debt, however, is due to swing transactions with West Germany.

Five Western industrial nations have been the main parties in 80 percent of the agreements (amounting to $21.4 billion): France ($5.66 billion), the Federal Republic of Germany ($5.3 billion), Great Britain ($2.9 billion), Italy ($1.8 billion), and Japan ($1.6 billion).[53]

7. Is Eastern Bloc Indebtedness Too High?

In September 1976, international bank credits reached $500 billion.[54] The Eastern bloc's share (7-8 percent) is relatively modest. Its indebtedness is not much higher than Great Britain's ($45 billion), and the Soviet Union's obligations are lower than Brazil's ($18.4 billion) or Mexico's ($16.8 billion).

Credit relations in the planned economies, however, have features all their own. In intra-bloc trade, which makes up more than 60 percent of total foreign trade and is settled bilaterally by institutionalized policy, credits are used merely as stopgap measures. Major discrepancies between imports and exports are tolerated only in trade with the West and, moreover, are financed by Western banks, which are also increasingly being used to finance large capital investment projects.

Even the two CMEA banks turn to the Western market to obtain the necessary credit funds, which they then distribute within the Eastern bloc. West-East credit relations are a one-way street.

The structure of the Eastern economies is geared to the division of labor within the bloc. Exchange quotas for intra-CMEA trade are set for relatively long periods, and the instruments of economic policy ensure that these commitments are fulfilled. At present the Eastern countries have no sufficient export structure to meet Western demand. Hence, the most telling index of the size of debt in the East is not the ratio of credits to total exports, but the amount of credits relative to the volume of exports to the West.

Net Indebtedness Relative to Exports to Western
Industrial Countries (exports = 1)

	Bulgaria	GDR	Poland	Romania	Czechoslo-vakia	Hungary	USSR	Eastern Europe
1974	2.1	1.4	1.4	1.0	0.4	1.3	0.3	0.9
1975	3.1	1.9	2.0	1.1	0.6	1.6	1.0	1.5
1977	4.3	2.2	3.6	1.5	1.0	3.0	1.4	2.5

Source: Statistics from Chase Manhattan Bank, December 30, 1976; Chase World Information, East-West Markets, May 29, 1978.

Money, Credit, and Prices in Foreign Trade

The average CMEA indebtedness in 1975 was 50 percent
higher than the volume of exports to hard-currency countries,
while in 1974 it was 10 percent lower and in 1977, 2.5 percent
higher. This indicator was poorest for Bulgaria (4.3) and best
for Czechoslovakia, which is the only CMEA country in which
the debt equals the annual export volume. Poland's situation
has deteriorated considerably: its debt to the West is equal to
3.5 years' exports. The Soviet debt is relatively half as great.
The debt of the German Democratic Republic is almost as great as
Poland's, but repayments and interest rates are much lower than
for Poland owing to the high share of interest-free swing credits
in trade between the two Germanys. Credit terms are also
harder for Poland than for the other Eastern countries.

8. Credit Terms

Eastern bloc nations have always enjoyed a good reputation
on the world market and thus have received favorable repayment terms and low interest rates.[55] To promote business with
the East, France, Great Britain, and Italy have always been
willing to subsidize interest rates from the state budget. Eastern importers have been able to negotiate interest rates between 6 and 7 percent on these markets. West Germany was
the only nation unwilling to subsidize interest rates, except for
the credit of one billion deutsche marks granted to Poland in
Helsinki in June 1975; this loan bears an interest rate of 2.5
percent.

Since the balance of trade has deteriorated, the Eastern countries have become willing to pay higher interest than before.
Rates for suppliers' credits are 7 to 7.5 percent. The USSR,
which formerly would pay no more than 6 percent per annum,
is now willing to pay 7 percent, while the German Democratic
Republic will pay 7 to 7.5 percent (in trade between the two
Germanys, in which the interest rate is tied to the Bundesbank
discount rate, GDR credits bear 3.5 to 4.0 percent interest).
Czechoslovakia also pays 7 percent; Bulgaria has paid as high
as 7.7 percent; Romania pays 7.5 to 8.0 percent; while Poland,

which has the greatest payments difficulties, has paid 8 or 9 percent in some cases and tries to get as long repayment terms as possible. Formerly, Poland paid off its loans at semi-annual rates, but it now wants to pay off about 80 percent of a credit after the term of payment begins.[56] Credit terms also vary on the Euromarket, which before had tended to deal with all the Eastern countries on an equal basis. Since mid-1973, interest rates have been tied to the LIBOR and have varied depending on the borrower's capacity to pay and on liquidity of the capital market.

Interest Range Paid by CMEA Countries
over the LIBOR, 1973-76

	1973	1974	1975	1976
Bulgaria	—	1.25	1.5	1.375
GDR	—	.75	1.375	1.25
Poland	.75	1.125	1.5	1.5
Czechoslovakia	—	.75	1.375	1.25
Hungary	.5-.75	1.375	1.375-1.5	1.25
USSR	—	—	1.25	1.25
CMEA bank	.5	1.125	1.5	1.25-1.375
Non-CMEA borrowers	.375-1.5	1-1.125	1.25-1.375	.875-1.125

Source: Financial Market Trends, No. 14, December 1976.

In addition, a 0.25-0.5 percent fee is levied on syndicate credits. The table above shows that Poland and Bulgaria have generally paid above-average interest rates. On the whole, however, Eastern nations are treated no worse than non-CMEA best borrowers. The terms of trade with the East show a slight deterioration only for 1975 and 1976. CMEA countries that have been given poorer terms — Bulgaria and Poland — have therefore made more use of the IBEC than the others as a mediator to obtain loans. In 1978, the interest rate for credits extended to the Soviet Union, Hungary, and the GDR were only 0.75 percent over the LIBOR.

9. The Economic and Political Risks

The Eastern nations cannot be regarded as a homogeneous

bloc — that is, as a collective borrower with a collective responsibility — as far as estimating economic risk is concerned. It would also be wrong to assume that the Soviet Union is ready to step in to assist an Eastern nation that gets into payments difficulties. The credit worthiness of each country must be assessed separately.

The payments difficulties of the Soviet Union are of no concern, since its production of raw materials and fuels is steadily growing, further stimulated by Western loans and the financial assistance of the other Eastern countries in erecting large investment projects. The massive grain purchases that have driven up its debt considerably in the past few years could be put to an end with a few good harvests. In addition, the USSR has gold reserves (estimated at 2,000 to 3,000 tons) and produces about 200 to 250 tons of gold annually, which it could put up if needed. The Soviet Union is also in the process of improving its situation at the expense of its CMEA partners by pushing up oil prices and adopting other economic measures, for example, shifting the burden of defense expenses onto its allies.

The other Eastern countries are in a relatively poorer situation. They have a much narrower range in which to maneuver than the Soviet Union, and they can expand their export structure only with finished products, which have always been difficult to establish on the world market because of inferior quality and poor marketing and service. The smaller Eastern nations have always felt their isolation from the world market and the world monetary system more acutely than the Soviet Union, and this handicap can be expected to grow. In addition, each Eastern country has its own particular payments difficulties determined by its special economic situation.

Poland is a special case. It has relied most on Western credits for its economic development. Western imports have increased enormously in volume in the past three years, yet its export structure has been less tuned to the needs of the Western market than those of the other Eastern countries. The West accounted for 50.5 percent of total imports in 1974 and 49.4 percent in 1975. In the five-year period of 1971-75, however, Western imports were only 62.1 percent covered by exports (as little as 56.2 percent for 1974 and 51.8 percent for 1975). The foreign trade deficit with the West was $6,971 million for the five-year period 1971-75 ($2,290 million in 1974 and $3,104 million in 1975). Poland's problem therefore has been structural imbalance, not a cyclic depression

A conference of Polish foreign trade experts in late 1975 made quite explicit the country's difficulties in building up its export structure. Attempts to expand exports, partly at the expense of internal needs (especially coal, meat, and sugar), have failed. Supply problems have grown worse and public resistance has made it impossible to ease the demand pull and cost push by means of drastic price rises (in 1975, prices were subsidized with 165 billion zlotys from the state budget — that is, 20.8 percent of total budget expenditures).[57] Between 1970 and 1977, price subsidies rose by sevenfold. The Polish government is faced with chronic problems that reduce its range of maneuver.

The debt service ranged from 14 percent in 1972 to 18 percent in 1974, and reached 25 percent — about $1 billion — in 1976.[58]

Repayment periods are scheduled to lapse on a large scale during the last years of this decade, and chances are slim that an even balance of payments plus a 30 percent surplus will have been reached by that time to cover the credits due.

In the period from 1976 to 1980, exports to the West are expected to increase more rapidly than imports. Tentative figures for 1976, however, show that, despite cutbacks on imports, the trade deficit with the West was $2 billion — that is, only $0.3 billion less than the previous year — while the total deficit ($2.8 billion) was even higher than in 1975 ($2.3 billion).

Bulgaria will also have payments difficulties; Bulgaria has had the largest debt in the CMEA when measured against exports: its total trade deficit rose from $448 million in 1974 to $837 million in 1975. Steps have already been taken, however, to reduce the trade deficit with the West; exports to nonsocialist countries rose by 13 percent over 1975, while imports decreased by 15.3 percent,[59] and the trade deficit fell from $800 million to $400 million.

Although the German Democratic Republic is deeply in debt, its payments burden is lighter, since more than one-fourth of its debt is in the form of swing credits that are both long term and interest free. The GDR's position in trade between the two Germanys improved considerably in 1976: East German exports rose by 16 percent, while imports rose by only 11 percent; exports of machinery increased by as much as 32.2 percent.[60] The German Democratic Republic also has a wider range of export goods to offer than the other Eastern nations, and has had more success in finding markets for them in the West.

Neither is Hungary's payments situation any cause for concern. Because of its excellent relations with the world market, Hungary is better able to bridge payments difficulties than are the other Eastern countries. It reduced its trade deficit from $600 million in 1975 to $400 million in 1976. In the five-year period of 1976-80, exports to the West should increase by 60 percent and imports by 35 percent, with an even balance of trade with the West expected by 1980. Most of Hungary's debt consists of middle-term and long-term credits, and the first major repayment — $197 million — is not due until 1979.[61]

Romania's payments situation is for the present difficult to assess, although Romania was able to reduce its trade deficit from $480 million in 1975 to $20 million in 1976 by cutting back 15 percent on imports and increasing exports by 60 percent. The earthquake of March 4, 1977, the worst in European history, did considerable damage to Romania's economy, and it will be many years before the country has completely recovered. Loans falling due in the next few years probably will be rescheduled.

In assessing creditworthiness, each Eastern country must be regarded in the final analysis as a collective debtor, regardless of the degree of decentralization of economic control. The view that detailed information on the purpose of a loan will prevent errors in assessments — a notion especially common in American economic circles — is exaggerated. Payments difficulties are totally independent of the success or failure of the project

financed with Western credits. The state, which controls all
foreign exchange reserves, decides on the final product and its
allocation for internal use, for intra-bloc trade, and for trade
with the West. The overall economic situation, not the performance of a particular venture, is the deciding factor in the
creditworthiness of an Eastern country.

A Western firm or bank is seldom able to obtain a clear picture of the Eastern country's economy. More than is usually
the case, therefore, foreign trade and credit relations with an
Eastern bloc nation must be the affair of the government of the
Western nation.

Credit relations with the East are still not free of political
considerations, and for the foreseeable future East-West economic relations must continue to be viewed as relations between two competing political world systems, opposed both economically and politically.

The political risk is not just that, in a conflict situation, the
borrower can refuse payment. There is also the chance that
technology exported to the East and financed with Western credits will benefit a potential adversary in some future conflict.
This risk can be eliminated only if détente leads to disarma-
ment and if the political confrontation between the two systems
can be made negligible.

10. A Unified World Monetary System

Isolation of the economic mechanisms of the Eastern countries and of their money and price relations from the world market is an inherent aspect of their system. As long as trade with
the West was only a marginal activity of the Eastern nations,
this was of no importance, but now the situation has changed:
trade with the West presently comprises 30 to 50 percent of
total Eastern foreign trade. Integration of the foreign trade
system is now a sine qua non for attaining a position of equal
standing in business with the West, and the East has a particular interest in achieving that status.

The integration, and hence de-ideologization, of East-West

trade presumes convertibility — that is, integration of the Eastern currencies into the world monetary system — not the incorporation of Western currencies into the clearing systems of the Eastern bloc, as suggested by the Forty-third Session of the IBEC council in October 1976.

The Eastern countries are already integrated into the world economic order in many respects: Poland, Romania, Czechoslovakia, and Hungary are members of the GATT, all Eastern European countries are members of the Economic Commission for Europe, UNIDO, and so on, and particular progress has been made toward integration with the expanding network of Eastern banks in the West and Western in the East.

Eastern bank branches have developed from information and contact bureaus into full-fledged institutions operating on the international money market. They facilitate East-West credit relations, issue Eurodollar loans together with Western banking syndicates, and finance Eastern trade with the West with funds raised in the country in which they are located.

The largest and oldest of these banks is the Moscow Narodny Bank, founded in London in 1916; it has enlarged its staff from 30 to 300, and its activity has grown by leaps and bounds. Its assets have risen from £549 million at the end of 1972 to £1,212 million at the end of 1975. The declared capital was raised to £20 billion and paid-in capital to £15.5 million; in 1975 net earnings were £1,214,829.[62] The Banque Commerciale pour L'Europe du Nord (Eurobank) is also expanding. Its balance sheet total rose from 8.8 billion francs in 1972 to 13.6 billion francs at the end of 1975; clear earnings rose from 24.1 million to 40 million francs, and declared capital was raised to 250 million francs in May 1975.

The Voskhod Commerce Bank AG founded in Zurich in 1966, the East-West Commerce Bank AG established in Frankfurt am Main in 1972, and the Danube Bank active in Vienna since 1974 are also doing well. The other Eastern nations have also expanded their bank network in the West.

At the beginning of 1972, Hungary gave an extensive facelifting to the Centralwechselstube AG, operating in Vienna since

Money, Banking, and Credit

1918, and renamed it the Central Wechsel and Creditbank AG. On October 18, 1973, the Hungarian National Bank, Ltd., was opened in London with a founding capital of £1 million. The Hungarian National Bank has representatives in Zurich, Paris, and Beirut and, since October 1974, in Frankfurt as well. A subsidiary of the Hungarian bank was established in New York at the beginning of 1978.

In March 1972, Poland opened a joint bank with the Federal Republic of Germany — the Central European Bank AG in Frankfurt; the partners are the Bank Handlowy of Warsaw (70 percent) and the Hessische Landesbank Girozentrale (30 percent).

A French-Romanian bank was established in February 1972 with a founding capital of 20 million francs; eight major French banks participated. In the same year, a Romanian-British bank was founded with a capital of $7 million.

In August 1976, the Romania Foreign Trade Bank, the Banque Franco-Roumaine, S.A., Paris, and the DG Bank and BHF Bank, both of Frankfurt, agreed to establish the Frankfurt-Bucharest Bank AG in Frankfurt. The new bank will have a founding capital of 20 million deutsche marks, to be raised by the Romanian Foreign Trade Bank (52 percent), the Banque Franco-Roumaine (8 percent), the DG Bank (24 percent), and the BHF Bank (16 percent).

The expanding network of Eastern bank branches in the West is developing into a cornerstone of West-East economic relations as well as an influential factor in its own right in the international monetary system.

Western banks have also been expanding their network in the East for some time now. At the end of 1976, twenty-one branches were operating in Moscow, four each in the German Democratic Republic and Poland, two in Hungary, and one each in Bulgaria and Romania. They do not engage in usual banking business, however, but limit their activities to establishing contacts and providing information. Balance sheet data of the banks of the CMEA countries in Western Europe and representative offices of Western banks in the Eastern countries are given in the tables on the following pages.

The fact that Eastern banks have been able to integrate into the Western banking system, while it has proved impossible to

Representative Offices of Western Banks
in the Eastern Countries

Western bank*	Location of office**
Banca Commerciale Italiana (Italy)	Moscow (1975), Warsaw (1975), East Berlin (1976), Belgrade (1978)
Banco di Napoli (Italy)	Sofia (1974), Moscow (1975)
Banco di Roma (Italy)	Moscow (1975)
Banco di Sicilia (Italy)	Budapest (1977)
Bank of America (USA)	Moscow (1973)
Bank of Tokyo (Japan)	Moscow (1975)
Banque de Paris et des Pays Bas (France)	Moscow (1974)
Banque Nationale de Paris (France)	Moscow (1974), Warsaw (1974)
Barclays Bank (UK)	Moscow (1974)
Chase Manhattan Bank (USA)	Moscow (1973)
Citibank (USA)	Moscow (1974), Budapest (1975)
Commerzbank (Fed. Rep. of Germany)	Moscow (1975)
Crédit Industriel et Commercial (France)	Warsaw (1975)
Crédit Lyonnais (France)	Moscow (1973), East Berlin (1975)
Creditanstalt-Bankverein (Austria)	Budapest (1975)
Credito Italiano (Italy)	Moscow (1975)
Deutsche Bank (Fed. Rep. of Germany)	Moscow (1973)
Dresdner Bank (Fed. Rep. of Germany)	Moscow (1973)
Export-Import Bank (Japan)	Moscow (1975)
First National Bank of Chicago (USA)	Moscow (1974), Warsaw (1974)
Kansallis-Osake Pankki (Finland)	Moscow (1973)
Lloyds Bank (UK)	Moscow (1975)
Manufacturers Hanover Trust (USA)	Bucharest*** (1974)
Midland Bank (UK)	Moscow (1975)
National Westminster Bank (UK)	Moscow (1975)
Schweizerische Kreditanstalt (Switzerland)	Moscow (1975)
Société Générale (France)	Moscow (1975), East Berlin (1975), Warsaw (1976), Belgrade (1978)
Société Générale Alsacienne de Banque (France)	East Berlin (1975)
Standard Chartered Bank (UK)	Shanghai*** (1853)
Svenska Handelsbanken (Sweden)	Moscow (1974)
Union Bank of Finland (Finland)	Moscow (1976)

*Parent country is given in parentheses.
**Year of establishment or authorization is given in parentheses.
***Nominally a branch.
Source: Jozef Wilczynski, East-West Banking and Finance and Their Relevance to Australian and Canadian Interests, Ottawa, Carleton University, 1978.

Money, Banking, and Credit

Balance Sheet Data of the Banks of the CMEA Countries
in Western Europe (as of December 31, 1976; in million U.S. dollars)

Country	Bank	Capital	Balance sheet figure	Profit and reserve	Granted credits and deposits	Received credits and deposits
Czechoslovakia	Zivnostenska Banka, London	(not published — branch of Head Office in Prague)				
Hungary	Central Wechsel und Credit Bank, Vienna	4	237	2.4	191	226
	Hungarian International Bank, London	2.5	107	2.8	73	94
Poland	Centro Internationale Handelsbank AG, Vienna	5	91	0.6	78	81
	Mitteleuropäische Handelsbank, Frankfurt am Main	6.8	141	0.3	131	132
	Bank PKO, Paris	4.4	415	0.6	395	396
Romania	Banque Franco-Roumaine, Paris	6	461	2.2	399	433
	Anglo Romanian Bank, London	4.1	131	0.8	129	140
	Frankfurt Bucharest Bank, Frankfurt	(active since April 1, 1977)				
Soviet Union	Moscow Narodny Bank, London*	34	2,062	12	1,535	1,977
	Ost-West Handels-Bank, Frankfurt am Main	25.5	757	6.5	555	714
	Banque Commerciale pour l'Europe du Nord	50.7	2,848	13.7	2,197	2,672
	Donaubank, Vienna	6	217	5	195	203
	East-West United Bank, Luxemburg	13.9	690	2.3	649	661
	Wozchod Handelsbank, Zurich*	26.6	248	9.4	100	178
Total		189.5	8,405	58.6	6,627	7,907

*Balance sheet as of December 31, 1975.
Note: Exchange rate, December 31, 1976, for 1 U.S.dollar: pound sterling, 1.70; French franc, 4.93; deutsche mark, 2.35; Austrian schilling, 16.65; Belgian franc, 35.75: Swiss franc, 2.44.
Source: K. Głażewski, "Banks of CMEA Countries in Western Europe," Report for the Workshop on East-West European Economic Interaction, Budapest, October 16-20, 1977.

208

integrate Western branches into the Eastern system, shows clearly how the world monetary system is going as far as adaptation is concerned.

A banking system without developed monetary relations is unable to create the necessary conditions for internationalization and multilateralization of economic relations. Without a developed monetary system, partnership on an equal footing remains an alien concept.

The view that monetary relations based on worldwide currency convertibility are a precondition for flourishing foreign trade is a debated issue. East-West trade will have a stable foundation only when the foreign trade apparatus of both systems is able to operate with equal effect; that is; when the planned economies, with full-blooded monetary systems, are incorporated into the world market. The structure and scope of East-West trade will then be able to reflect the existing economic structures.

Partnership is not just a most-favored-nation clause for all: it also means a situation in which Eastern countries can function as lenders as well as borrowers on the world market, and in which the only real driving force of the international division of labor — comparative cost advantage — will be able to operate with full effect.

The monetary systems also require a common center of control if they are to operate on an equal footing. The Bretton Woods agreement could serve as the institutional framework for a unified world monetary system; indeed, when it was created, the Soviet Union was one of the participants. Although its current regulations are vulnerable to crisis, there can be no doubt that this agreement could provide a sound basis for a future reformed world monetary system in which the planned economies also had an important role to play.

It is also clear that the membership of the Eastern countries in a well-structured world monetary system will create much better conditions for their equitable participation in world trade and for their own economic development than their insistent reliance on traditional steering mechanisms which, over the long

Money, Banking, and Credit

term, are condemned to the importation of technological progress. The planned economies will adapt their steering mechanisms to the requirements of a unified world monetary system, just as the latter will have to give special consideration to the peculiarities of the planned economies. Currency convertibility, however, must be regarded as absolutely indispensable for an organized, equitable foreign trade; the latter, in turn, is essential for balanced and flourishing economic growth — which is in the interests of all. A unified world monetary system, viewed as part of a worldwide economic order, is also a precondition for an integrated world no longer divided into two separate systems, in which the division of labor will promote growth, not hasten decline.

NOTES

1. See Alec Nove, An Economic History of the USSR, Middlesex England, 1969, p. 187.

2. Vneshniaia torgovlia, SSSR s 1918-1940, Moscow, 1960, p. 14.

3. The Hungarian expert has this to say: "There are countries where these categories and the economic laws associated with them will be permitted to assert themselves in the framework of a market mechanism planned and regulated by the state; and others where they are intended to be utilized to a greater extent than in the past as incentives promoting the fulfillment of direct central instructions." See S. Ausch, "International Division of Labor and the Present Forms of Economic Mechanism in the CMEA countries," in Reform of the Economic Mechanism in Hungary, Budapest, 1969, p. 231.

4. The Hungarian expert J. Bognar comments as follows: "In Czechoslovakia, the German Democratic Republic and Hungary, for instance, several industrial branches have been created or expanded to many times their former capacity in compliance with the needs of the Soviet market. Later, however, the industrially less advanced countries embarked on an import-saving road of development, building up the manufacture of products they had earlier imported from other socialist countries." A Contemporary Approach to East-West Economic Relations, Budapest, 1969, p. 7.

5. A. Schüller observes: "[In Hungary] there exists no sound idea as to how a socialist market management openly oriented toward the efficiency of capitalist enterprise can be created while at the same time socialist ownership of the means of production is maintained"; but this view seems to be unfounded. See Osthandelspolitik als problem der Wettbewerbpolitik, Frankfurt am Main, 1973, p. 54.

6. Polish expert M. Orłowski describes the anchoring of the monopoly on

Money, Credit, and Prices in Foreign Trade

foreign exchange in the planning system as follows: "Under socialist conditions, a monopoly over foreign exchange, like the monopoly over foreign trade, is an intrinsic part of a socialist planned economy and a permanent instrument in the socialist social order." See Kursy walutowe, pieniądz, kapitał, Warsaw, 1973, p. 165.

7. "All proceeds in foreign exchange are handed over to the state where they accumulate in a state account, which allocates the funds required for planned imports and other expenditures." See S. Rączkowski, Międzynarodowe stosunki finansowe, Warsaw, 1972, p. 24.

8. Polish monetary expert Wesołowski says: "This system immunized individual enterprises from the effects of world prices, but not the economy as a whole. As a consequence, world prices, just as domestic prices have, repercussions on the state budget." Bilans złotwoy wymiany z zagranicą, Warsaw, 1973, p. 10.

9. See Schüller, op. cit., p. 212.

10. The vice-president of the Polish National Bank writes: "Multilateralization of monetary transactions has created the preconditions for multilateralization of trade in goods and services. It must be conceded, however, that the latter takes place only to a minimal degree. The great majority of deliveries (98 percent) are cleared bilaterally." Z. Fedorowicz, Podstawy teorii pieniądza w gospodarce socjalistycznej, Warsaw, 1975, p. 291.

11. J. Schumpeter says: "Since money volumes and monetary processes have meaning only to the extent that they reflect volumes of commodities and processes in the commodity world, an understanding of monetary processes presupposes an understanding of processes in the world of commodities." Das Wesen des Geldes, Göttingen, 1970, p. 119.

12. From the resolution of the Twenty-fifth Session of the CMEA on the Comprehensive Program. See Neues Deutschland, August 7, 1971.

13. Fedorowicz, cited above, notes: "The conversion of world prices into transferable rubles does not make the ruble an independent yardstick of value, even when cyclic and speculative fluctuations are excluded." Op. cit., p. 293.

14. See A. Zwass, "Die Internationale Investitionsbank des Rates für gegenseitige Wirtschaftshilfe," Konjunkturpolitik (Berlin), 1972, No. 3.

15. Fedorowicz agrees with this view: "Although obligations are paid in monetary transactions, the creditor still will demand the undelivered goods," and "the limited monetary functions of the transferable ruble show up especially clearly when one wants to use interest rates, distribute profits, or put credits allocated in transferable rubles to concrete use." Op. cit., pp. 291,295.

16. See W. Karpich in Mezhdunarodnaia sotsialisticheskaia valuta stran chlenov SEV, Moscow, 1973, p. 55.

17. Ekonomicheskaia gazeta, April 1976, p. 21.

18. S. Rączkowski, "International Money of the Socialist Countries," in op. cit., p. 326.

19. The resolutions of the Forty-third Session of the IBEC board are published in the Press Bulletin of the Moscow Narodny Bank, 1976. No. 788, Vol. 8, XII.

Money, Banking, and Credit

20. GDR experts G. Brendel and E. Faude have this to say: "World market prices are oriented toward achieving world indicators with regard to the productivity of labor, level of scientific and technological progress, product quality, and costs of production." See "Wesenszüge und Entwicklungstendenzen des RGW-Preisbildungssystems," Wirtschaftswissenschaft, 1973, Vol. 9, p. 1286.

21. J. F. Kormnov, Specialisierung und Kooperation der Produktion der RGW-Länder [Specialization and Cooperation in Production among the CMEA Nations], East Berlin, 1974, p. 200.

22. See A. W. Sijthooff, Socialist World Market Prices, Leyden, 1969, p. 109.

23. Polish expert S. Rączkowski has this to say: "In these circumstances none of the national currencies of the CMEA countries can now perform the function of international money. None can be used internationally as a measure of value, because conversion to such a currency ... does not adequately reflect economic relationships, as the differences in the domestic price structures of the countries involved are too great." Op. cit., p. 317.

24. Martin J. Kohn is cited in this context: "Because of the prevalence of disequilibrium domestic prices combined with disequilibrium exchange rates, the resort to other yardsticks for determining intra-CMEA trade prices is understandable." See "Developments in Soviet Eastern European Terms of Trade, 1971-1975," in Soviet Economy in a New Perspective, Joint Economic Committee of the Congress of the United States, October 14, 1976, p. 71.

25. Sijthooff, op. cit., p. 181.

26. See Wochenbericht des Deutschen Institutes für Wirtschaftsforschung, January 13, 1977, p. 11, and Monthly Bulletin of Statistics, October 1976, p. 169.

27. See Monatsberichte des Osterreichschen Institutes für Wirtschafts-forchung, 12/1976, survey 13.

28. At the beginning of the seventies, oil prices were $1.05 per ton in Libya, $0.75 per ton in Saudi Arabia, $0.49 per ton in Iran, and $0.35 per ton in Iraq.

29. See Information Service of the Swiss Bank Society, Zurich, June 8, 1976.

30. The Eastern countries are currently involved in the construction of ten major projects of common interest, mainly in the USSR: in particular, the construction of the 2,750 kilometer long Orenburg gas pipeline; the expansion of the "Mir" energy association from Vinnitsa (USSR) to Albertisa (Hungary); the expansion of a second oil pipeline from Polotsk to the Western border of the USSR; the construction of a cellulose plant in Ust-Ulim and an asbestos plant in Kizhembaev; and so on.

31. Taken from the report of Prime Minister Strougal at the Fifteenth Party Congress, April 13, 1976.

32. See Neues Deutschland, January 15, 1976.

33. See Mirovaia ekonomika i mezhdunarodnye otnosheniia, Moscow, 6/1976, p. 25.

34. See Życie gospodarcze, April 20, 1976.

35. See J. Rutkowski, "Stabilność i elastyczność cen w obrotach wzajemnych krajów RWPG" [Stability and Flexibility of intra-CMEA Trading Prices], Handel zagraniczny (Warsaw), 1/1977, p. 4.

36. Ibid.

37. Ibid.

38. Says Polish expert Rączkowski: "The realism of the exchange rate of the transferable ruble in relation to other currencies now raises considerable doubt." Op. cit., p. 325.

39. The vice finance minister of Hungary, Imre Vincze says: "Exchange rates for the CMEA countries' national currencies in terms of transferable rubles are not necessary for the formation of foreign trade prices ... exchange rates for the CMEA countries' national currencies in terms of transferable rubles were used only on a relatively narrow scale in 1975." Figyelö, May 1976, translated into English in JPRS, June 22, 1976, pp. 4, 6.

40. Zbigniew Brzezinski's view is worth considering here: "Indebtedness often increases the leverage of the debtor and decreases the leverage of the creditor." In an interview for Business Week, May 1976, Vol. 3.

41. Hungarian economist J. Bognár says: "During the past decades, the socialist countries have developed an advanced industry whose structural (macrostructural) changes have followed — in the form of tendencies — the trends evolved in the world economy." A Contemporary Approach to East-West Economic Relations, Budapest, 1969, p. 4.

42. See Wochenbericht, 39/1976; DIW, September 30, 1976, p. 360.

43. Handelsblatt, January 5, 1974.

44. East-West Market, October 4, 1976.

45. L. J. Brainard says: "They are in large part borrowed funds which are held as deposits. They serve as trade clearing accounts and fulfill an essential liquidity reserve function." "Criteria for Financing East-West Trade," in Tariff, Legal and Credit Constraints on East-West Commercial Relations, edited by John P. Hardt, May 1975, p. 12.

46. There are nine banks of Western Europe (Belgium, Germany, France, Great Britain, Italy, Luxemburg, the Netherlands, Sweden, and Switzerland) and Canada, Japan, the United States, and foreign branches of American banks in the Caribbean, Hong Kong, and Singapore.

47. See Handelsblatt, February 25-26, 1977.

48. Direct borrowing from firms is usually encouraged by the Western banks, which in this way try to get around internal ceilings and also get an insight into the business dealings of the firm. See F. Guiles, "L'endettement des pays socialistes," Le Monde, February 8, 1977.

49. Data from the director of the Vneshtorgbank, A. M. Maslow, in an interview for Euromoney, March 1977.

50. See Handelsblatt, March 1, 1977.

51. See Handelsblatt, February 10, 1977; Guiles, op. cit.

52. See East-West Market, Chase World Information, October 4, 1976.

53. See East-West Market, September 20, 1976, and October 4, 1976.

54. See Handelsblatt, March 1, 1977.

55. S. F. Porter states in her report, published in September 1976: "Soviet and East European buyers consistently insist on the lowest possible interest rates for medium- and long-term export credits, claiming their excellent credit standing entitles them to what in today's capital markets are preferential

rates." East-West Trade Financing, U. S. Dept. of Commerce, IX, 1976, p. 45.

56. See J. Struminski, "Harter Poker um Konditionen im Ostgeschäft" [Hard Bargaining on Terms in Eastern Trade], Handelsblatt, January 5, 1977.

57. Statistisches Jahrbuch, 1976, p. 494.

58. H. Horsmeyer, "Poland Seeks to Limit Western Indebtedness," an interview with the Polish vice-minister of foreign affairs, M. Krzak, Journal of Commerce, December 15, 1976, pp. 2-3.

59. See Handelsblatt, February 4, 1977.

60. See Handelsblatt, March 3, 1977; but the machinery deliveries of West Germany in 1975 were still three times as great (1.2 billion deutsche marks) as those of the German Democratic Republic (313 million deutsche marks). See FAZ, March 3, 1977.

61. See FAZ, January 20, 1977.

62. See Financial Times, May 28, 1976.

Chapter 7

SUMMARY: PERSPECTIVES FOR INCORPORATING CMEA CURRENCIES INTO INTERNATIONAL TRADE

The invitation extended to Western industrial nations by the Forty-third Session of the Council of the International Bank for Economic Cooperation in October 1976 to settle East-West trade either partially or wholly in transferable rubles, aroused the hope in many economic circles in Europe and America that a major breakthrough in monetary relations had been achieved in the CMEA. The headlines of the Western papers proclaimed a new era in the clearing system of world trade, in which a Europa-ruble or transfer-ruble would become a major instrument in trade with the West.

Two years have now passed since then with no discernible change in clearing practices in East-West trade. No Western nation has accepted the invitation to settle its transactions with the East in a clearing instead of a hard currency. The transferable ruble has remained an internal currency of the CMEA, and is not even partly convertible into the hard currencies of the Western countries.

One thing has changed, however: even the CMEA nations now prefer to be paid by their Eastern bloc partners in hard currencies in cases where they have hardware to deliver beyond established quota exchange.

But the October decision of the IBEC was not new: the October 1963 agreement concerning multilateral settlements in transferable rubles and the founding of the IBEC had invited nonmembers of the CMEA to participate in the CMEA clearing system. The conditions necessary for such participation were

not created, however, either between the time of the agreement
and the renewed offer in 1976, nor after October 1976, although
the invitation to Western nations to clear their trade with the
East in transferable rubles had come from such an authoritative
quarter as Prime Minister Kosygin, who extended this offer to
Austrian Minister of Trade J. Staribacher on the occasion of the
latter's visit to Moscow in February 1978.

1. Inherent Obstacles of the System

The principal obstacle preventing the collective CMEA currency, the transferable ruble, from acquiring international va-
lidity lies in the fact that it is a creation of the planned economies, which have so far been unable to establish the necessary
conditions in their individual monetary systems to make even
their own domestic currencies transferable on a worldwide basis. The ability of the collective CMEA currency to function
as money in international transactions can be no greater than
that of the domestic currencies of each of the CMEA member
nations; the international CMEA market can create no broader
basis for a convertible currency than can the domestic markets
of the individual CMEA countries.

Bilateralism is built into the system in the planned economies. Institutional agreements in the settlement system alone
are incapable of effecting a breakthrough in the conduct of foreign trade as long as foreign trade quotas are strictly regulated
and the market for a free flow of goods and money is not open.

Developments after the establishment of multilateral clearing
institutions — first a clearinghouse at the Soviet Gosbank in
1957 and then an independently operating international CMEA
bank in 1964 — speak an unequivocal language: the CMEA countries have so far been unable to do away with bilateralism. According to their own estimates, multilateral intrabloc trade
amounts to no more than 2 or 3 percent of the total trade.

The search for better clearing procedures also indicates,
however, that multilateral foreign trade is as attractive a prop-
osition for the planned economies as it is for the West. Never-

theless, the clearing system is only an instrument suited to existing economic relations; it is by no means a pacesetting or determining factor.

2. Distrust of the "Invisible Hand" of the Market in Centrally Steered Economies

In a centrally steered economy — even that of a somewhat looser and more liberalized form, as in Hungary — money, credit, prices, and profits exercise more controlling and economic accounting functions than business and allocation functions. In the traditional steering system, the state-owned enterprise is provided with a sum from the state budget, its "own fund," which it can then dispose of as it sees fit; the enterprise transfers most of its profits to the budget, which then in centralized fashion allocates it for capital investment projects and general state purposes. In Hungary, where decision making has been decentralized and much greater play is given to the market mechanism than in the traditional planned economies, the enterprise is still only one part of the state-run economy in which the power structures accord greater status to political priorities than to market imperatives.

Authentic monetary categories can come only from an authentic market, and only a genuine market can really use market monetary relations. The quasi-market of the planned economies entails only quasi-monetary categories, for that is the only kind it can use.

A modern industrial society, however, cannot function as a natural economy. If commodities are sold, not distributed, they must have a price expressed in money. The planned economies as well have found no better yardstick than profit for assessing the efficiency of an enterprise, and workers have only their wages as appropriate recompense for their effort.

All the concepts of the market — such as money, credit, price, and profits — are used in the planned economies, but the economic content these categories traditionally have on the market is operative within the planned economies only to the extent made necessary by the existing system of production and distribution.

In every planned economy in the CMEA, even in the widely reformed steering system found in Hungary, the economy is regulated more by state command than by anonymous mechanisms. In no case are market mechanisms employed to such an extent that they could come into conflict with the priorities spelled out in the state plan, and, if ever such a danger should loom, suitable measures are taken to correct the situation.

Capital goods are no longer distributed in the traditional sense, but they are not sold in the market sense of the term either. The capital goods market persists as a seller's market par excellence, in which the commands of the planning authorities play a more important role than market criteria. Prices are no longer symbolic measures of value for capital goods, but they are by no means equilibrium prices either. Capital goods prices are relatively lower than consumer goods prices. They contain a margin of profit, but as a rule no tax component. In 1976, the turnover tax made up 6.9 percent of the wholesale prices of Soviet heavy industry (i.e., in consumer goods production in this sector), while it constituted 21.5 percent of wholesale prices in light industry and the foodstuffs industry.[1]

Profit is still primarily an officially prescribed efficiency norm of the central planners rather than a market category; this is true even now, when profit is calculated as a component of the "production price" in the form of a percentage of enterprise capital and at least outwardly resembles market profit, in contrast to formerly, when it was built into the sale price as an add-on to production costs. What is more, profit will continue to be only a calculation term and a yardstick of efficiency as long as enterprises are not permitted to dispose over it as they see fit. In 1976, Soviet industrial enterprises employed no more than 11 percent of profits for their own investment purposes,[2] while Polish industry, which is much more decentralized, transfers no less than 80 percent of accumulated profits to the state budget,[3] and Czech enterprises cover only 14.7 percent of their own needs with their own resources.[4] Even in

Hungary, where the micro level has been granted a broader range of decision making than anywhere else, enterprise profits are only a component of state resources, which like other components is planned and allocated in accordance with state-set priorities.

The consumer goods market is taking on more genuine market features than the capital goods market, since distribution is not rationed. But consumer goods prices are not authentic or uniform either. They are too high for luxury goods and too low for basic foodstuffs. In addition, a planned economy is as vulnerable to inflationary pressures as a market economy. Production costs cannot always be kept within the limits of the plan target to avoid a cost push. Demand pull, the second most powerful component of inflationary pressure, has been an invariable companion of the planned economies from their inception.

Disproportionate capital investment activity has been the contributing factor: because of lags in project completion (in the Soviet Union incompleted investment projects made up 80 percent, and in Poland as much as 170 percent of total annual outlays in 1976), there has been no commensurate supply of goods to meet the total purchasing power created through these investment activities.

Another factor contributing to the discrepancy between supply and demand is excessive inventories; nevertheless, these stockpiles are unable to cover real needs. More than 10 percent of the USSR national product for 1973-76 and about 7 percent of that of Poland ends up as stockpiled inventories, yet insufficient supply remains a chronic problem.

Excess demand — at one time institutionalized as a law of development in the planned economy, which had made demand pull into a permanent feature — is not reflected adequately, if at all, in price trends, since most planned economies prefer to keep the prices of basic foodstuffs stable. Cost push is financed through budget subsidies, which in Poland made up one-fifth of the state budget outlays for 1976 (700 percent more than in 1971). The German Democratic Republic had to spend about 13 billion deutsche marks — 780 deutsche marks per capita in

219

1976 alone — just to maintain stable consumer prices and fees for consumer services. Subsidies to public transport (2.5 billion deutsche marks) constitute 60 percent of actual transport costs. The Hungarian approach to maintaining equilibrium and cost-covering prices is, if anything, an exception in the CMEA.

A planned economy relies neither on real and authentic independent initiative on the part of the enterprises, nor on the "Invisible Hand" of the market, to use Adam Smith's well-known expression.

3. The Development of Foreign Trade and Its Instruments

The national currencies are of necessity reduced to a domestic role. No planned economy has so far dared to put convertible currency — a world market good par excellence — into international trade, although the inferiority of a currency restricted to domestic functions is generally acknowledged.

The traditional steering system for foreign trade with an autonomous price structure and nonconvertible currency — which historically has been defined in the planned economies as "state monopoly of foreign trade and foreign exchange" — was one time quite suited to the original model of a central planned economy; now, however, it has come into conflict with the needs of a vigorously growing foreign trade.

The planned economies have long ago abandoned autarkic growth; imports are no longer viewed as stopgaps for internal supplies, and exports are no longer regarded merely as a source of funds for financing imports. The traditional steering model of foreign trade has also been reformed — to be sure, mainly in Hungary, though to a certain extent in Poland as well. The reforms in these countries have given major enterprises the authority to handle their foreign trade transactions themselves or through their sales organizations. Conditions have been created so that enterprises no longer view foreign trade as a domestic transaction in which goods are paid for and received at domestic prices, but as an activity to be transacted at prices shaped under the influence of the world market. In the other Eastern nations, however, the traditional steering system still prevails: enterprises are shielded from foreign markets by the instrument of the foreign trade monopoly — namely, the foreign trade organization — and the state budget carries full responsibility for the financial returns accruing from foreign trade.

In every planned economy, however, the tendency toward bilateralism persists, even where substantial reforms have been introduced into the foreign trade system. Two interrelated factors are responsible for this situation: in every CMEA country, foreign trade is included into input-output balances and into material and financial parameters as an organic component of a planned economy. Foreign trade cannot be much more market oriented than the domestic economy itself. Economic control in the domain of both foreign trade and foreign exchange is total.

Since the currency of a planned economy cannot be based on authentic prices, neither can it be linked organically with other currencies through realistic exchange rates. It will therefore lack the attributes of convertibility which are indispensable for a currency to be able to function in foreign trade.

Although the planned economies have now abandoned the path of autarkic growth, they are still more autonomous and introverted than any other economic system in the world. They lack viable means and channels of communication for both economic relations with the West and intra-CMEA trade.

4. The Clearing Functions of the Transferable Ruble and the IBEC

The agreement of October 22, 1963, on "Multilateral Settlements in Transferable Rubles and the Establishment of the IBEC" was from its inception no more than a compromise between those CMEA nations that, following the example of the European Payments Union, had set their sights on currency convertibility as a precondition for effective international bank activity and multilateral foreign trade, and those countries that wanted no more than a streamlined settlements system.

Though Poland, and later Hungary, expended considerable efforts to make the transferable ruble at least partly convertible,
the IBEC developed in accordance with the wishes of the majority. The reformers were destined to see their efforts come to
naught, for the CMEA could create no better conditions for multilateral trade than could the national economies. Monetary relations within the CMEA evolved in accordance with Gresham's
Law, in which it was the more backward monetary system of
the defenders of the traditional steering system, not the system
of the reform-inclined members, which determined the functionability of the collective CMEA currency.

Given that the desire was merely to continue with bilateral
foreign trade — and this was documented unequivocally by the
Comprehensive Program of 1971 — a multilateral clearing institution such as the IBEC represented, no matter how perfect,
was of no use.

In the fourteen years since the establishment of the IBEC,
foreign trade practice has shown unmistakably that the common
CMEA market is even less willing or able to rely on the "Invisible Hand" of the market than the domestic economies of its
member nations.

The monetary holdings of the IBEC members cannot be used
to procure any goods except those determined by quotas established beforehand through mutual agreement between buyer and
supplier. The monetary holdings and settlement credits of the
IBEC members are no more than a reflection of divergences
from the planned supplies. The accumulation of monetary assets has no purpose, since such assets cannot be used to procure anything beyond established quotas; nor will credit achieve
anything more than to offset the negative balance of an IBEC
member that has received more from a partner than it has delivered.

The transferable ruble represents neither a genuine purchasing power nor a measure of value in the usual sense of the term,
for the autonomous and widely varying price structures of the
member nations provide no basis for an equivalent goods exchange.

All efforts of the CMEA to evolve its own averaged price structure based on internal cost relations, pursuant to the decision of the Ninth Session of the CMEA in 1958, have foundered. Rather than neutralizing the shortcomings of the national price systems, the CMEA average would in fact have subsumed them all. There appeared to be no way out except to retain world market prices as a price basis.

Until 1975, the average, appropriately adjusted world market prices for the preceding five-year period were taken as a price basis for the current five-year period (the average prices for 1960-64 for the five year-period from 1966 to 1970, and the average prices for 1965-69 for the five-year period 1971-75). The price basis for the five-year period from 1971 to 1975 was discarded one year earlier than scheduled in connection with the price rises for fuel and raw materials; now the prices for intra-CMEA trade are adjusted annually to the five-year average.

A currency that can neither have a genuine purchasing power nor function as a measure of value is likewise incapable of exercising any of the other essential functions of money. Neither the IBEC nor the International Investment Bank (founded in 1971) were able to create an effective bank capital in transferable rubles on the basis of this clearing currency. After two years of operation, both banks ceased receiving inpayments of subscribed capital in transferable rubles.

Practice so far has shown that the transferable ruble is suitable only for providing technical clearing credits. Effective credit activities utilize funds raised on the world market.

5. The Exchange Rate of the Transferable Ruble

The transferable ruble was no more able than the national currencies of the CMEA to develop the attributes of "moneyness" that are indispensable for the establishment of organic links with the other currencies of the world, including the CMEA currencies. But, unlike the latter, it cannot use the internal CMEA price structures as a value basis for its common currency. The CMEA market is constrained to employ a price

223

basis that has nothing to do with production relations within the CMEA, for which a common CMEA denominator must be created. This is accomplished by means of a conversion coefficient (the official exchange rates between the transferable ruble and the Western currencies). The transferable ruble, then, can be connected neither with the hard currencies of the West nor with the national currencies of the CMEA, with exchange rates corresponding to economic realities as a basis for convertibility.

The rates of exchange computed between the transferable ruble and the national currencies have brought no advantages since, to quote Imre Vincze, Hungary's vice-minister of finance and former CMEA secretary, "the ratios of the CMEA countries' producer prices show significant variations among countries as well as in relation to foreign trade prices." [5]

The official exchange rate of the transferable ruble is equivalent to that of the Soviet ruble, and over the past few years has ranged between 1.30 and 1.35 U.S. dollars. This rate is remote from expressing any real value relationship to Western currencies, however, as is evidenced by the calculations of the CMEA countries, which have worked out exchange coefficients between the transferable ruble and the national currencies for internal settlement purposes on the basis of purchasing power parity. For example, Hungary calculates 39.80 forints for 1 U.S. dollar for foreign transactions, but only 35 forints for one transferable ruble. Thus, at 0.88 = 1 U.S. dollar, the transferable ruble was valued at one-third less than the official rate.

If one considers that the CMEA countries still trade on the basis of bilaterally established quotas in which hardware is exchanged for hardware and software for software, and that in such transactions the transferable ruble represents neither universal purchasing power nor a uniform measure of value, it will be clear why the project to make the transferable ruble at least partially convertible — first proposed by Poland in 1964 and later supported by Hungary — could never be realized. The same fate awaited the September 1, 1973, agreement among a few IBEC countries to allow a very limited exchange of holdings and credits in transferable rubles against hard currencies —

an agreement which, had it been realizable, was later to have been extended to the other CMEA countries.

National CMEA currencies are converted into transferable rubles only within the framework of the February 9, 1963, Prague agreement regarding noncommercial payments (tourism, fees, etc.). Ordinarily, the outstanding bilateral balance of non-commercial transactions is transferred annually to the transferable ruble accounts of the CMEA member nations in the IBEC on the basis of an exchange rate between the national currencies and the Soviet ruble, which is calculated especially for this purpose and employs the conversion coefficient between the Soviet ruble and the transferable ruble (currently, 2.3 Soviet rubles are exchanged for 1 transferable ruble under conditions where official rates of exchange between the two currencies and the Western currencies are identical).

The official exchange rate of the transferable ruble with the Western currencies is used only as a purely technical instrument to compile bank balance sheets. Both CMEA banks carry out their transactions in transferable rubles (settlement of intra-CMEA foreign trade and related extension of clearing credits and deposit operations, as well as the extension of credits for capital investment projects within the means allowed by the modest ruble capital of the IIB), as well as in convertible currencies (receipt and distribution of middle-term and long-term credits, raised mainly in the West, and short-term money deposits). These operations take place on a parallel basis without any connection with one another. Bank balances, however, are compiled only in transferable rubles. For this purpose only, the foreign exchange transactions are converted into transferable rubles on the basis of the official exchange rate.

6. The Attempt to Attract Third Countries to Settlements in Transferable Rubles

Efforts to involve third countries in ruble settlements have paralleled in time the discussion concerning the possibility of making the transferable ruble at least partly convertible. Initially, however, it was the developing countries that were targeted as settlement partners. Achievements in this area have been very modest to say the least: as of the end of 1976, settlement agreements in transferable rubles had been signed only between the USSR, Czechoslovakia, and Morocco, and between a few other IBEC countries and Iraq and Finland, and only a very minor volume of business has been transacted on that basis. Furthermore, the applications of Peru, Colombia, and Panama to settle exchanges of bananas for Eastern machinery in transferable rubles have been tabled indefinitely. Nonetheless, although no success had been achieved in this area, the Forty-third Session of the IBEC Council in October 1976 extended an invitation to the industrial nations of the West to settle their accounts with the CMEA countries partly or wholly in transferable rubles.

As a rule, the Eastern nations have a chronic deficit in their foreign trade relations with the West. The consequence of such a switchover to settlements in transferable rubles would therefore be to express the collective assets in this functionally limited currency. Western nations can achieve no more in the CMEA with transferable ruble holdings than can CMEA members themselves, however, for the decisive factor in foreign trade on this market is not money as a universal purchasing power but deliveries, agreed upon bilaterally between individual partners.

Although theoretically the transition from value magnitudes on the Western market to those on the CMEA market is technically feasible (the official exchange rates set by the IBEC for the transferable ruble could be used), any organic connection between the balances in transferable rubles of the Western nations and the balances of the IBEC nations is scarcely conceivable. The value of the assets of a Western nation, expressed in transferable rubles, would not be commensurate with the value of the transferable ruble assets of its CMEA partner — among other reasons, because the prices for intra-CMEA trade, which are determined on the basis of a five-year average of the world market prices, diverge considerably from the current

226

prices on Western markets. For example, the Soviet price for crude oil to the Eastern nations in 1978 was one-fifth lower than the price demanded by the USSR from a Western partner.

One can hardly expect that a Western partner could continue to enjoy the advantage of a reduced price for oil as a participant in IBEC settlements, nor could a Western nation be expected to pay higher prices for certain CMEA machinery than the price in force on the Western market. Further, it must be taken into account that the commodity structure of East-West trade differs substantially from that of intra-bloc trade.

The lack of two components of moneyness — namely, the ability to function as a universal purchasing power and the ability to function as a standard of value — which distinguishes the transferable ruble from functional money, would prevent the Western outsider from the normal use of its transferable ruble holdings.

Transferable ruble holdings, whose use is limited even within the CMEA market, would be of no advantage whatsoever outside this market. The transferable ruble is not convertible into hard currencies, and the IBEC, which in its October 1976 decision declared itself willing to accept hard currencies to cover transferable ruble credits, promises no reciprocity — that is, no conversion of transferable ruble assets into hard currencies.

The IBEC members themselves do not seem to place too great stock in the October 1976 decision of the bank council. A CMEA country that has a surplus in trade with the West would prefer to materialize it in hard currencies and not in transferable rubles, that is, in goods of an Eastern partner with a deficit in trade with the West. The Soviet Union, for example, would be reluctant to exchange its surplus in trade with Austria for Polish goods — Poland is a chronic debtor of Austria — since it could buy any goods on any market with schillings, but in Poland it could purchase only what the Polish market had to offer, and the Soviet Union already imports the best of the lot.

Although the possibility that a Western country might also conduct a few transactions with an Eastern partner in transferable rubles cannot be ruled out, it would be more advantageous

for East-West trade for an Eastern country to switch over to
the hard currency system, with all the terms attached to it, than
for a hard currency country to participate in a clearing system,
with all its attendant limitations.

7. Foreign Exchange Settlements in East-West Trade

Although the Eastern countries have gradually switched over
from bilateral clearing to settlements in foreign exchange since
the mid-sixties, they have created even fewer of the conditions
necessary for multilateralization in East-West trade than in
intra-CMEA trade. The disadvantages of bilateral clearing have
largely been eliminated, but no progress at all has been made
toward multilateralization of economic relations with the West.
The preconditions for multilateral foreign trade still exist only
in the West. Eastern markets are no more open to multilateral
trade than they have ever been; moreover, the domestic currencies of the planned economies have not been redesigned to
function as business currencies. The proclivity of the planned
economy for clearing trade has not diminished to any appreciable degree, and the commodity structure of East-West trade
still resembles the structure of trade between developing countries and the industrial nations.

East-West trade has grown vigorously in the seventies, although Eastern exports to the West during 1971-76 covered no
more than 73 percent of their imports from the West, with a
figure of 55 percent for Bulgaria and 54 percent for Poland.

The switch to settlements in hard currency has proven useful, however, since negative balances no longer need to be
covered by switch and transit transactions, so costly for the
East, as during the days of bilateral clearing; supplies credits
and bank credits may now be used, and these have proven themselves to be much cheaper than the facilities available for
covering clearing deficits because of the persistent — though
now somewhat moderated — inflation.

Settlement in foreign exchange frees the Eastern nations
from the limitations of bilateralism and allows them to enjoy

the customary mobility of multilateral settlements.

In the meantime, however, although East-West trade has grown vigorously, it has not been balanced; a worrisome mountain of debt has built up, reaching such magnitudes that it would take Poland or the German Democratic Republic, for example, the foreign exchange earnings of three years of exports to cover their deficits.

This development could benefit both sides only if the Eastern nations were able to utilize advanced technology and know-how imported from the West and co-financed with Western credits to enlarge upon a commodity structure acceptable to the West and, at the same time, create suitable conditions for commodity and currency convertibility.

These two organically interrelated components of a fair and equal international division of labor have never materialized, however. The Eastern nations therefore have been forced to take a step backwards rather than a move ahead. To prevent a further increase in debt, they have turned once again to barter transactions in even larger volume than in the sixties and at the same time cut back drastically on imports from the West.

In the first half of the seventies, the growth rate of imports from the West was more than twice as high as that of exports to the West, but in 1977 a reversal of this trend was already discernible. Imports stagnated or declined, but exports to the West increased more than in the preceding year. The extraordinary increase in compensation transactions is primarily responsible for this dynamic growth in Eastern exports, and this turn of events may perhaps be considered even more dangerous than the pileup of debt.

In one recent planned compensation deal, Krupp-Koppers, Sachgitter, and Klöckner were to build a petrochemical plant worth $3 billion in the Soviet Union in return for chemical products in the amount of $400 million annually. Commented Manfred Krüper, economic expert of the West German trade union, "It is more than the market can absorb."

Dissatisfaction is widespread in Great Britain and even more so in France, whose machinery manufacturers are to be compensated with chemical products that the French chemical industry is already producing in surfeit. To protect themselves against barter transactions, which often require a 130 percent compensation in return, the French have set up an interest group, the ACECO, consisting of bankers, industrial managers, and representatives of the government.

Imperial Chemical Industries, Ltd., submitted a protest letter against the expansion of barter transactions in the Common Market, and a USA delegate to the Belgrade followup conference observed: "We understand their hard currency problems but believe that barter deals as a policy could be stifling."[6]

Indeed, barter deals provide no real future for the development and growth of East-West trade. On the other hand, the expansion of facilities and factors that would contribute to multilateralization could provide a powerful stimulus to growth and at the same time promote equalization of trade relations; but this is dependent primarily on the Eastern nations.

8. Prospects

Economic relations with the West in terms of foreign trade, cooperation transactions, and credits have already reached such scope that it is now in the interests of both systems to create the economic conditions for a division of labor that provides both sides with equal facilities and hence equal chances in competition on the world market.

The most promising precondition for a fair and equal division of labor between the two systems would be an integration of the Eastern market into the world market and collaboration within a worldwide trade and currency system whose basic principles would be worked out jointly.

An organically integrated world market, embracing both world systems, would not have to lead to the breakup of the integration groupings as they now exist. The division of labor between the two systems can be successful, however, only if the conditions of trade within each bloc do not differ very greatly from the conditions obtaining between the two blocs. Intra-

CMEA Currencies and International Trade

CMEA trade based on clearing and quotas existing alongside an East-West trade based on settlements in foreign exchange offers no prospects for success over the long term.

An appropriate goal would be multilateral foreign trade on an international scale, in which the only real measure of competition — namely, comparative cost advantage — would be applied in full measure.

Orientation toward an integrated world market would demand a proper contribution from both world systems: from the West, the gradual elimination of crisis phenomena in the world monetary system so that it can function on a worldwide basis, and, until such time as that can be achieved, a coordination of foreign trade and credit policy toward the East in order to put an end to unfair competition; from the East, the adaptation of steering mechanisms to the needs of an effective international division of labor.

NOTES

1. Narodnoe khoziaistvo SSSR za 60 let [Sixty Years of the Soviet Economy], p. 200.
2. Ibid., p. 636.
3. Życie gospodarcze, November 2, 1976.
4. Financial Times, February 16, 1978.
5. "Exchange Rates in the CMEA Monetary System Discussed," Figyelö, May 26, 1976; translated by JPRS, June 22, 1976.
6. See Business Week, January 23, 1978, p. 42.

About the Author

Born in Poland, Adam Zwass for many years held managerial positions in the central banking systems of Poland and the USSR. From 1963 to 1968 he was Councellor in the CMEA Secretariat in Moscow, where he was responsible for financial settlements and the work of the International Bank for Economic Cooperation.

Since his emigration to Vienna in 1969, Dr. Zwass has been affiliated with the German Institute of Economic Research (West Berlin), the Austrian Institute of Economic Research (Vienna), and the Viennese Institute for Comparative Economic Studies, where he is currently a research associate.

Dr. Zwass is the author of numerous articles on monetary questions, banking, and problems of integration, which have been published in Europe and in the United States. His books include Wielkość i struktura obiegu pieniężnego (Warsaw, 1962), Pieniądz dwóch rynków (Warsaw 1968), and Zur Problematik der Währungsbeziehungen zwischen Ost und West (Vienna 1974; published in English as Monetary Cooperation Between East and West by M. E. Sharpe, Inc., White Plains, New York, 1975).

DATE DUE

FEB 5 1981			
FEB 1 1 1982			
MAR 3 1982			
MAR 1 7 1982			
MAR 3 1 1982			
GAYLORD			PRINTED IN U.S.A